S0-BSD-070

Unless Recalled Earlier
Date Due

DEC 28 1991			
MAY 31 1991			
FEB 7 1992			
MAR 15 1992			

BRODART, INC. Cat. No. 23 233 Printed in U.S.A.

Sociology for Whom?

Sociology for Whom?

ALFRED McCLUNG LEE

New York
Oxford University Press
1978

Copyright © 1978 by Oxford University Press, Inc.

Library of Congress Cataloging in Publication Data

Lee, Alfred McClung, 1906–
  Sociology for whom?

  Includes index.
  1. Sociology. I. Title.
HM51.L353   301   77-13653
ISBN 0-19-502336-6
ISBN 0-19-502335-8 pbk.

To my wife and fellow sociologist,
Dr. Elizabeth Briant Lee

Acknowledgments

The ideas in this book were discussed over the years with many friends. Without in any way wishing to shift onto them responsibility for views I have stated, I want to express my debt to those who have stimulated and enriched my thinking. I remember especially Ernest W. Burgess, Maurice Rea Davie, John Kosa, Abraham H. Maslow, Francis E. Merrill, Robert E. Park, Hugh H. Smythe, and Willard Waller, all now gone. It would be impossible to list all those friends now living who have been helpful, but I want to express a special indebtedness to a few.

Throughout our long association, Miriam and Leo P. Chall of *Sociological Abstracts* have contributed substantially to this and other of my projects.

Sidney H. Aronson, currently chairperson of the Sociology Department, Brooklyn College, and long-time colleague, aided me in this and other projects in many ways. James Michael O'Kane, in the chair of the Sociology Department of Drew University, Madison, New Jersey, made helpful facilities and services available to me. Franco Ferrarotti, Charles P. C. Flynn, Sidney Leonard Greenblatt, Glenn Jacobs, S. M. Miller, Pamela Roby, and Kenneth T. Skelton, as friends and fellow sociologists, sustained me in many ways, as they often have, during the preparation of this book. This research was supported (in part) by a grant from The City University of New York PSC-BHE Research Award Program.

A. McC. L.

Contents

Sociology for Whom?

introduction

The Challenge of People-Based Power

Concerned Americans are now re-examining our common human values more probingly than ever before. The events of Vietnam, Angola, Kent State, South Boston, Northern Ireland, Watergate, India, the Middle East, South Africa, and many other places haunt us with problems of the extent to which human values are not shared. They suggest how often such allegedly shared values as those associated with patriotism, religion, ethnicity, and "race" are used to mask such antisocial manipulations and conspiracies as wars, struggles among multinational business corporations, and the rigging of elections. Might not our personal and collective goals be delusory and of service merely to cynical financial and political "operators"? What goals can we set for ourselves and for our society with some assurance that they may reasonably be attainable—at least in part—and worth attaining?

Ours is a day of growing pessimism. For example, the philosopher Rubin Gotesky predicts that the "advanced productive systems cannot control the rate at which they are exhausting human and material resources. Their inability to control the utilization of resources is resulting in the pollution of the air, the ocean, and the earth and the destruction of the plant and animal life essential for human survival." And from this doom, the writer sees no escape for the human race: "There exist no social groups, elites, or social classes capable of taking over world control of existing productive systems in order to prevent these consequences."[1]

Unrest, violence, and other symptoms of revolt among the unemployed, underemployed, and oppressed continue to grow in many parts of the world. They are extremes to which people are driven in an effort to deal with (or to forget) our disintegrating physical environment and our chaotic interclass, interethnic, and international relations. Dissatisfaction spreads in rural as well as in urban and suburban areas. Vandalism, liquor and drug excesses, gang plots, riots, rape, thievery, and even bombings and arson plague high schools and colleges. The pools of unemployed and underemployed continue to grow. Agitation among the young against "straight" ways of life and against business and government is not so open or frequent as it was during the 1960s. Revolt is taking other forms that include increasing runaways of both male and female teenagers, retreats into mysticism and other cult beliefs and activities, as well as political action. Are these symptoms of change or are they signals of forthcoming doom? If they are symptoms of change, can we be optimistic about the character of that change?

No definition or list of social problems is acceptable to more than a limited constituency. A so-called "scientific" definition of social problems has to be highly adaptive and flexible; it has to reflect the multivalent character of human society.

Great differences exist among the perspectives on human life and living as they are seen by dwellers in slums, in carefully guarded urban highrises, in white-suburban developments, in exurban estates, and in farming areas. Status as oppressors or oppressed as well as membership in class, occupation, race, ethnic segment, sex, age level, and state-of-health groups all affect how people perceive social issues and problems. Regardless of identity or locale, however, the nature of the control and use of social power in a given situation and more generally is crucial to the study of social problems, the formation of policy, the shaping of opinion of individuals and publics, the organization of society, and action toward social change.

When one attempts to diagnose and cope with social problems from the standpoint of any social group, the character of operation of concerned power brokers and manipulators becomes a focal consideration. These brokers and manipulators are financiers, industrialists, merchandizers, union officials, religious leaders, politicians, governmental administrators, and top professionals. How can we predict with any accuracy the uses to which astute power brokers will put an enacted law or a constitutional provision, a charismatic leader or an international confrontation? How can we foresee what advantages such manipulators might derive from modifications in climate, in intercorporate competition, in an election struggle, or in civil strife? All social developments have this common basis: all social power derives from people as individuals, as groups, and as a whole. The control of social power, as the English philosopher Bertrand Russell defines it, is the ability to produce "intended effects."[2] Power is "social" when its "intended effects" involve human thought or behavior or are otherwise relevant to human concerns. People emotionally, traditionally, or rationally transfer to and thus concentrate their power in those with whom they have some dependency relationship. As people have undergone their long-term and spreading struggles toward literacy, social understanding, and politicization, power-seekers have had to concentrate more and more effort upon the finding of effective methods to gain and maintain their control and thus their ability to direct this people-based power.

Whatever optimism or pessimism we might have about the future of the human lot depends upon the relative speed with which broader popular participation may be achieved in the control and employment of social power. Will people learn how to participate in time to save themselves from the short-sightedness and greed of entrepreneurs? Will people discover in time how to control themselves and their resources for humane ends? Or will they continue to serve mostly as pawns in the vast and hazardous game-plans of self-serving manipulators while the earth's resources are being exhausted and the human population continues to increase? As the English psychologist Havelock Ellis remarked, years before people had sent probes to other planets, "the sun and the moon and the stars would have disappeared long ago . . . had they happened to be within the reach of predatory human hands."[3] Now human hands are searching even those possible resources.

It is fashionable to be a pessimist along the lines of the philosopher's conclusions quoted at the outset. To take an optimistic position as to the future of humanity appears to many to be naïve, sentimental, or propagandistic, but that is the view taken here. This is done after having compared, as in the seventh chapter, major positive and negative tendencies now operating in our country and in the world.

Social power may be controlled by force, by the adoration or fear of a dominant person, by customary mythology, rhetoric, ritual, and organization, by acquiescence to the status quo or lack of an alternative, or even by conscious and well-informed consent. However social power is controlled, "it is necessary for a prince to possess the friendship of the people; otherwise he has no resource in times of adversity,"[4] as Niccolò Machiavelli advised the leaders of the sixteenth century.

Look at the vast expenditures of modern capitalistic enterprises made directly and at their behest by controlled governmental units, foundations, and voluntary agencies to improve their popular "image." Look at the similarly vast expenditures of communist and socialist governmental and party organizations used to develop and maintain loyalty—or at least acquiescence.

Techniques and ideologies vary, but all efforts to reach people's minds indicate the persistence of this basic challenge: the control of social power depends upon the manipulation of values that people attach at the time to structures, personalities, rituals, and resources. Bureaucracies, armies, armaments, property rights, markets, media of communication and of transportation, and technology are all built upon and remain useful in consequence of popular acceptance, support, and action.

Modern societies contain a confusing array of seemingly autonomous agencies which serve political, economic, religious, family, recreational, and other personal and social needs and desires. They include organizations of health specialists, educators, amateur and professional sports participants, and various types of artists and artisans. However, those who search thoroughly enough can learn, as did the social analyst Walter Lippmann, that "the whole economic life of this country . . . is controlled by groups of men whose influence extends like a web to smaller, tributary groups, cutting across all official boundaries and designations, making short work of all legal formulae, and exercising sovereignty regardless of the little fences we erect to keep it in bounds." What is especially insidious about this "invisible government" is "that we do not see it, cannot use it, and are compelled to submit to it."[5]

Lippmann made those generalizations before the outbreak of World War I. Since then, corporations have become tremendously large and more comprehensive of human activities. Americans had too long neglected Thomas Jefferson's "warning" to learn from the English example of plutocratic corruption "and crush in its birth the aristocracy of our monied corporations which dare already [in 1816] to challenge our government to a trial of strength and bid defiance to the laws of our country."[6]

Groups of corporate key specialists refine ever more the effectiveness of "public relations" and other power-manipulating strategies and facilities. Aided by this sophisticating process, corporations linked themselves into vast conglomerates. They learned to "live" with and to utilize functionaries on many levels of local and national government, as well as heads of labor unions and trade associations, executives of social service, professional, and religious societies and agencies, foundation administrators, crime entrepreneurs, and foreign communist and socialist leaders. Their plutocratic operations thus became ever more complicated as well as extensive. Consequences of decisions in one board room can now sweep beyond the bounds of any one country and circulate around the world to influence the lives of thousands and even of millions of people.

As the social scientist William Graham Sumner points out, "Capital, as it grows larger, takes on new increments with greater and greater ease. It acquires a kind of momentum."[7] This is especially the case with capital employed plutocratically in the contemporary world. Sumner describes plutocracy as "a political form in which the real controlling force is wealth." He contends that wealth's current character is "the thing which seems to me to be really new and really threatening." He recalls "states in which there have been large plutocratic elements, but none in which wealth seemed to have such absorbing and controlling power as it threatens us. . . . In its motive, its processes, its code, and its sanctions it is infinitely corrupting to all the institutions which ought to preserve and protect society." The instruments of the plutocrats, in Sumner's perception, he spoke of as people "on the make." Such a person "does not think of himself as dishonest, but only as a man of the world." Thus, as Sumner concludes, "Modern plutocrats buy their way through elections and legislatures, in the confidence of being able to get powers which will recoup them for all the outlay and yield an ample surplus besides."[8]

As the modern American and worldwide plutocracy expanded, knowledge of people—psychology and sociology—became key factors in developing and exploiting the rising imperial fabric. Sumner foresaw that this would become all the more the situation when he wrote in 1882 that "classes and groups are thrown against each other in such a way as to produce class hatreds and hostilities."[9] As national or ethnic jealousies diminished, he sensed that "class jealousies threaten to take their place," and that "Forces which come into action in one part of human society rest not until they have reached all human society. The brotherhood of man is coming to be a reality of such distinct and positive character that we find it a practical question of the greatest moment what kind of creatures some of these hitherto neglected brethren are."[10] That ethnic, religious, and so-called "racial" biases would continue to reenforce as well as to disguise interclass antagonisms was perhaps not so clear a century ago as it is today.[11]

The variously named subsidiaries of capitalist and communist multinational operations make the locus of control nearly invisible and difficult or impossible to trace. Not that politicians in any country find it worth their while to publicize such factors behind their own power. Little wonder that capitalist corporations spend billions in various currencies on strategy "think tanks" and on "contract research" among intellectuals and technologists both inside and outside of universities, on the staging of opinion-influencing "news" events, on the control of news reports and their interpretation, on "good will" advertising, on bribery of people with power who are not already under their control, on subversion of those who are not available for purchase or other influence, and on other efforts at social manipulation, at "public relations" or "image management," and at "evaluation research."

As our national "statesmen" speak of their efforts to defend the "free" world of "representative democracies," they bring to mind the sardonic advice given long ago by Lincoln Steffens[12] to a hard-pressed Russian Czar: Why not try the American scheme of government? Steffens later summarized that scheme as being a "Government of the people by the politicians for the businessmen."[13] The Czar's successors tried something other than a capitalistic republic. It differs from our plutocratic republic chiefly by providing more simplistic controls: government of the people by the party faithful for the commissars.

The integration of industrial, governmental, and military power, so exaggerated in our century, makes instruments for the control of publics of increasing strategic importance to top decision-makers and their close collaborators. Such power wielders utilize not only the obvious organizational facilities and mechanical devices available to them, but they experiment as well with a variety of technicians and professionals who might help to improve such instruments and their use. The increasingly literate masses at the same time tend to become more politicized and more activist, especially in times of crisis—and times of crisis now appear to be coming more and more frequently, and to be having ever broader ramifications.

During the nineteenth century, corporations and governmental agencies nurtured the development of press agents, lobbyists, law firms, political bosses (as power brokers on various levels), and analysts of markets and of political constituencies.[14] During the present century these entities developed and used more sophisticated market surveyors and testers, public opinion pollsters, political campaign managers, tax manipulators, and public relations specialists. In a similar vein, such interests minimized their difficulties with the deprived segments of society by transforming charity and reform efforts into "social welfare programs," some of which were smoothly planned and guided by professional social workers.[15] They also continued to enjoy the services of the highly class-slanted "criminal justice system" that fills our prisons with a disproportionate percentage of the deprived and treats with cautious "understanding" the crimes of professionals, managers, and entrepreneurs.

Sociologists, especially those who are social-engineers-for-hire, arose out of all the needs and pressures that had produced the more obviously commercialized specialists. Sociologists as such arrived relatively recently on the commercial scene because it seemed to many both in business and in academia that sociology might open too many unnecessary doors exposing intimate, speculative, and probably disturbing aspects of life, especially those involving social relationships. Sociologists might even suggest "radical" notions in spite of the fact that much academic sociology has been inspired as an answer to such frightening writers as Karl Marx. The sturdy columns of numbers, the equations, and the graphs of orthodox economists, the plausible theories of "establishment" social philosophers, and the dependable casuistries of lawyers, "political scientists," and the clergy had long offered dependable enough answers.

Sociologists at first seemed too remote from the worlds of people "on the make" to have practical significance. In their eagerness to achieve the status of "scientists" rather than to continue to be labeled "philosophers" or "reformers" or "do-gooders" and thus to ride into academic and social respectability, sociologists came to speak a scientistic jargon not commonly heard in the marketplace. The way-breakers for commercial sociology were thus the products of business organizations and of schools of commerce—market researchers, public opinion pollsters, and social welfare surveyors.

The vastly expanding colleges and universities turn more and more from adaptable education for living (in the liberal arts and sciences) to training for specific and available jobs. Sociologists like many other academic specialists thus become more assimilated into the "real world" of business, politics, and government—in other words, into the military-industrial network. Especially during the depressed 1930s and World War II, social engineers put aside the common sociological exercise of restating in plausible scientistic terms traditional and respectable bourgeois social formulas. They "came of age" as "value free"—allegedly uncommitted and wholly objective—practitioners who might do impressive work on a social problem in behalf of any available sponsor.

We do continue to have a great many curious-minded sociologists who explore human relationships and try to diagnose social problems with a sense of responsibility only to their own ideals of accuracy and of human service. At the same time, entrepreneurial social engineers move with increasing frequency into positions of administrative, policymaking, and discipline-defining power in sociology, the "central policy science," as these engineers like to call it.

Thus, in spite of various value colorations, something called "sociology" strikes many members of power elites and also of intellectual groups as somehow containing a significant key to understanding and perhaps to controlling people-based power. Just how a relation between an intellectual and a would-be utilizer of sociology sometimes works out can be illustrated by a personal experience:

A college classmate of mine became an executive for some years of one of the largest public relations agencies serving industrial organizations. Our ways of life and our ideologies became quite different, and I had no interest in being retained as his consultant, but we both found it amusing and perhaps instructive to talk together from time to time. He looked curiously upon my preoccupation with free-ranging sociological inquiry, and I liked to glimpse through him intimate scenes in his tense world. In some of our talks he told me about his experiences in attempting to contract sociological investigators to aid him with projects for his agency's clients.

"When I get someone to do some sociological research for one of my clients," he would say, "I want either propaganda or honest guidance and sound information, and I want to know clearly which of the two I am supposed to be getting. The trouble with the sociologists I talk with is that when they come to me to sell their services, they are just too damned anxious to give me what they think I want regardless of what I tell them I need. They think I am so naïve about their activities that I won't be able to distinguish among bootlicking, case-making, and sound data."

I replied that, as he well knew, the mores of businessmen and the idealizations of social scientists do contrast rather sharply. Then I added that the typical sociologist has had so little field-clinical experience and so little exposure to non-academic life that his gaucherie in a practical setting should be anticipated. To this the public relations executive retorted: "Then what kind of sociologists are now being trained? How can anyone learn about people for any purpose only by using standardized research instruments and IBM machines without actually taking part in social competition and conflict?"

He was posing two pressing problems that sociologists must confront. They are problems for both "applied" and "theoretical" sociologists—if there is any tenable difference between the two. For one thing, too many sociologists lack intimate and varied field-clinical experiences.[16] For another, too many lack a clear conception of for whom and in what manner a sociologist can actually do defensible scientific work. These problems penetrate deeply into the character of sociology as a scientific discipline and into the integrity and responsibility of sociologists as persons, as scientists, and as citizens.

To be a sociologist equipped to contribute guidance in dealing with social problems through research and through accumulated and critically examined social wisdom, one cannot be a creature ruled by standard formulas for avoiding issues. A few of the common formulas can be labeled (1) neo-scholastic, (2) methodological, and (3) "further research."

Neo-scholasticism in sociology wraps conclusions in such complex theories and jargons that the person advised is either naïvely impressed or rightly disgusted. After a barrage of such rhetoric, the listener or reader might even be convinced by a simple restatement in English of what is alleged to be the "main point"—regardless of how confused, obvious, or even useless that point might actually be!

An emphasis upon overwrought methodology becomes a way of excusing a lack of aid in problem-solving. It arises from a sociologist's realization that she/he may not have learned much or perhaps has discovered material, such as medical malpractice, embarrassing for a middle-class intellectual to report. She/he can then fall back on and elaborate her/his methodological presuppositions. She/he can put together a murky picture adorned by learned references to the standardized and fashionable methods selected and employed in the particular research project. The scant results are then said to be important as tests of those methods even though they may yield nothing in increased social understanding. The barrage of rhetoric flowing from this type of effort might also bring the person or group served to accept some simple bit of alleged wisdom after being bored by a parade of ritualistic jargon.

The third issue-dodging formula, "further research," is an old standby. It appears in almost every research report. It is the customary plea to keep the research funds coming. Those using it contend that someday, somehow, in some way the problem in hand will be conclusively solved by someone. They often find it helpful to excuse superficiality, a lack of exploratory digging, formula-bound thinking, an absence of background, or dependence upon routine procedures.

In situations requiring decisions for which sociological information and theories might be useful as well as in the development of a more accurate conception of the nature of society, people look for the best approximations for guidance that they can obtain. They want answers, rough and tentative though they may be, not contributions to abstract sociological theory or experiments in methodology or case-making for "further research." They want more accurate perspectives on social situations and estimates of probable consequences of policy decisions that they may have to make.

All this means that sociologists who hope to engage in sociological practice as teachers, as researchers, or as consultants not only need formal training in theory and in research methods; they also need the kind of orientation to diverse ethnic cultures and especially to diverse social-class subcultures that only extensive and intimate field-clinical work can provide. They cannot assume that their discipline's formal literature and the infighting in their corner of academia or their home neighborhood have adequately informed them of the nuances of human controls, manipulations, competitions, and combats. Sociological classrooms and computer rooms must lose the opacity of their walls—even the sense they give of confinement within walls.

Such cult-centric reflections of middle-class prejudice as the terms "social pathology," "delinquency," "crime," "alienation," and "social deviation" dissipate before a realization of the multi-valency of society and of its members, the omnipresence of "deviations" more or less sanctioned by the disparate groups of society. What would our society be without "deviants" who defy pressures toward placid normality and make creative artistic, scientific, or ideological contributions or have the courage to agitate for change? At the same time, it is no accident that police and judiciary officials fill our prisons chiefly with lower-class and minority people and fail to investigate or treat with leniency large-scale swindlers. The class and ethnic biases in the use of intelligence tests are notorious.

As part of all this, social conspiracies—some moral and some immoral, all rooted in group mores—abound in board rooms, social work agencies, faculty clubs, government bureaus, and trade union halls as well as in pool rooms, churches, business sales conferences, prisons, and brothels. Such conspiracies surface as blocks to the upgrading of women and minorities in employment, as bribery scandals, and as many other schemes of political and business corruption. As Frank Church, head of the U.S. Senate Foreign Relations subcommittee on multinational corporations, asserts: "A cancer is eating away at the vitals of western society, and that cancer is corruption . . . in big business as well as in politics"[17] and, it is to be added, at all levels.

All this is not intended to give the impression that something called sociology can be made available to clients or to students without regard for the roles and aims of the client or of any other given public. This problem in recent decades has taken on a new aspect for, as the sociologist Gertrud Lenzer[18] observes, "There are signs to be seen everywhere that mounting social as well as economic pressures are leading to the initiation of large-scale efforts for the systematic planning and managing of the social R&D [research and development] efforts that might leave in their wake a profound restructuring of the social sciences as we know them today. . . . [The] so-called clients of our knowledge have now begun to insist openly upon the true nature and prerogatives of their role in this relationship, namely, that of being the owners of the means and, therefore, of the products of mental production." To what extent can a sociologist maintain her/his autonomy and integrity in the face of such pressures as they expand and have widening repercussions in the discipline? The exploitative, vicious, and authoritarian members of society sometimes can and do use social strategies based upon sociological research to help them gain immediate goals.

For at least four reasons, sociological scientists who wish to continue to function as creative contributors to their discipline do not sell or knowingly give their services to those whose activities they diagnose as antisocial: (1) the credibility of any scientist rests upon integrity, upon a reputation for serving the public interest broadly conceived; (2) a scientist's findings may turn out to be quite contrary to the findings desired by a client; (3) the exploitative want lackeys and want to reserve to themselves the right to

14   Sociology for Whom?

tamper with research methods and conclusions; and (4) research for an antisocial interest may be either self-defeating or socially destructive.

In connection with the latter, think of all the efforts racists have made to inspire "scientific" studies to support their contentions. Even though at times they gain sensational backing from so-called scientists and from racist popular media and politicians (the extent of racist oppression in our society has to be faced frankly), such efforts to make racism "scientifically respectable" are not acceptable to social scientists of integrity. The most spectacular current examples of such case-making are in the struggles over the use of busing as a means of upgrading educational opportunities for Blacks and other minorities and over the use of class-centered and racist I.Q. criteria.[19]

Admittedly, once accurate social knowledge on some subject is available in print, it can conceivably serve the interests of any reader who can accept and understand it and to whom it may be useful. But there are those who cannot accept it. They brush it aside as "fanciful" or "academic," perhaps "soft-headed." It would require them to make too many great changes in their goals and attitudes as well as in their "game plans." Thus many times they refuse to apply it.[20]

Now to tell the rest of the story about my college classmate who became a public relations executive: He never did find a sociologist of integrity willing to spend the time and effort to get him the basic and unbiased social data he thought he needed. He found only those who would "manufacture some fairly plausible propaganda" or who would do some routine fact-gathering. Other than for those services, he had to limp along with what aid he could obtain from indoctrinated "specialists" produced by business administration "finishing schools."

For sociology to contribute to the future of human welfare, I trust that such "operators" as my former classmate continue to have similarly frustrating results. While he was unusual in that he knew what "sociologists" were trying to sell to him, he did not realize that he could not provide the kinds of problems or the broad degree of freedom within which sociologists can do creative work. He was not unusual among hired strategists in that he presumed that an accurate report on a social situation in all its relevant ramifications and discoverable possibilities would enable him to work out a winning scenario for his client.

Sociologists can appropriately and enthusiastically engage in sociological practice for many organizations and purposes dedicated to human service. These are people-oriented projects in education, politics, consumer protection, anti-imperialism, public and private health, propaganda analysis, nonviolent strategies for social change, and other concerns which they may look upon as socially constructive.

To the extent to which sociologists can aid social leaders to be more accurately representative of all the people's needs and desires, they help to make a more livable and longer persistent human society possible. They serve to amplify popular participation in the implementation of the people's own power. To the extent to which sociologists merely try to strengthen control over people-based power for selfish ends either by plutocrats or by their communist or socialist equivalents, they abet the observable trend toward the destruction of our social and physical environment, a course along which so much of the world is now heedlessly traveling.

The following chapters in this book first take a look at the struggle over the control of sociologists' roles in social competition and conflict and at how we can demystify our thinking about human life and living. Why do common social concerns lead to feuds between sociologists and members of such other disciplines as social work? From these discussions, then, what emerge as key issues in sociologies as weapons utilized in social struggles and adaptations? In what senses are manipulable "normal" social behavior patterns the chief stakes in such struggles and adaptations? The concluding chapters then outline strategies useful in stimulating and adapting to social change. They offer a sociological perspective on the chances for human survival. They delve into basic problems related to the nature of professional sociological responsibility. Finally they speculate about the possible future of a humane sociology and thus also of a more humane society.

The wonder and mysteries of human creativity, love, and venturesomeness and the threatening problems of human oppression and of sheer persistence beckon and involve those with the curiosity and courage to be called sociologists. Only those who choose to serve humanity rather than to get caught up in the scramble for all the immediate rewards of finance and status can know the pleasures and lasting rewards of such a pursuit.[21]

notes

[1]Rubin Gotesky, "Social Force, Social Power, and Social Violence," in *Reason and Violence*, S. M. Stanage, ed. (Totowa, N.J.: Littlefield, Adams & Co., 1974), pp. 145-79; pp. 174-75 quoted.

[2]Bertrand Russell, *Power* (New York: Barnes & Noble, 1962), p. 25; see also A. McC. Lee, "Power-Seekers," in *Studies in Leadership*, A. W. Gouldner, ed. (New York: Harper & Brothers, 1950), pp. 667-78.

[3]Havelock Ellis, *The Dance of Life*, 1923 (New York: Modern Library, 1929), p. 336.

[4]Niccolò Machiavelli, "The Prince" (1513), trans. by Luigi Ricci, rev. by E.R.P. Vincent, in *The Prince and the Discourses* (New York: Modern Library, 1940), pp. 1-98; p. 38 quoted.

[5]Walter Lippmann, *A Preface to Politics*, 1913 (Ann Arbor: University of Michigan Press, 1962), pp. 21-22.

[6]Thomas Jefferson, letter to George Logan, 1816, in *Thomas Jefferson on Democracy*, S. K. Padover, ed. (New York: D. Appleton-Century Co., 1939), p. 138.

[7]W. G. Sumner, "What Makes the Rich Richer and the Poor Poorer?" 1887, in Sumner, *Essays*, A. G. Keller, ed., vol. 3 (New Haven: Yale University Press, 1914), pp. 65-77; pp. 74-75 quoted.

[8]W. G. Sumner, "Definitions of Democracy and Plutocracy," 1888, in Sumner, *Essays*, A. G. Keller and M. R. Davie, eds., vol. 2 (New Haven: Yale University Press, 1934), pp. 220-25; pp. 223-25 quoted.

[9]W. G. Sumner, "The Science of Sociology," 1882, in Sumner, *Essays*, A. G. Keller, ed., vol. 4 (New Haven: Yale University Press, 1919), pp. 401-5; pp. 402-3.

[10]Ibid., p. 403.

[11]A. McC. Lee, "To What Is Northern Ireland's Civil War Relevant?" *Holy Cross Quarterly*, vol. 6 (1974), pp. 94-100.

[12]Lincoln Steffens, "Dedication to His Majesty, Nicholas the Second," in *The Struggle for Self-Government* (New York: McClure, Phillips & Co., 1906), pp. v-xxii.

[13]Lincoln Steffens, "Midnight in Russia," 1918, in *The World of Lincoln Steffens*, Ella Winter and Herbert Shapiro, eds. (New York: Hill and Wang, 1962), pp. 34-51; p. 47.

[14]A. McC. Lee, *The Daily Newspaper in America*, 1937 (New York: Octagon Books, 1973), esp. chaps. 10 and 12, and *How to Understand Propaganda* (New York: Rinehart & Co., 1952).

[15]See chapter 3.

[16]A. McC. Lee, "Sociology, clinical," in *Dictionary of Sociology*, H. P. Fairchild, ed. (New York: Philosophical Library, 1944), p. 303; "The Clinical Study of Society," *American Sociological Review*, vol. 20 (1955), pp. 648-53; *Multivalent Man*, 2nd ed. (New York: Braziller, 1970), chap. 22.

[17]Frank Church quoted by J. M. Shevis, "The Web of Corporate Corruption," *New York Teacher Magazine*, November 30, 1975, pp. 15-18, at p. 15.

[18]Gertrude Lenzer, "Policies of the Social Sciences," *Social Research*, vol. 43 (1976), pp. 153–68, at pp. 167–68.

[19]T. F. Pettigrew and R. L. Green, "School Desegregation in Large Cities: A Critique of the Coleman 'White Flight' Thesis," *Harvard Educational Review*, vol. 46 (1976), pp. 1–53; F. H. Levinsohn and B. D. Wright, eds., *School Desegregation: Shadow and Substance* (Chicago: University of Chicago Press, 1976); W. H. Form, Secretary, "Minutes of the Third Meeting of the 1976 ASA Council," *ASA Footnotes*, vol. 4, no. 5 (May 1976), pp. 8–9; Nicholas Wade, "IQ and Heredity: Suspicion of Fraud Beclouds Classic Experiment," *Science*, vol. 194 (1976), pp. 916–19; J. J. Butler, "Inequality in the Military," *American Sociological Review*, vol. 41 (1976), pp. 807–18.

[20]See materials on ignoring of research findings in Mirra Komarovsky, ed., *Sociology and Public Policy: The Case of Presidential Commissions* (New York: Elsevier, 1975).

[21]Parts of this introduction are adapted from A. McC. Lee, "Human Values in a Changing Society," in *Proceedings of the Conference on Planning and Public Policy in the Regional Setting*, F. J. Costa, ed. (Akron, Ohio: University of Akron, October 1975), pp. 54–70; and "Letter to the Editors," *Sociological Practice*, vol. 1, no. 1 (Spring 1976), pp. 7–9.

one

*Sociology
for Whom?*

"Sociology for whom?" is not a new question. It is one that is eternally fresh—as well as controversial. Keen members of each new undergraduate generation rediscover it. When trained sociologists recognize it as a question, it can either trouble them or open up new vistas for intellectual exploration, self awareness, and historical perspective.

The character of any sociological inquiry depends upon by whom it is conceived and for whom, but it also depends upon by whom it is carried out as well as for whom. This means that the credibility, privileges, and opportunities of sociological work constitute a territory over which professional practitioners and, to a lesser extent, politico-economic interest groups contend for influence and control. It also suggests that sociologists, being people, often do not transcend their own habitual intellectual orientations related to their sexual, social class, ethnic, racial, and other identities.

Professional sociologists as individuals and as members of "schools" or like-minded cults struggle to obtain a hold upon more of the discipline. They do this through accepting, elaborating, and pushing an orientation or ideologized version of sociology.

They propagate followers and convince others to accept their group's views as having special claims upon accuracy, authority, and vendibility. They demonstrate to adherents and to potential sources of funds what they believe to be the technical and theoretical serviceability of their sociology. Too many come to believe that "truth" and "scientific objectivity" are things to be packaged for the tastes and services of "important" denizens of the worlds of commerce and politics.

"Respectable" sociological professionals shore up the legitimacy of their kind of sociology through use of existing scientistic symbols, philosophies, and methodologies known to be acceptable to ruling politico-economic-academic elites. Some who differ with the "respectable" attempt to relate to an existing rebel cult. Still others, even fewer in number, take the more difficult path of individual investigation, conceptualization, and expression. Interestingly enough, even though individual ways are the most difficult ones professionally, some of the few taking such a path have out-produced the respectables as well as the rebel cult members. W. G. Sumner,[1] W.E.B. Du Bois,[2] P. A. Sorokin,[3] W. I. Thomas,[4] R. S. and H. M. Lynd,[5] O. C. Cox,[6] R. E. Park,[7] Willard Waller,[8] and C. W. Mills[9] exemplify such creative individuals. Whether working within or outside an academic setting, they are the ones who rise to what heights there are in sociology. The trivialization and neglect to which the works of these scholars have been subjected evidence the ideological censorship and organizational repression that operate so widely in the profession.

To the extent to which politico-economic interest groups find sociology to be of possible use or concern, such groups try to influence the techniques, findings, and credibility of sociologists who cooperate with them as well as of those who do not cooperate.[10] Through dispensing foundation grants and consultation fees as well as through controlling universities of repute and other employers, these groups have impacts that outweigh their actual interest in or use of the discipline. The great foundations and family fortunes "are the masters of much of the country's prestige and status system," points out the newspaper columnist Nicholas von Hoffman. "They hand out the goodies and they don't have any civil service commission to attempt to make the distribution equitable."[11] Or, as the sociologist Irving Louis Horowitz notes:

the "sources of funds for research tend to be exclusively concentrated in the upper classes. . . . This fusion of government and corporate wealth makes it difficult to bring about a countervailing pluralistic system of power with respect to social science funding."[12]

Sociological scientists as such presumably serve only their own curiosity. They contend that in doing so they perform a useful social role. Somehow they try to devote themselves to "science for its own sake." Such a "purely scientific" sociological attitude is often alleged to be a value-neutral or a naïve one. It may yield results ranging in social significance from dilettantish verbal fretworks to radical syntheses of existing social knowledge.

Fellow professionals and academic institutions support or at least put up with the work of sociological scientists because of the useful possibilities they think might come out of such research. Those who subsidize research do not usually intend or even desire critical revisions and other innovations in existing knowledge—unless such changes appear obviously to further the subsidizer's vested interests.[13] The subsidizers invest in props and/or ornaments for the *status quo,* but occasionally the research they sponsor has unforeseen by-products they may not desire. This occurs even though they use project and personnel screenings and other precautions at their disposal to avoid such failures. The fate of such scholars as W. G. Sumner,[14] P. A. Sorokin,[15] and C. Wright Mills[16] in conservative or "establishment" texts testifies to the success of repressive efforts to compensate for mistaken subsidization by prestigious universities. All three were academically canonized only after they were safely dead and their work bowdlerized or rationalized. This was not due to any deliberate plot against such innovators. The sociologist Robert S. Lynd states clearly the nature of the repressive pressures at work as follows:

Liberal democracy has never dared face the fact that industrial capitalism is an intensely coercive form of organization of society that cumulatively constrains men and all of their institutions to work the will of the minority who hold and wield economic power; and that this relentless warping of men's lives and forms of association becomes less and less the result of voluntary decisions by "bad" or "good" men and more and more an impersonal web of coercions dictated by the need to keep "the system" running.[17]

Sociology for Whom? 21

In American society, sociological scientists are almost always limited in their research by professionalism. They are caught up in the practical exigencies and expediencies of careerism. They are therefore inclined to act like robots to meet the mandates of the marketplace. They obligate themselves to the demands of academic administrators, to political and business establishments that operate educational and research organizations, to publishers, and to those who provide subsidies for special projects of research, writing, and consultation. Such relationships do provide opportunities for creative expression to the fortunate few, but they subtly shackle the many. Perhaps the most repressing influence against creativity is the professional's fear of not being looked upon favorably by other professionals, what Lynd referred to as "an impersonal web of coercions dictated by the need to keep 'the system' running."[17]

There is an alternative to the pretense of value neutrality. There is also an alternative to the uncritical acceptance of conventional wisdom in one's discipline and in the larger society. Sociologists can go beyond merely copying or celebrating the latest fashions that sweep across the discipline.[18] They can go beyond such "fads and foibles" as those P. A. Sorokin discussed in his book of that title: "sociological operationalism," "testomania," "quantophrenia," "social physics," and their ilk.[19] They can comprehend the significance of contrasts among sociologies and perceive their own relatedness to the major conflicts over "sociological turf."

Those who become assimilated into the profession usually learn soon enough that variations in sociological orientation are not to be tolerated as equally useful or valid or perhaps even equally "stimulating." All orientations but the one locally called "scientific" are to be taken to be distortions. The "unscientific" sociologies of other schools of thought result at best from misperception and at worst from prejudice or from lack of data. At the same time, the hegemony of the "scientific" sociology locally sanctioned by a given group involves chiefly fidelity to a label, to an associated rhetoric, and to a network of persons. It is not recognized as the meandering trail or contrived pathway to professional status (but not scientific accomplishment) that it might be. It is claimed to be the careerist's highway to sociological success.

From such maneuverings, as Francis Bacon noted as long ago as

1620, "proceed sciences which may be called 'sciences as one would.'" And so, as Bacon continues, their promulgators reject "difficult things from impatience of research, sober things because they narrow hope, the deeper things of nature from superstition, the light of experience from arrogance and pride." In short, he concludes, "Numberless . . . are the ways, and sometimes imperceptible, in which the affections colour and infect the understanding."[20] Among the many groups dedicated to a pretentious scientism, this means an orthodox sociology that can be expressed in abstract symbols and formulas. It is to be tested with computerized and thus highly simplified or even caricatured data—the data so proudly called "hard."

Aspiring students and untenured teachers often perceive and want to discuss the professional intrigues and conspiracies their tenured mentors gloss over with proper academic disquisitions from behind moralistic façades. The mentors make it clear that lack of respect for the local orthodoxy leads inevitably to something called either "the revolving door" or "the tomb of the untenured teacher." Thus too often tenured statistical technicians or abstract theorists dictate to students their dehumanized manner of perceiving and living with society in the same way that welfare and unemployment caseworkers and counselors dictate how those under their control shall live.[21] This common emphasis upon "quantophrenia" and other intellectual rituals turns away from sociology many persons who might develop into sensitive observers and literate recorders and interpreters of social behavior. Unless such persons are fortunate in their selection of a graduate department and of professional guides and sponsors, they may find that their persistent curiosity will be stigmatized as "unprofessional."

Novices quickly grasp the scenario, the ceremonials, the ideas that courtiers to the tenured need to "understand." In too many graduate schools, they come to sense that they are being initiated into a kind of secular religion replete with revered personages, revealed doctrines, rites of passage, and ceremonials performed by the ordained. Early on in most sociology curricula, fledglings come to take for granted that they have only these options: (1) commitment to an orthodoxy, (2) cynical acceptance of an orthodoxy as a cover for a life of hustling, of entrepreneurism, (3) training in enough dehumanized techniques to fit themselves for a bureaucratic slot in government or industry, (4) autonomous creativity accidentally protected by university tenure or supported by independent resources,[22] or (5) some other discipline or way of life. The fledgling's usual choice among these alternatives is not a simple one. That is to say, it is a "mature," a multivalent one. She/he may be idealistically committed to an orthodoxy or to autonomous creativity, but she/he may reserve other options as possible practical steps toward that career goal.

When fledglings are performing in terms of the role expectations of the first three alternatives, they take the position that only the obtuse or immature or malcontented pry too sympathetically into unfashionable doctrines.[23] These future professionals convince their sponsors that they will conform and not naïvely face an individualistic struggle. Like prison trusties, American slave-time "house boys," and Irish "castle Catholics," they indicate that they know their "place" and "proper functions" in a society controlled by others.[24] Some even promise themselves that once they gain the power to act independently they really will be autonomously creative.[25]

In other words, would-be sociological professionals try to have as many career options open to themselves as they feel they safely can. They learn to serve as rationalizers and propagandists for the *status quo* and thus to perform as typical middle-class instruments of social control often with little consciousness of the hypocrisy of their stance or their rigidifying influence upon society. They learn to do "research" that helps elites cope with rebels against the current "social system" and with other problematic deviants from normalcy and stability by buttressing the undefinable and changing myths of that "social system." They learn to promulgate theories and text materials that reassure students, interpreters for the mass media, and sociologists themselves that nothing at all is gained from "radicalism," from anything more disturbing than cosmetic changes in social theory and in society. The "system" is allegedly great, albeit wobbly, cannibalistic, and carelessly destructive of its own increasingly exhausted resources, but sociological jargon can provide "the spurious resolution of problems by naming them."[26]

Thus, despite their idealized goals, many sociologists take on tasks differing notably from what they say they would like to do. Viewing such rhetorical gymnastics of professionals, Francis Bacon observes that "words plainly force and overrule the understanding, and throw into confusion, and lead men away into numerous empty controversies and idle fancies"![27] Or as the belletrist T. H. Middleton observes: How often "the simple translation of a statement in clear English into its counterpart in sociologese will be hailed by the uncritical as creative thinking, whereas it is nothing but highflown tautology"![28] Or consider the statement of a wise modern scientist, Henry Eyring, that individual success in research is associated with "a shedding of any undue veneration for embalmed science of the past." This scientist, a chemist, contends "that if one wanted to become a creative chemist one should certainly learn all he could about chemistry. He should then decide to refuse to believe any of it. From then on he would be free to select on the basis of his own thinking the relevant ideas and reject the irrelevant."[29]

How many nascent sociologists are so encouraged? The advice is at least as pertinent to sociology as it is to chemistry. Sociologists-in-training have to be recognized as people already long conditioned by their environment in a set of social values. They often assume that the first contradictions with their views they perceive are due to their own lack of understanding. If they are sensitive, however, Eyring points out that "glaring inconsistencies . . . bring [their] conceptual world into serious question. The necessary reconstruction is the beginning of a creative process limited only by the expertness of the innovator and the time devoted to it."[30] Those who wish to pursue this process in sociology as well as it has been taken in disciplines less obviously entangled with the social *status quo* might remember characterizations of Charles Darwin and of Albert Einstein. A Darwin biographer tells how young Charles "insisted on seeing, for himself," and he adds: "The more I ponder that boyish skepticism, the more amazing it seems. . . . That is the rarest impulse of the intellect. The human mind almost always prefers two other ways of solving problems—either to ask an authority or to use pure reason."[31] And Einstein "never lost his early childlike sense of awe and wonder."[32] He was either unable or refused to comprehend the obvious in the manner others did. As a student, "he even preferred to suffer punishment rather than to repeat something he had learned by rote without understanding."[33] He, too, had to find things out for himself.

Two former presidents of the largest United States sociological organization commented sharply on this point. In his 1946 presidential address before the American Sociological Society, Carl C. Taylor asserted that it takes young sociologists "from five to ten years to recover from what happens to them in their graduate training." The process, he contended, makes many "incapable of patient, painstaking analyses of living social phenomena."[34] Seventeen years later, Everett C. Hughes in his presidential address before the body said much the same thing: "While professionalizing an activity may raise the competence of some who pursue it by standardizing methods and giving license only to those who meet the standard, it also may limit creative activity, by denying license to some who let their imagination and their observations run far afield and by putting candidates for the license (Ph.D.) so long in a straightjacket that they never move freely again." The problem of sociologists, "in the next few years," Hughes continued, "will be to resist the drive for professionalizing, and to maintain broad tolerance for all who would study societies, no matter what their methods."[35] Now I can do no better than to underline what my two predecessors in that office have said. Fortunate are the undergraduates and graduate students who participate in irresponsible "rap" sessions with stimulating associates, in "radical caucuses" organized within and outside of professional societies, and in the academic seminars of the occasional offbeat professor.

But professionally it is a gamble—albeit an enticing one to free spirits—to look forward to a career devoted to reconstructing social ideas and society. This "heritage of treason," as an interpreter of science, Gerard Piel, calls it, is an "honorable distinction" of the Western intellectual. The Western intellectual, he continues, "has ever been a heretic and political dissenter; the subverter, again and again, of the institutions and arrangements of arbitrary power. His most revolutionary enterprise, by far, is science."[36] It is unfortunate that this legacy of the Enlightenment is so often suppressed or forgotten in the contemporary social sciences.[37]

To be a conformist is indefensible as an intellectual stance for a scientist of any kind, but it is a practical and comfortable characteristic of a profitable professional role pattern. A reputation for originality or cleverness or erudition or critical thought can always be acquired in sociology by offering fresh embroiderings of established "classical theories" or plausible defusings of explosive facts or conceptions. The theories are "classical" and respected because the ruling elites they tend to support or ornament favor those who conform to such ways of thought and action—as evidenced by the career patterns and policy decisions of editorial and employment gatekeepers and other functionaries.

To reinforce this point, one needs only to read an assortment of "standard" introductory texts or the papers typically published in the periodicals of the American Sociological Association. Reading them reminds me of Mark Twain's remark: "You tell me whar a man gits his corn-pone, en I'll tell you what his 'pinions is."[38] The usual excuse for the jargonized superficiality and "quantophrenia" of the ASA periodicals is thus set forth by Lee Freese, an ASA editorial board member, thus: "Any editor is no better than the papers that are submitted to him and the referees on which [sic] he relies to evaluate them." An editor lists as members of her/his editorial board those she/he knows to be dependable or whose published work she/he admires. The previous work of the editor and of the editorial board members thus gives the journal a certain public image. In consequence, as Freese admits, "Certain kinds of papers are not submitted because of a belief that 'this editor will not publish that sort of thing' and, since few thus are submitted, indeed that editor rarely publishes that sort of thing for lack of much opportunity to do so." I have heard the same sentiment expressed many times in the few meetings of the ASA Publications Committee I have attended. He further states that ASA periodicals actually do "provide a mirror for what the sociological profession is doing."[39] Actually those periodicals reflect the ideological coloration dominant among the ASA committee members who select the editors. The "mirror" theory is an expedient rationalization.

The national coordinating editor of the Federal Writers' Project in 1937-1939[40] gives a quite different perspective upon creativity. In that stimulating and relatively permissive program of the depression years, writers blossomed who might otherwise never have had the courage or an incentive to make such an effort. We do not know how much innovative sociology dies aborning for want of an incentive for its creation and of a medium for its publication.

What I am saying is that individuals and groups put sociologies together to represent their own interests and concerns. Their products reflect what they understand human relations to be within the social arrangements—the so-called social structures[41]—they experience or learn about by report. They write out such understandings in the context of the competition and conflict of interest groups within which they live and work. Despite their eagerness to preserve their scientistic status distinct from that of "politicians" and from that of the "mere journalists" of the mass media, they remain quite mindful of issues uppermost in the mass media and thus in the decision-making processes of grant donors and research contractors. That is how they make their applications for support fresh and fashionable! In consequence, we have a variety of sociologies born of diverse definitions of social situations.[42] Many of them bear labels—functional, structural-functional, cultural, ethnomethodological, biosocial, socio-biological, ethological, symbolic-interactionist, Marxist, neo-positivist, humanist—to mention only certain prominent ones.

This diversity of sociologies—some fairly distinct, some modest variations or translations of others—presents disparate definitions of terms, contrasting methodologies, and assorted theories that may or may not appear to deal with the same genus *homo sapiens* considered socially. Even dehumanized scientists—if there should really be any such—and their computers could not develop a single sociology that would transcend group concerns and values and still be useful as a social instrument. Dehumanized abstractions in social theory lack a sufficient sense of nearness to human affairs, sufficient focus, to yield a comprehension of actual social processes. To the extent that sociologists have approached such an "ideal" sociology they have contributed chiefly to the complexities of the rhetorical and statistical games so many academicians and other researchers now play. These games become pretentious substitutes for trying to perceive and understand both social ideas about the nature of social "reality" and whatever lies behind or stimulates those ideas.

Can sociologists—as so many claim to be—have it both ways? Can there be scientists who may be trusted as reasonably dependable sources for accurate data and for useful theories when at the same time they are professional careerists organizing to raise their status and income in the commercial scramble within society? Vernon Parrington, a historian of literature, spoke of "the imperious subjection of the individual to a standardizing order, the stripping away of the slack frontier freedoms in the routine of the factory, the substitution of the ideal of plutocracy for the ideal of Jacksonian democracy."[43] How many sociological scientists can somehow withstand that pressure and maintain their creative drive?

The basic issue is not at all unique to sociologists. It is the basic issue of freedom to perceive, to express, to create, to question, to promulgate, whether as an artist or as a scientist. The basic issue is whether or not so many sociologists must follow the same hypocritical career pattern as have many clergymen, lawyers, merchants, educators, labor union officers, and manufacturers. Must sociologists use the moral or ethical pretensions of sociology as a cloak or a mask for their role in a social conspiracy to maintain the *status quo*? Must sociologists share in the control and manipulation of the masses by appearing to practice a humanity-serving discipline while actually serving—whether they know it or not—the narrow interests of society's ruling elites? In other words, to what extent are sociologists part of a culturally enslaved instrument of exploitative control and of technocratic manipulation? As Henry David Thoreau characterized such a relationship, slavery "exists wherever men are bought and sold, wherever a man allows himself to be made a mere thing or a tool, and surrenders his inalienable rights of reason and conscience. Indeed, this slavery is more complete than that which enslaves the body alone."[44]

For sociologists the issue of autonomy raises a host of related questions, such as: How freely can dissident and critical sociologists, including those working outside the mainstream of current institutionalized sociology, gain access to the principal media of communication in the discipline? These media are controlled by formal and visible as well as by informal and invisible networks of professional influence and persuasion. When we learn this, why do so many of us continue to attribute so much *intellectual* distinction to the formality of publication in an allegedly prestigious medium? After all, there are a great many—at least some two hundred—periodicals of a substantial sort now available to sociologists for serious contributions.

Gregor Johann Mendel[45] (1822–1884) is only one of many whose outstanding contributions to physical, biological, and behavioral science first appeared in an obscure periodical. That is one reason why the editors of the principal science abstracting services[46]—including Leo P. Chall[47] of *Sociological Abstracts*—insist upon being inclusive rather than selective of the periodicals and papers of the discipline they cover. Fortunately for the development of sociology as a humanity-enhancing discipline, regional, state, university, and independent journals are multiplying in number in spite of poor financial prospects.

What biases are typically prevalent among the profession's gatekeepers to academic degrees, to employment, to promotion, to distribution of acclaim, grants, and prizes, to honorific lectureships, and to other kinds of professional preferment? Why do people so often fail to see those biases behind institutional façades? What do these and other transmitters of influence do to sociologists as scientists and even more importantly to sociologists as human beings? To what extent and by what standards do they select the imaginative, the excellent, or the mediocre, the predictable? To what degree do they blunt or sharpen, muffle or free, distort or extend the development of sociology as a field of inquiry? To what degree do they recognize the social utility of sociology as a human instrument and not merely as an instrument for manipulative elites?

To complicate even further the changing patchwork proclaimed in academic catalogs and professional society labels to be a single discipline, sociologists in trying to be both scientists and professionals intertwine conflicting conceptions of science and professionalism. It is little wonder that a variety of positivistic cults are offered as an attractive basis for intellectual comfort and practical success. Such cultists claim that they are busily constructing "the" single, all-purpose, "scientific" sociology. This is to be a sociology comparable in comprehensiveness and in systematization to an ideally fabricated, verifiable physical or biological science.[48] Albeit man-created, this would be a sociology so reflective of "nature" as to be beyond human manipulation, considerations of human values, and wishful thinking.[49] On the contrary, to

30   Sociology for Whom?

judge from the healthy controversies still raging in physics and biology, these disciplines themselves have not reached such a finished stage of development. They include among their practitioners skeptics like the thoughtful chemist quoted, and they thus continue to unfold and to change. They still bear traces of their human creators, of their sponsors, and of their social settings.[50]

The questions raised about trying to be both a scientist and a professional suggest that ideological struggle, manipulation, and rationalization or in other words politicization are integral parts of a mixed career. They also point to the operation of the scientist's own attitudinal multivalency, that complex product of her/his assimilation into a variety of contrasting social groups and social roles.[51] In public pronouncements, she/he may reject vehemently the notion that her/his work cannot help but be part of politico-economic and other social processes. Personal politicization and even more the political maneuvers of others are profane, vulgar, anti-intellectual. Years of deprivation and discipline as a neophyte in a cult are required to obtain certification and to build personal relations that lead to prestige in a science. Any other procedure is said to undermine the very bases of the scientist's psychological and professional integrity, security, and autonomy. Political maneuvers substitute something other than "rational" criteria for policymaking decisions as to academic admissions, employment, upgrading of status, certification, publication, subsidization of study and research, and other professional facilitations and recognitions. Such maneuvers loom as attempts to change or even to brush aside the rules of the intellectual's traditional life plan and to allot to others rewards for which she or he sacrificed so much. And yet, few who gain recognition in sociology as in other sciences do not join in what they look upon as appropriate political procedures.

To those who have taken active part in a variety of social organizations, differences from the academic are likely to have been experienced as more those of superficialities than of basic interests and concerns. Moral, legal, and technical frameworks vary to fit tasks peculiar to a given organization or discipline, but within most of the status groups of a given social class, in-group mores of mutual understanding and operation, of competition and cooperation are fairly well set for a given time and place and are not too dissimilar. Exploitations of financial and/or political controls for personal and group gains pervade almost all types of social organization in our society. When something gives way, it is rarely in replacement or reorganization of obvious aspects such as moral façade and rhetorical symbols. It is not in the mores of operation of groups that continue to be powerful. It is chiefly in the rationalized reinterpretation of moral symbols that change takes place. Only groups consisting of offbeat marginals of whatever class deviate notably from the slightly contrasting mores typical of groups of entrepreneurs, bureaucrats, and technicians, whether of the academic or of some other middle-class field.[52]

Especially in the social sciences, politicization distracts attention from the pronouncements of experts possessing only academic status and influence. It often places academicians at a disadvantage in competition for authority with spokesmen openly identified with special interests. Whether within or outside the academies, those with access to kinds of social power other than the academic overshadow the influence of those who exhibit mere academic accomplishment as a basis for their authority. A researcher is thus most often valued not for her/his intellectual impact upon a discipline but for the hundreds of thousands of dollars she/he attracts in the form of research grants or contracts, by the volume of consultantships and the power they imply, and by appointments to corporate boards or governmental commissions.[53]

Struggling sociologists pull in many directions. The numerous groups in all sorts of departments who constitute aggressive ideological cults or what the sociologist Willard Waller called "the compacts of incompetents"[54] try to erect bulwarks against what they often term "uncollegial behavior" as well as against administrative pressures and incursions and against interdepartmental efforts at building empires. "Uncollegial behavior" might be anything from a disagreeable personality to ideological nonconformism or to notable virtuosity in teaching, research, community work, or other professional activities. Those bulwarks include academic tenure and grievance procedures often bolstered by trade-unionism. Such recourses do protect the jobs of the vindictive and the vegetative, but they can also provide some of the freedom we have to produce controversial innovations. Few enough of the creative and disputatious who manage to transcend graduate school indoctrination, even exploitation, survive the years of untenured courtiership that precede the magical "continuing contract" of the tenured and eventually the full professorship.

The current contraction of teaching and research budgets now makes politicization a most pressing consideration for all concerned with the future of higher education. This contraction is pushing many sociologists to become aggressively defensive about their claims to reputable and legitimate authority. They are less secure concerning the viability of our discipline. Thus they lean all the more on the purloined sham of legitimacy provided by scientism and by investigative assignments serving the special interests of profit and power.

Traditionally, the academic pattern idealized the individualistic artisan-researcher who spent her/his spare time and summers (perhaps aided now and then by small grants for expenses) on projects designed to strengthen the discipline. These projects included both personal research and the encouragement of graduate students to write autonomous dissertations. For some time now, this ideal has been overshadowed by that of the big-time grantsperson who is excused from much or all teaching responsibilities in order to direct the work of junior staff assistants and of graduate students who are given the "opportunity" to use part of a subsidized group project as a Ph.D. dissertation.

But now grantspersonship is giving way more and more to contractspersonship! Administrators of funds for "research" grants often worry about the "irresponsibility" of academic research institutes or individual grantees. Such grantees are said sometimes to be too free-wheeling, too much interested in combining a gain in academic prestige with work on a grantor's problem. What might be produced often cannot be predicted clearly enough. So the academic "research" institute or individual grantee—as well as the non-academic—may now have to become more precisely exploitable in order to survive these austere times. "Research" may become even more a routinized factory situation and provide even less opportunity for exploratory work. And what will the dissertation writers whom such a contract subsidizes and controls know about autonomous, curious, probing investigation? As an official of the U.S. Department of Health, Education, and Welfare, Keith Baker, bluntly sums up the matter:

The academician must learn to live with contracts if he wants the applied research dollar. . . . Compared to a grant, a contract gives the agency more control over the research. . . . Further, if the investigator fails to do what is specified in the statement of work the government is not obliged to pay him.[55]

In other words, when the sociologist agrees to be bought by such a contract, she or he must stay bought and produce the agreed results—or else! No wonder the sociological "research" institutes have produced more and more complicated methodological ploys and gimmicks.[56]

A physical scientist, H. T. Hudson, outlines the academic competition scenario that now emerges: "The most dangerous act a nontenured faculty member can perform is to receive recognition as an outstanding teacher. Tenured faculty who devote too much time to the students are denied salary increments and promotion." He contends:

Merit is equated solely with money in grants, and publications which result from activity that does not generate overhead [payments for expenses to the institution] is criticized. The value of publication to the scientific or intellectual community is of little consequence.

This is expecially the case in the privately controlled "research" universities.

This scientist is replying to accusations of students cheating in such ways as using cribs for examinations and purchasing term papers and even dissertations. He asserts: "The student is not to blame. His teachers spend their time trying to second-guess who will give money for what. In the classroom, the faculty are preoccupied with survival problems." He insists that we not "blame the student. He is only modeling."[57]

The traditional academic pattern—to the lessening though still dominant extent that it exists— not only gives us dilettantes, tired job holders, and kindly parent substitutes; it also provides us with a wealth of the products of artisan scientists and artists. Some of those artisans in sociology—like W. I. Thomas[58] and Thorstein Veblen[59]—cared much more for their intellectual preoccupation than they did for the meeting of the requirements of an academic or other position's formalities. Some grantspeople have also created impressive products—as in the cases of the Middletown projects of Helen M. and Robert S. Lynd[60]—so long as they remained artisan scientists and did not become mere entrepreneurs. As sociologist

Florian Znaniecki puts it: "All new developments in the history of knowledge have been due to those scientists who did more in their social roles than their circles wanted and expected them to do."[61]

The professional's concern with career-insurance gives advantage not only to the merely conservative but also to the stodgy. It is increasingly difficult now to attract the experimentally minded, the perceptive, and the literate into sociology. Once they are enticed, it becomes more and more unlikely that they will obtain academic positions and remain in the discipline.

How many free intellectual spirits will devote their lives to working on controlled assignments, to using hackneyed scientistic analogies as standards not at all necessarily applicable to sociology, and to conforming to "establishment" social science terms, theories, and procedures? As the social psychologist, A. H. Maslow, observes:

One must sometimes talk to one's graduate students in the social and psychological sciences as if they were going off to war. One must speak of bravery, of morals and ethics, of strategy and tactics. The psychological or social scientist must *fight* to bring truth about the hot subjects.[62]

That is the kind of orientation a sociological teacher and researcher requires. If continuing tenure becomes even more difficult to obtain or is eliminated, how many will survive as creative people for endless years in the toadying world of short-term appointments and of contract pandering?

To take another perspective on some of the critical judgments outlined, let me ask: How can sociology survive and thrive unless sociologists see themselves as part of the social and intellectual struggles to make possible more satisfying human life and living for our grandchildren? Consider how much sociologists now owe to suggestions and criticisms from members of other disciplines. Merely mentioning the names of Marx and Freud is enough without adding those of outstanding psychologists, cultural anthropologists, historians, economists, political scientists, human geographers, journalists, belletrists, and philosophers. Sociologists cannot be persons apart from the human condition they presumably seek to understand. They commingle with the other specialists in the general intellectual and cultural stream. Social scientists might well make special pleas for intellectualism in general and for sociology in particular so that separately and together they might bring to humanity broad-ranging, daring, adapting, and varying instruments useful in search, discovery, problem solving, model building, and hypothesis construction and testing as well as in enlightening and easing the social struggle.[63]

Basically, then, the problem of "Sociology for whom?" can be perceived as the struggle of would-be sociologists—creative and otherwise—to function somehow in a necessarily institutionalized discipline. An institutionalized discipline is one that is bureaucratized, served chiefly by routine technicians, and subject to entrepreneurial manipulation. It may possibly be kept alive and fresh in spite of the foregoing by participants who are questioning, dissenting, and creative.

The excuse for the existence of sociologists is not simply the maintenance of academic employment and research funding. The chief excuse is the answering of the question, "Sociology for whom?" in this manner: Sociology for the service of humanity. This answer refers to the need to develop knowledge of direct service to all classes of people as citizens, as consumers, and as neighbors. This means knowledge of social behavior that can and will be communicated by its developers through all appropriate media to those who can best use it. It includes studies of ways in which people can protect themselves from undesirable manipulation by those in positions of power, of how to achieve more livable homes and communities, of constructive alternatives to family, civil, and international violence, and of much more.

In serving humanity, sociologists act principally as critics, demystifiers, reporters, and clarifiers. They review critically the folk wisdom and other theories by which people try to live. In doing so, they strip away some of the outworn clutter of fictions about life and living that make the human lot even more difficult than it might be. Then they try to report more accurate information about the changing social scene and with it to help clarify ways of understanding human relations and of coping with personal and social problems.[64]

notes

[1] M. R. Davie, *William Graham Sumner* (New York: Thomas Y. Crowell Co., 1963).
[2] H. L. Moon, ed., *The Emerging Thought of W.E.B. Du Bois* (New York: Simon and Schuster, 1972).

36   Sociology for Whom?

[3]F. R. Cowell, *Values in Human Society: The Contributions of Pitirim A. Sorokin to Sociology* (Boston: Porter Sargent, 1970).

[4]H. E. Barnes, "William Isaac Thomas," in *An Introduction to the History of Sociology*, Barnes, ed. (Chicago: University of Chicago Press, 1948), chap. 40; Kimball Young, "The Contribution of William Isaac Thomas to Sociology," *Sociology and Social Research*, vol. 47 (1962-1963), pp. 3-24, 123-37, 251-72, 381-97.

[5]R. S. and H. M. Lynd, *Middletown* and *Middletown in Transition* (New York: Harcourt, Brace, 1929, 1937); R. S. Lynd, *Knowledge for What?* (Princeton: Princeton University Press, 1939).

[6]O. C. Cox, *Caste, Class and Race* (Garden City, N.Y.: Doubleday, 1948) and *Race Relations* (Detroit: Wayne State University Press, 1976); E. E. Harris, "Oliver C. Cox," and R. L. Goldstein, "Another Memory of Oliver C. Cox," *ASA Footnotes*, vol. 3, no. 8 (November 1975), p. 3.

[7]R. E. Park, *Race and Culture, Human Communities,* and *Society* (Glencoe, Ill.: Free Press, 1950, 1952, 1955).

[8]Willard Waller, *On the Family, Education and War,* ed. with intro. by W. J. Goode, F. F. Furstenberg, Jr., and L. R. Mitchell (Chicago: University of Chicago Press, 1970).

[9]C. W. Mills, *Power, Politics and People,* ed. with an intro. by I. L. Horowitz (New York: Oxford University Press, 1963).

[10]T. F. Pettigrew and R. L. Green, "School Desegregation in Large Cities: A Critique of the Coleman 'White Flight' Thesis," *Harvard Educational Review*, vol. 46 (1976), pp. 1-53; see also the cases of Cyril Burt and of P. J. Nyden in chap. 8 below.

[11]Nicholas von Hoffman, editorial column, *Washington* (D.C.) *Post* and other newspapers, October 23, 1975; cf. Ferdinand Lundberg, *The Rich and the Super-Rich* and *The Rockefeller Syndrome* (New York: Lyle Stuart, 1968, 1975).

[12]I. L. Horowitz, *Professing Sociology* (Chicago: Aldine, 1968), p. 271; cf. P. F. Lazarsfeld, "Reflections on Business," *American Journal of Sociology*, vol. 65 (1959-1960), pp. 1-31.

[13]D. C. Blaisdell, *Economic Power and Political Pressures,* Temporary National Economic Committee Monograph No. 26 (Washington: Government Printing Office, 1941), pp. 154-56; John Dewey, "Liberating the Social Scientist," *Commentary*, vol. 4 (1947), pp. 378-85; R. S. Lynd, "The Science of Inhuman Relations," *New Republic*, August 27, 1949, pp. 22-25; I. L. Horowitz, *Professing Sociology,* op. cit., chaps. 10, 11, 14; C. W. Mills, *The Sociological Imagination* (New York: Oxford University Press, 1959), chaps. 4 and 5.

[14]A. G. Keller, *Reminiscences (Mainly Personal) of William Graham Sumner* (New Haven: Yale University Press, 1933); B. J. Stern, "William Graham Sumner," *Encyclopaedia of the Social Sciences*, vol. 14 (1934), pp. 463-64.

[15]P. J. Allen, *Pitirim A. Sorokin in Review* (Durham, N.C.: Duke University Press, 1963); F. R. Cowell, *Values in Human Society* (Boston: Porter Sargent, 1970); Talcott Parsons, *Structure of Social Action* (New York: McGraw-Hill, 1937), pp. 552-53, 576, 631-33, 680.

[16]G. W. Domhoff and H. B. Ballard, eds., *C. Wright Mills and the Power Elite* (Boston: Beacon Press, 1968); I. L. Horowitz, "Introduction," to C. W. Mills, *Power, Politics and People,* Horowitz, ed. (New York: Oxford University Press, 1963), pp. 1-20.

[17]R. S. Lynd, "Foreword," to R. A. Brady, *Business as a System of Power* (New York: Columbia University Press, 1943), pp. vii-xviii; p. xii quoted.

[18]Irwin Sperber, *Fashions in Science* (Ph.D. dissertation, University of California at Berkeley, 1975).

[19]P. A. Sorokin, *Fads and Foibles in Modern Sociology and Related Sciences* (Chicago: Regnery, 1956).

[20]Francis Bacon, "Magna Instauratio," 1620, in *Essays, Advancement of Learning, New Atlantis, and Other Pieces*, R. F. Jones, ed. (New York: Odyssey, 1937), pp. 237–363; p. 283 quoted.

[21]Glenn Jacobs, ed., *The Participant Observer* (New York: George Braziller, 1970), chap. 11; Frederick Wiseman, "Welfare" (film) (Boston: Zipporah Films, 1975).

[22]Florian Znaniecki, *The Social Role of the Man of Knowledge* (New York: Columbia University Press, 1940), chap. 4.

[23]Edward Shils, "The Calling of Sociology," in *Theories of Society*, Talcott Parsons *et al.*, eds. (New York: Free Press, 1961), pp. 1405–48; esp. pp. 1421–24.

[24]A. McC. Lee, *Toward Humanist Sociology* (Englewood Cliffs, N. J.: Prentice-Hall, 1973), p. 12.

[25]Sinclair Lewis, *Arrowsmith* (1925) and introduction by William Soskin (New York: Modern Library, 1933), pp. v–x.

[26]T. H. Middleton, "Light Refractions: Name Your Problem," *Saturday Review*, April 17, 1976, p. 58; cf. P. A. Sorokin, *Fads and Foibles in Modern Sociology and Related Sciences*, chap. 2.

[27]Francis Bacon, op. cit., p. 280.

[28]T. H. Middleton, op. cit.; cf. Joseph Gusfield, "The Literary Rhetoric of Science," *American Sociological Review*, vol. 41 (1976), pp. 16–34.

[29]Henry Eyring, "Scientific Creativity," in *Creativity and Its Cultivation*, H. H. Anderson, ed. (New York: Harper, 1959), pp. 1–11; p. 10, and as summarized by Anderson, p. 125.

[30]Eyring, op. cit., p. 1.

[31]C. H. Ward, *Charles Darwin* (Indianapolis: Bobbs-Merrill, 1927), p. 13.

[32]Banesh Hoffman with Helen Dukas, *Albert Einstein Creator and Rebel* (London: Hart-Davis, MacGibbon, 1972), p. 18.

[33]Philipp Frank, *Einstein*, trans. by George Rosen, Shuichi Kusaka, ed. (New York: Alfred A. Knopf, 1947), p. 16.

[34]C. C. Taylor, "Sociology and Common Sense," *American Sociological Review*, vol. 12 (1947), pp. 1–9; p. 8 quoted.

[35]E. C. Hughes, "Race Relations and the Sociological Imagination," *American Sociological Review*, vol. 28 (1963), pp. 879–90; p. 890 quoted.

[36]Gerard Piel, "The Treason of the Clerks," *Proceedings of the American Philosophical Society*, vol. 109 (1965), pp. 259–66; p. 259 quoted.

[37]H. J. Muller, *The Uses of the Past* (New York: Oxford University Press, 1952), pp. 277–87.

[38]Mark Twain (S. L. Clemens), "Corn-Pone Opinions," 1900, pp. 214–18 in *Mark Twain & the Three R's*, Maxwell Geismar, ed. (Indianapolis: Bobbs-Merrill, 1973), p. 214.

[39]Lee Freese, "ASA Editors Not Paradigm Enforcers: Mirror Work of Profession," *ASA Footnotes*, vol. 3, no. 6 (August 1975), p. 2; cf. [Morris Zelditch, Jr.] "Items," *American Sociological Review*, vol. 41 (1976), pp. 924, 1094.

[40]Jerre Mangione, *The Dream and the Deal* (New York: Little, Brown, 1972).

[41]A. McC. Lee, *Multivalent Man*, new ed. (New York: George Braziller, 1970), chap. 14.

[42]H. W. Odum, *American Sociology* (New York: Longmans, Green, 1951), pp. 442–44; Florian Znaniecki, *Cultural Sciences* (Urbana: University of Illinois Press, 1952), p. 243.

[43]Vernon Parrington, *Main Currents in American Thought* (New York: Harcourt, Brace, 1930), vol. 3, p. 189.

[44]H. D. Thoreau, *Journal*, 1860, Bradford Torrey, ed. (New York: AMS Press, 1968), vol. 14, p. 292.

[45]G. J. Mendel, "Experiments in Plant Hybridization," 1866, trans. by William Bateson, in Bateson, *Mendel's Principles of Heredity* (Cambridge: University Press, 1930), pp. 335-79.

[46]R. J. Rowlett, Jr., "Key to World's Chemical Knowledge," *Chemistry*, vol. 41 (1968), pp. 12-17; D. B. Baker, "Chemical Abstracts Service," *Encyclopedia of Library and Information Service*, vol. 2 (1969), pp. 479-99; P. V. Parkins, "Bioscience Information Service of Biological Abstracts," *Encyclopedia of Library and Information Science*, vol. 2 (1969), pp. 603-21; Parkins and H. E. Kennedy, "Secondary Information Services," *Annual Review of Information Science and Technology*, vol. 6 (1971), pp. 247-75.

[47]L. P. Chall, ed., *Sociological Abstracts*, vols. 1-(1953-).

[48]G. A. Lundberg, *Can Science Save Us?* 2nd ed. (Longmans, Green, 1961), chap. 7.

[49]P. M. Hauser, "The Chaotic Society," *American Sociological Review*, vol. 34 (1969), pp. 1-18; cf. J. D. Colfax, "Knowledge for Whom?" *Sociological Inquiry*, vol. 40 (1970), pp. 73-84.

[50]C. P. C. Flynn, "Quantification: No Substitute for Insight," *ASA Footnotes*, vol. 3, no. 4 (April 1975), pp. 2-3.

[51]A. McC. Lee, *Multivalent Man*, new ed. (New York: Braziller, 1970).

[52]Ibid., chaps. 15-16; Lee, *Toward Humanist Sociology* (Englewood Cliffs, N. J.: Prentice-Hall, 1973), chap. 7.

[53]P. F. Lazarsfeld, "The Sociology of Empirical Social Research," *American Sociological Review*, vol. 27 (1962), pp. 757-67; Howard Hillman and Karin Ararbanel, *The Art of Winning Foundation Grants* (New York: Vanguard, 1975); Keith Baker, "A New Gamesmanship," *American Sociologist*, vol. 10 (1975), pp. 206-19.

[54]Willard Waller quoted by A. McC. Lee, *Multivalent Man*, p. 317.

[55]Keith Baker, op. cit., p. 211.

[56]I. L. Horowitz, *Professing Sociology* (Chicago: Aldine Publishing Co., 1968), chaps. 11, 14.

[57]H. T. Hudson, "Paper Mills and Campus Ethics," *Science*, vol. 193 (1976), p. 274.

[58]W. I. Thomas, *Social Behavior and Personality*, ed. by E. H. Volkart (New York: Social Science Research Council, 1951); Herbert Blumer, *An Appraisal of Thomas and Znaniecki's The Polish Peasant in Europe and America* (New York: Social Science Research Council, 1946).

[59]Thorstein Veblen, *The Higher Education in America* (New York: Huebsch, 1918); C. W. Mills, "Introduction," in Veblen, *The Theory of the Leisure Class* (New York: Mentor, 1953), pp. vi-xix; D. F. Dowd, ed., *Thorstein Veblen* (Ithaca, N.Y.: Cornell University Press, 1958).

[60]R. S. and H. M. Lynd, *Middletown* and *Middletown in Transition* (New York: Harcourt, Brace, 1929, 1937).

[61]Florian Znaniecki, *The Social Role of the Man of Knowledge* (New York: Columbia University Press, 1940), p. 164.

[62]A. H. Maslow, *The Psychology of Science* (New York: Harper & Row, 1966), p. 17.

[63]C. W. Mills, *The Sociological Imagination* (New York: Oxford University Press, 1959), pp. 195-226; S. M. Miller, "Prospects: The Applied Sociology of the Inner City," in *Applied Sociology*, A. W. Gouldner and S. M. Miller, eds. (New York: Free Press, 1965), pp. 441-56; A. McC. Lee, "On Context and Relevance," in *The Participant Observer*, Glenn Jacobs, ed. (New York: Braziller, 1970), pp. 3-16; E. B. and A. McC. Lee, "The Society for the Study of Social Problems: Visions of Its Founders," *SSSP Newsletter*, vol. 5 (1973-74), pp. 2-5, and "The Society for the

Study of Social Problems: Parental Recollections and Hopes," *Social Problems,* vol. 24 (1976–77), pp. 4–14.

[64]Chapter adapted and amplified from 1976 presidential address August 30 before American Sociological Association, New York, N. Y., published with the same title in *American Sociological Review,* vol. 41 (1976), pp. 925–36.

two

Demystifying Theories about Human Life and Living

Fresh and vivid experiences tend to unsettle pre-existing beliefs and behavior patterns, at least to place them in new perspectives. Under a variety of labels, many academic disciplines discuss the implications of such experiences and especially their contribution to the demystification of ideas about human life and living.

Such experiences give rise to philosophies termed sophist and humanist. Historians perceive these influences especially in frontier situations. Anthropologists find that such experiences give rise to culture shock and thus contribute to culture change. Psychiatrists discover how such unanticipated experiences require them to develop and learn from their patients through perceptive listening and empathy. And sociologists approach fresh and vivid experiences through such studies as those of marginal or peripheral or deviant groups, through using life-history and participant observation data, and through making field-clinical studies of social behavior.

A significant similarity of all these studies of fresh and vivid experiences lies in the manner in which they are all efforts to relate the immediate, specific, and personal to existing theory even though such theory may be distant and abstract. These studies thus may throw traditional theories into contrast with current thought and behavior and also with the quite different ideas traditional among various other groups. Social scientists thus discover, to quote the sociologist George Simpson, that "personal experiences can themselves open up areas for field research undreamed of by wholly 'objective' behaviorism."[1] Social scientists thus can become, he adds, "critics of the very social process which tries to make them merely technicians."[2]

When this demystifying impact can be constructively absorbed, it moves individuals away from—even tears them out of—a cultural context. It furnishes opportunities to re-examine value commitments, ways of viewing oneself and others, and ways of behaving. The philosopher B.A.G. Fuller notes that it draws attention "to the relative, unstable and conflicting character of political institutions, social usages, religious beliefs and even moral standards and ideals."[3] It makes for greater creativity, rebelliousness, and cosmopolitanism—when it is constructively absorbed. It can stimulate others to cynicism or irresponsible antisocial acts.

One of the fragments remaining from the extensive writings of Protagoras of Abdera is often said to encapsulate the fifth century B.C. humanist and sophist viewpoint: "Man is the measure of all things, of the existence of things that are, and of the nonexistence of things that are not."[4] The first clause of this statement in particular has been echoed down through the ages by humanists as well as by their critics. Because of the contrast of this humanism with his own commitment to essences and absolutes, Plato quotes Socrates as speaking satirically about sophists, who, he says, argue out of the "superfluity of their wits."[5] Plato also has Socrates caustically pontificate that for Protagoras—secretly, among his own disciples only and not in statements "to the common herd"— "all things are said to be relative . . . out of motion and change and admixture all things are becoming relatively to one another, which 'becoming' is by us incorrectly called being, but is really becoming, for nothing ever is, but all things are becoming."[6] This Platonic sneering, this anti-intellectualism, is a sample of the innuendoes with which elitist philosophers have tried to destroy the teachings of such sophists as Protagoras, the one who, according to the historian Gilbert Murray, "gave a philosophic basis to [Periclean] Democracy,"[7] and his successors.

Who were these people? Those called sophists, the "wise ones," began coming to Athens some five centuries before the Christian era and then later to Alexandria, chiefly from the Greek frontiers in Ionia (Asia Minor) and Magna Graecia (South Italy). Greek settlers on those frontiers had been adventurers and fugitives from wars against invaders of Greece. Generations there had had culture-stripping and culture-building experiences in their relations with diverse tribes. They had had direct participation in social change—in other words, field-clinical experiences with social and cultural reorganization—thrust upon them. This gave to at least a few of them a creative marginality in their intellectual stances which became identified as "sophism," especially when they went to the great centers of commerce and of learning. Theirs was intelligence colored by culture shock, a reflection of perceptive listening to others from quite different backgrounds. They had involved themselves in expanding trade and colonization and in diverse personal intimacies that included exogamy. For them, traditional tribal values had been mediated or replaced by more cosmopolitan interpersonal and community identifications.

The main mission of the sophists, as it appears to Gilbert Murray, "was to teach, to clear up the mind of Greece, to put an end to bad myths and unproven cosmogenies, to turn thought into fruitful paths. . . . The whole movement was moral as well as intellectual, and was singularly free from . . . corruption and lawlessness."[8] According to the psychologist Havelock Ellis, their "monition to us [is] that we cannot to the measurement of life apply our instruments of precision, and cut life down to their graduated marks." Such instruments have "their immensely valuable uses, but it is strictly as instruments and not as ends of living or criteria of the worth of life."[9] Toward the gods, the sophists could be at least agnostic. As Protagoras put it, "With regard to the gods I cannot feel sure either that they are or that they are not, nor what they are like in figure; for there are many things that hinder sure knowledge, the obscurity of the subject and the shortness of human life."[10]

Protagoras's ideas were as outrageous to the Platonists as they have been ever since to anxious seekers after dependable bases for authority upon which to erect controlling and controllable ideologies. As the social historian Harry Elmer Barnes concludes, "The truly modern attitude towards most questions singularly resembles the general point of view of the Sophists. It has taken humanity well over two thousand years to recover from the influence of post-Sophistic thought and to get back into this salutary frame of mind."[11] Sophist ideas, such as those mentioned, contain the main thrusts of humanizing experiences, the experiences that have from time to time in human history contributed invigorating and demystifying impacts upon social thought.

During its long subsequent history in social thought, humanism as a term succeeding sophism has shared the following characteristics with those used to label other major generalities: It is shifty, and it is sticky. It has had many definitions. It has been alleged to adhere to almost all sorts of other ideas, and it has also been shown to be opposed to each of them—whatever they were. These problems of the term can best be seen by realizing that humanism most accurately labels not a body of doctrine but a kind of mind-changing social experience. It is a recurrent ingredient in social movements, not a specific idea or social philosophy.[12]

Basic to this sense of humanism as humanizing social experience are one-to-one confrontations and then friendships among quite different sorts of people. This experience depends upon those relations being continuing enough and egalitarian enough to result in the development of a degree of efficiency in communication and at the same time of a reciprocated ability to empathize. Granted such relatively intimate relations, this type of friendly experience tends to dissipate notions of personal and group superiority. It opens new perspectives on human talent and worth. It even reveals to those who are patient the human bases upon which mankind fumblingly strives to develop the beginnings of participatory democracy.

Humanism has figured in a wide range of religious, political, and academic movements. As such, it has been identified with atheism, capitalism (especially of the *laissez-faire* brand), classicism, communism, democracy, egalitarianism, populism, naturalism, positivism, pragmatism, relativism, science, scientism, socialism, statism, symbolic-interactionism,[13] and supernaturalism, including versions of ancient paganisms, Hinduism, Buddhism, Judaism, Roman Catholicism, Protestantism, and Mohammedanism. It has also been rationalized as being opposed to each of these. It has served as an ingredient in movements against each.

And these terms do not at all suggest all of humanism's ideological and social associations.

That humanism has had so many adventures is a tribute to the recurring human inclination to suspect or to perceive that the problems of life are actually human responsibilities—for better or for worse and whether or not they can be solved. This recurring tendency, at the same time, has preoccupied generations of theorizers who have tried to anaesthetize the humanistically-tempted into depending rather upon either a supernatural agency or, as that imagery has grown pale, upon an all-dominating natural order far beyond human control or manipulation.

When defined as simply and as etymologically as possible, humanism refers to "thought or action in which human interests, values, and dignity are taken to be of primary importance."[14] It is thus a preoccupation with conditions and problems most relevant, significant, and important to human beings. It is concerned primarily with individuals, with human expression and creativity, with human society and socializing, and with people's ability to persist and to flourish. This kind of thinking has emerged and has had great influence at times when international migrations and commerce were bringing people of diverse backgrounds into close contact with one another—in situations of participant observation and of perceptive listening. Ancient Phoenician, Greek, and Roman colonizations in the Mediterranean area provide classic examples of this cosmopolitanizing influence. In discussing the vast American experience, the historian F. J. Turner recounts how the frontiersman "must accept the conditions which it [the environment] furnishes, or perish, and so he fits himself into the Indian clearings and follows the Indian trails. Little by little he transforms the wilderness, but the outcome is not the old Europe. . . . here is a new product that is American."[15] Our ethnically mixed neighborhoods and schools continue to make a similarly stimulating contribution to American life.

Along with supernaturalism and naturalism, humanism has been called by the philosopher E. P. Cheyney "one of three rival claimants to philosophic allegiance."[16] Notions of anthropomorphic agency, notions of an unconscious and automatically acting natural system, and notions of humanism are three germinal threads that run through recorded human thought. Each implies a basis for its own authentication as well as a criterion for the rejection, reinterpretation, or incorporation of the two others. Since social theorists often find it plausible and rewarding to mix two or three of these threads, their separate characters are difficult to detect, spell out, and discuss. To a degree, it can be done—if it is to be done at all—rather arbitrarily, in terms of ideal types. At any rate, in its simplest notion, humanism as a fresh and more accurate expression of interpersonal experience typically has implications unsettling to the *status quo* in any society. It is critical of and often antagonistic to both supernaturalism and naturalism in their myriad forms. Especially in this century, humanism provides bases in the uniquely individual with which to criticize the dehumanizing and depersonalizing implications of both the natural sciences and absolutist metaphysics.[17] When humanist perceptions are absorbed into a supernatural or a nature-centered ideology, they lose this annoyingly critical potential. In such an unstable mix of two or more of these philosophical threads, the composite can appear to become a prop for the *status quo*.

Supernaturalism concerns itself with ways to cope with aleatory elements in life through providing recourses to magical, spiritual, or divine powers. In doing so, it offers explanations of life and nature that go beyond objective verification through sense experiences. It develops notions of a more or less integrated supernatural agency rationally in control and available for special dispensations to those satisfying the prescriptions of the related cult. Verification arises from fantasies, dogmatic claims, and coincidences. On such bases, leaders have erected poetic and powerful structures of theory, ritual, organization, and enticing promises and services, and have thus achieved control over the thoughts and behavior of adherents.[18] With the growth of democratic and scientific tendencies, supernaturalists have also taken up selected naturalistic rhetorics. This is an attempt to cope with the critical and anti-authoritarian potentials of existential humanism. Religion thus becomes identified with human welfare on earth as well as in the hereafter, and scientific findings are claimed to be congruent with newly re-rationalized "divine" laws. In this latter sense, "natural law" is "divine law."[19]

Naturalism focuses upon the perception of nature and the discovery of nature's laws. In this perspective, even though it be that of an enterprise necessarily carried on by and presumably for people, men and women have no special place within it. They are merely members of a passing animal species, sometime parasites on a small planet. In order to soften the starkness of the view they put forward, individual advocates of naturalism often suggest identities and relations with supernaturalism and humanism. Impersonal nature thus becomes slightly anthropomorphized into something "not too different" as it were from "enlightened views of divinity." They may even use the term, "God." Curiously enough, that anti-humanist advocate of naturalistic determinism, the psychologist B. F. Skinner, has so rationalized his behavioristic position that he was hailed as "1972 Humanist of the Year" by the American Humanist Association.[20]

In Skinner's philosophy, "What is being abolished [by the nature-centered] is autonomous man—the inner man, the homunculus, the possessing demon, the man defended by the literature of freedom and dignity."[21] He approves this effort and has joined in it as one of its leaders. Just how such a dedication can be squared with something to be called "humanism," with human aspirations and humanizing experiences, it is difficult to understand. Since people are parasites on a small planet, their preoccupation has to be with their own needs in confrontation with cosmic processes. They should not merely acquiesce to the mandates of processes now only imperfectly glimpsed.

Both naturalism and humanism are now based on scientific findings, as principal current exponents of both contend. To emphasize this point, many humanists like to refer to themselves as scientific or naturalistic humanists in order to avoid confusion with Roman Catholic, Protestant, Jewish, academic,[22] or other humanists. The term naturalistic humanism does not at all imply an acceptance of such a position as that of Skinner. Both the nature-centered and the people-centered theorists interpret scientific findings in terms of their own needs and aspirations. The egalitarian and libertarian temptations of humanist experiences and their demonstration of the relativity of values to individual, group, and changing subculture and culture scare many psychologically and socially insecure people. Like supernaturalism, nature-centeredness places responsibility outside the individual, outside of humanity. The "will of God" becomes the consequence of

Demystifying Theories about Human Life and Living 47

natural processes as perhaps revealed by "the utterly impersonal problem solutions of the computer," to quote the engineer R. Buckminster Fuller's naïve statement of faith. Fuller then adds: "Only to their [the computers'] superhuman range of calculative capabilities can and may all political, scientific, and religious leaders face-savingly acquiesce."[23]

Humanism is heady stuff. As social experience, it can tempt thoughtful men and women to throw into question their cultural heritage of supernaturalism or nature-centeredness as an exclusive or predominant frame of reference for thought and action. When they attempt to do so, however, they often try to carry along as much of their previous intellectual baggage as they can, and this often gets in the way of their new orientation to life and living. Compromise statements compound themselves and eliminate the controversial and even revolutionary aspects of the humanist temptation. Belief in the controlling power of the supernatural is so great that many skeptical theorists, with little or no faith in a deity themselves, agree with the Florentine Niccolò Machiavelli that "there is no greater indication of the ruin of a country than to see religion condemned." He asserted that, with rulers maintaining religious forms in a convincing manner, "it is easy to keep their people religious, and consequently well conducted and united."[24]

It was only with the emergence of a statist need for unity *in spite of* religious diversity that that eighteenth century child of the Enlightenment, the United States of America, adopted the separation of church and state as a constitutional principle.[25] Thomas Jefferson, the principle's main sponsor and advocate, had reduced divinity in his own thinking to an abstract naturalism labeled theism. In effect, a secular religion of statism was to replace in the United States such awkward, emotionally divisive, and outworn instruments of social control as the Church of England and its competitors with their state-subsidized schools. As is currently evidenced by the religious-sectarian colorations of interclass and intraclass struggles in Northern Ireland, in Canada, and even in the English and Scottish industrial cities, the British have yet to follow the salutary United States precedent of trying to free religion from political and economic involvements. As imperfectly implemented as it is in the United States, the principle of the separation of church and state has still freed the country from much anguish in religious terms.[26]

48　Sociology for Whom?

As has been indicated above, the outset of humanism is usually placed, for lack of more ancient documentation, in ancient Greece five centuries before our era. As taught by those wandering teachers, the sophists, humanism helped to give Greek literature as exemplified by the dramatists Euripides and Aristophanes its people-centered, secular, realistic character. Gilbert Murray calls these teachers "the spiritual and intellectual representatives of the age of Pericles."[27]

After humanism's great days in Athens and in Alexandria,[28] its second and more continuing center, there are jumps to the Muslim and Jewish flowerings in North Africa during the fourteenth century and to Italy during the fourteenth and fifteenth centuries. Greek learning and the findings of such inveterate travelers, readers, and commentators as Ibn Batuta and Ibn Khaldun made the North Africans a bridge between the humanist past and the Renaissance.[29] The Italians Petrarch, Boccaccio, and others of the fourteenth century expressed humanist views in part through reviving interest in Greek classics and in part through their own imageries and theories.[30]

But in those periods, in the Enlightenment of the eighteenth century, and in recent times in humanist-oriented literature, painting, philosophy, social science, and even "religion," humanism has resisted thoroughgoing conceptualization as a philosophical system. It has not yielded such ideological constructions as have supernaturalism and naturalism. On the contrary, it has frequently intruded on such ideology-building and unsettled or even destroyed it. This demonstrates the critical and change-oriented nature of humanizing experiences and humanist philosophizings. These experiences and thoughts are parts of intellectual and social processes in constant flux. They are consequences of intimate exposure to diverse types of human beings. They stimulate human empathy and sympathy, awareness of common humanity and a common fate. They unfold knowledge and appreciation of and concern for human affairs through direct practical or field-clinical involvement in social change.[31]

This may all seem very well when viewed historically and in rather abstract terms. What does humanism mean in social thought today? Why is it still so controversial even among students of human sciences such as sociology and social psychology? What does it do to the security some of us find in pretentious methodologies, fancy terminologies, and elegant theoretical constructs? As the social psychologist A. H. Maslow observes, "being a full human being is difficult, frightening, and problematical. While human beings love knowledge and seek it—they are curious—they also fear it. The closer to the personal it is, the more they fear it."[32]

Let us get at our questions by looking briefly at five somewhat related social developments, all called "humanist." These are: (1) liberal humanism, (2) Marxian humanism, (3) "religious" humanism, (4) humanistic psychology, and (5) humanist social science. It is useful to discuss the first two as background for the other three. "Religious" humanism, humanistic psychology, and humanist social science arose out of liberal humanism and Marxian humanism and have problems somewhat similar to them. There is no point in going so far afield here as to discuss Roman Catholic[33] and Protestant[34] "humanism." It would be much more relevant to add a discussion of the impact of humanizing experiences on painters and other artists and of humanist fine art upon social perception generally. From Pieter Bruegel (1525–1569), El Greco (Domenikos Theotocopoulos, 1541–1614), William Hogarth (1697–1764), and Francisco de Goya (1746–1828) to Diego Rivera (1886–1957) and the many great moderns (including outstanding newspaper and periodical cartoonists), the record is most impressive.[35]

1. *Liberal humanism* became, in the nineteenth century, a recourse for intellectuals who were repelled by naturalistic evolutionism as a justification for unbridled "free enterprise" capitalism as well as by supernaturalism and by communism. The position was and is a complicated one. It is compounded of values traditionally embedded in European-American middle-class ideals. These values glorify compromise, gradualism, civil liberties, and fair play. They are the values of those who would be both societal stabilizers and surrogates of societal morality.[36] In consequence, the adherents of liberal humanism find its more outspoken and critical exponents—albeit non-communist and non-capitalist extremist—difficult bed fellows. Illustrative of such thorny spokespersons are Anatole France (Anatole François Thibault, 1844–1924) and Mark Twain (Samuel Langhorne Clemens, 1835–1910). In contrast to their more culture-bound contemporaries, France

and Twain help to characterize liberal humanism. Others who would be useful to illustrate the nature of liberal humanism are John Dewey (1859–1952), Lillian Wald (1867–1940), Charles A. Beard (1874–1948), Thomas Mann (1875–1955), Mary Beard (1876–1958), Grace Abbott (1878–1939), Albert Einstein (1879–1955), Margaret Higgins Sanger (1883–1966), Eleanor Roosevelt (1884–1962), and Margaret Mead (1901–   ), to mention but a few of the many.

Anatole France and Mark Twain had deep and varied humanizing experiences. These experiences led them to rethink radically the views as to man's lot they had received in their early social environment. They then felt impelled to bespeak their criticisms of society and of man as they found them. Neither was handicapped much by formal education. France finally did pass his examinations for the university laureate, but his preparation was largely informal; he browsed in his father's bookstore and talked with all sorts of people in that store and in the streets and cafés of Paris. Twain was a grade-school dropout who educated himself in newspaper shops, river boats, bars, billiard parlors, and mining camps, and through all sorts of reading. As each grew older, his disillusionment with the *status quo* and his compassion for the oppressed and for all mankind increased. Each criticized not only avowed upholders of outworn social institutions but also other liberal humanists who took compromising stances. Toward the end, France even turned his back upon liberalism and became a communist of a somewhat free-wheeling kind. As human affairs have grown more chaotic in this century, liberal humanists have multiplied in numbers, and many have become increasingly caustic and radical. (For a recent list of leading "humanists" so labeled, see the multinational signers of "Humanist Manifesto II."[37])

In the great French tradition of Rabelais, Montaigne, Molière, Voltaire, and Renan, Anatole France gloried in his skepticism. As he saw it,

The word is used as synonymous with negation and futility. But our great skeptics were often the most affirmative and courageous of men. They repudiate only negations. They attack those who trammel intelligence and will. They fight against ignorance which debases, against error which oppresses, against hate which kills. . . . The most skeptical of thinkers, meditating on the futility of the eternal flux of the universal, on the ineffectualness of poor mankind and on the absurd sufferings which it inflicts on itself during its brief, dreamlike existence, are filled with a profound compassion for their fellows. From this compassion to a fraternal love is but a single step. Their pity is stirred, and those who believe themselves forever detached from everything lose themselves in the combat to rescue their unhappy brothers.[38]

Such was the *credo* and *apologia pro sua vita* of a great French novelist, the author of *Penguin Island* (1908) and of *The Revolt of the Angels* (1914), a staunch defender of Captain Alfred Dreyfus, and an opponent of World War I. Interestingly enough, both Anatole France and Mark Twain were authors of books dealing with Joan of Arc. That other skeptical humanist, George Bernard Shaw, made her the heroine of a play. Her glorification of the human spirit, her willingness to confront the decadence of church and state, thrilled them all.

In a sense, Twain was the most authentic product in literature of the American frontier. As background for his fresh and perceptive writing, it is instructive to consider the parallel in stimulating situations drawn by the historian F. J. Turner:

What the Mediterranean Sea was to the Greeks, breaking the bond of custom, offering new experiences, calling out new institutions and activities, that, and more, the ever retreating frontier has been to the United States directly, and to the nations of Europe more remotely.[39]

Like Anatole France, Twain built his popular fame upon his virtuosity as a storyteller. His thoroughgoing people-centeredness was the special ingredient with which he, like France, permeated all of his writings. In their ways, these novelists resemble those among scientists whom the sociologist Florian Znaniecki refers to as explorative thinkers, as people "who specialize . . . in doing the unexpected."[40] Both France's and Twain's skepticism made many intellectuals and even many liberal humanists react unfavorably to their writings.[41] The author of *Tom Sawyer* (1876) and *Huckleberry Finn* (1884) also wrote *The Mysterious Stranger* (1916),[42] a book which points up the adult implications of his "children's stories." Then, in the first decade of the twentieth century, he wrote his keenest commentary and analysis of the human lot as he experienced it during his lifetime, his *Autobiography*.[43] As a leading analyst of Mark Twain's work, Maxwell Geismar, asserts,

He was not merely the artist of American youth and the past; he was surely our most mature and wisest of artists whose acerbity and profundity alike were ringed about with the imperishable comic spirit. In his age he only became freer, bolder, more open and honest, more emancipated both socially and sexually, from the taboos of his epoch which, at base, his spirit had never accepted.[44]

Many who have attempted to shape what they call secular and liberal humanism in this century differ from such "irresponsible" writers as Anatole France and Mark Twain. The philosopher F.C.S. Schiller (1864-1937) tried to create an academically respectable humanism. He identified his doctrine as a variant of pragmatism, the movement launched by Charles S. Peirce (1839-1914) and William James (1842-1910). His humanism "was essentially," as he asserted, "a protest against the dehumanizing and depersonalizing procedure which seemed to characterize both the natural sciences and absolutist metaphysics." He located his metaphysics "intermediate . . . between naturalism and supernaturalism" and came to substitute the term "voluntarism" for "humanism" as a label for his philosophy.[45] On the other hand, such essayists as Paul Elmer More (1864-1937) and Irving Babbitt (1865-1933) shied away from the unsettling egalitarian implications of humanism. Both were preoccupied with the problem of order and its maintenance in social relations. They sought out compulsions toward such order in mystical inner experiences similar to those of religious devotees but stimulated nontheologically by tradition, interpersonal relations, and thought.[46] The contributions of Schiller, More, and Babbitt to the humanist movement in social thought have thus not been weighty.

2. *Marxian humanism* had among its starting points G.F.W. Hegel's "exaltation of man's endeavor 'to understand the world, to appropriate and subdue it to himself'" and his "clear willingness to commit the sin of pride in behalf of man."[47] It also owed much to Karl Marx's own awareness that the proletariat no longer need be written off as dependent and deferential. He took it to be the aggressive and dependable instrument for the revolutionary overthrow of capitalism.

The increasing popular appeal of natural science and its freedom from ecclesiastical controls apparently made naturalism most enticing to Marx. In his early exuberance he asserted: "Communism as a fully developed naturalism is humanism and as a fully developed humanism is naturalism. It is the *definitive* resolution of the antagonism between man and nature, and between man and man." He claimed that "atheism is humanism mediated to itself by the annulment of religion, while communism is humanism mediated to itself by the annulment of private property."[48] At this early stage, Marx thus appears to be people-centered and not yet to have moved on to a nature-centered societal determinism. It was in this early period of humanist preoccupation that Marx and Engels wrote their *German Ideology*,[49] based upon "men, not in any fantastic isolation or abstract definition, but in their actual, empirically perceptible process of development under definite conditions." This view made history cease to be for them "a collection of dead facts."[50]

The liberal humanisms discussed above have points in common with Marxian humanism, according to the Marxian theorist, George Novack, "just as the middle classes and the workers have certain interests in common. In so far as the [liberal] humanists combat obscurantism and reaction in any field, defend science and promote education, support progressive movements and measures, they will have found allies among the Marxists." Nevertheless, "this humanism is at most only a neighbor of Marxism." As Novack sees it, liberal humanists "depend primarily upon the effects of education, reasonable arguments, and appeals to the moral conscience of individuals to overcome the hostilities of contending forces. This is a secular version of the universal embrace of Christian brotherhood without the Fathership of God or the mediation of the Son-Savior."[51] A leading liberal humanist, Corliss Lamont, replies,

The Marxist materialists disagree . . . particularly in their ambiguous attitude toward democracy and their acceptance of determinism. They are, however, unquestionably humanistic in their major tenets of rejecting the supernatural and all religious authority, of setting up the welfare of mankind in this life as the supreme goal, and of relying on science and its techniques.[52]

A further discussion of Marx's position will point up this situation of similarity and contrast.

Two involvements appear to have diverted Marx from following out fully and without compromise implications of a people-centered orientation. These were (1) his vocation as an agitator for social change[53] and (2) his evident conviction that human considerations do not provide in themselves adequate bases for ideological authority or allegiance. He also needed—or had to accept—what he took to be the mandates of an overriding naturalistic determinism.[54]

Marx's vocation as an agitator of change led him to contend that the revolution of the proletariat would most likely begin in the British Isles. As he asserted, "The English have all the *material* prerequisites necessary for the social revolution. What they lack is the *spirit of generalisation* and *revolutionary* fervour." He predicted that an Irish revolt would provide the starting point and leverage for that revolution.[55] A more intimate knowledge of the English people and their accumulated and internalized social controls would have made him far less optimistic in his assessment of opportunities to agitate for revolution successfully in that country.[56] That communist revolutions would succeed in such industrially undeveloped countries as Russia and China was apparently not seriously entertained by Marx and Engels.

Once Marx had combined nature-centeredness or nature-determinism and its imperatives (as he saw them) with his humanism and had given that determinism greater weight than the people-centered viewpoint, he visualized historical processes as having sufficient precedence over individual potentialities, rights, and wishes to achieve the transformation of society he thought to be necessary. This gave his philosophy a kind of depersonalizing determinism in his more "mature" phase.[57] As he summarizes it, his dialectical process "regards every historically developed social form as in fluid movement, and therefore takes into account its transient nature not less than its momentary existence; . . . *it lets nothing impose upon it,* and it is in its essence critical and revolutionary."[58]

Nurtured by such skeptics as Anatole France and Mark Twain and by such revolutionary theorists as Marx and Engels, humanism survives in an increasingly objective and radical form to become the significant element in European-American intellectual currents. Three humanist developments, now to be examined briefly, have many of the problems of both liberal and Marxian humanism. These problems are chiefly the temptations of various scientistic determinisms and the resistance of middleclass people to the modification of their culturally entrenched and hence habitual values. Many of humanism's spokespersons have been so firmly molded in those culturally patterned values that they are intellectually limited and even distorted by them.

3. *Religious humanism,* an organizational offshoot of liberal humanism, was born chiefly of a need felt by educated parents to provide their children with a substitute for supernaturalistic church schools. It has grown as a friendly heresy within the Unitarian-Universalist denomination. In addition to those Unitarian-Universalist congregations and fellowships which are avowedly humanist, religious humanism's most ecclesiastical manifestations are the Ethical Culture Societies and the local units of the American Humanist Association.[59]

Like some Marxians, many religious humanist spokespeople have both nature-determinist and vocational biases. These biases complicate further their middleclass anxiety to be respectably plausible and to gain a kind of legitimacy through identifying with societal morality as they interpret it.

Reference has already been made to the nature-centered bias exhibited in an official act of the American Humanist Association. Readers of that organization's periodical, *The Humanist,* find that bias to be a persistent one. In contrast to that nature-centeredness, Curtis W. Reese, a respected leader of the general humanist movement, clearly observes that religious humanism "has withstood tons of volumes designed to show how man is in the grip of fate, or subject to the iron law of physical determinism, or molded by purposes of which he is unaware, or blown like a broken reed by the winds of the centuries." He affirms that "the nature of the world is such that human intention and activity may play the determining role in human enterprise, subject only to the conditioning factors of the environing situation."[60]

The vocational bias of religious humanists is a more subtle problem. Concern with it leads the author Paul Blanshard to warn against bringing "humanism under the sentimental, all-purpose umbrella of religion." He wants humanists to dedicate themselves rather to the promotion of such useful projects as birth control (including abortion at will) and legal equality for unbelievers, and to the struggle against parochiaid (tax support for church-related schools) and prayer and Bible reading in tax-supported schools.[61] He opposes such efforts as that of the philosopher J. H. Randall, Jr. to expand the vocation of the religious humanist to include "the humanistic interpretation of traditional religion." Randall wants "to bring into the forefront the relatively humanistic core that has been overlaid with supernatural ideas."[62] Perhaps even though such efforts as that proposed by Randall are likely to be sloppy intellectually, they may have their uses in social therapy, in the continuing struggle to liberate the minds of people.[63]

Religious-humanist organizations have remained small, but their relations with the great humanist intellectual and social movements and their contacts with organized supernaturalism have made them bridges of interpretation. Their greater freedom to take up proposals for social change has made their spokespersons sources of ferment in religious thought and social philosophy. They have thus helped to provide broad audiences for the creative voices of liberal and radical humanism and have furnished a degree of organizational support with which to withstand pressures from supernaturalist and other conservative organizations.[64]

4. *Humanistic psychology* is the creation of scientists influenced by humanistic social traditions and by their own humanizing experiences. They are ones who are nagged by questions of the relevance of their discipline's findings to the solution of personal and interpersonal problems. Humanistic psychology has roots in the pragmatism of Peirce and William James and in the psychic probings of Sigmund Freud, his followers, and some of his antagonists. In part it was a reaction against the biological determinism of such writers as Julian S. Huxley who saw humanism as a call to man "to do the best he can to manage the evolutionary process on this planet and to guide its future course in a desirable direction." To accomplish this, Huxley contends, "fuller realization of genetic possibilities becomes a major motivation for man's efforts, and eugenics is revealed as one of the basic human sciences."[65] On the contrary, an American leader in humanistic psychology, A. H. Maslow, calls the humanistic approach

a viable third alternative to objectivistic, behavioristic (mechano-morphic) psychology and to orthodox Freudianism . . . a revolution in the truest, oldest sense of the word, . . . i.e., new ways of perceiving and thinking, new images of man and of society, new conceptions of ethics and of values, new directions in which to move.[66]

In a debate, Carl Rogers as one of the principal current proponents of humanism in psychology agrees with B. F. Skinner "that the whole question of the scientific control of human behavior is a matter with which psychologists and the general public should concern themselves." As the sciences of biology and psychology develop, they are exhibiting frightening potentialities for human manipulation. Rogers focuses his differences with Skinner on answers to these questions: "Who will be controlled? Who will exercise control? What type of control will be exercised? Most important of all, toward what end or what purpose, or in the pursuit of what value, will control be exercised?"[67]

For Skinner, the answers to these questions lie within the mystique of science and of scientists. He asserts: "I cannot quite agree that the practice of science *requires* a prior decision about goals or a prior choice of values." Whether or not such a choice is *required*, he does not weigh adequately—nor did Huxley—the significance of the fact that such choice is made either for or by the would-be scientist: the choice always takes place. The unwitting acceptance of culturally or organizationally set goals is scarcely to be condoned in social science as a basis for avoiding responsibility for choice of goals in the name of an illusory, value-free ethical principle. Skinner contends that when we trust scientists the whole problem of the control of power is really on its way to being solved for the greater good of human survival. "If we are worthy of our democratic heritage we shall, of course, be ready to resist any tyrannical use of science for immediate or selfish purposes," Skinner naïvely insists. By the time such "tyrannical use of science"[68] becomes obvious to anyone, however, controls developed by psychologists or biologists might well have rendered mass resistance impossible.[69]

On the other hand, Rogers is vividly aware that scientists are people. He recalls how German rocket scientists worked for the Nazi Third Reich and then for whichever major power—the U.S.S.R. or the U.S.A.—captured them. As Rogers notes, "If behavioral scientists are concerned solely with advancing their science, it seems most probable that they will serve the purposes of whatever individual or group has the power." In other words, "the scientific control of human behavior" might permit or even encourage "the denial, misunderstanding, or gross underestimation of the place of ends, goals or values in their relationship to science." Rogers therefore contends that the choice of values "will forever lie outside the science which implements them; the goals we select, the purposes we wish to follow, must always be outside of the science which achieves them." To him this "has the encouraging meaning that the human person, with his capacity of subjective choice, can and will always exist, separate from and prior to any of his scientific undertakings."[70]

So as not to prolong these comments on a complex and promising scientific development, some summary statements by another exponent of humanistic psychology, Sidney M. Jourard, can be quoted: "When researchers are transparently pledged to further the freedom and self-actualizing of their subjects, rather than be unwitting servants to the leaders of institutions, then they will deserve *to be* and *to be seen* as recipients of the secrets of human being and possibility." Jourard then adds: "This is not the death of 'objective,' scientific psychology. Rather, it may prove to be the birth of a scientifically informed psychology of human persons—a humanistic psychology."[71]

In the early 1960s, the Association for Humanistic Psychology developed as an expression of this movement. Fortunately for the body's vitality, its officers and editors and authors involved in its many conferences and in its *Journal of Humanistic Psychology* and its *AHP Newsletter* have represented a wide range of viewpoints from the outset, and they continue to do so. An official statement carried in the *Journal of Humanistic Psychology* asserts that the A.H.P. is now "a world-wide network of people who value our distinctly human qualities and work toward the fulfilment of the innate potential of all people—individually and in society."

5. *Humanist social science* is not new. Like humanistic psychology, it is an offspring of intimate interpersonal experiences, of nagging problems of scientific relevance to every person's human concerns, of liberal and radical humanist movements, and of a scientific ethic dedicated to the satisfaction both of curiosity and of desire to serve people rather than merely to build a profitable cult or to exploit dependence upon an elite. By their very nature, humanist sociology, humanistic psychology, and humanist anthropology are closely related scientific movements and stimulate one another. They also have close ties with humanism in social history, in literature, and in social action. Like humanism generally, all three have constant struggles with the limiting influences of middleclass ideals, mores, and organizations, as well as with

pressures from other classes. Those who have tried to push sociology back toward its basic humanist orientation have had to confront the seductions of special interests, of scientism, of sentimentality, of humane panaceas, of irrelevant but prestigious methodologies, and of pretentious theoretical and rhetorical embroiderings. These are problems common to all humanist social scientists. As a humanist anthropologist notes, the major focus of a humanist social scientist "is on the individual and, more specifically, on the individual's striving for freedom and creativity within the confines and opportunities of nature, culture, and society."[72]

In his famous study of London at the end of the nineteenth century, the sociologist Charles Booth's[73] great contributions were not his statistics, according to the sociologist Robert E. Park, "but his realistic descriptions of the actual life of the occupational classes—the conditions under which they lived and labored, their passions, pastimes, domestic tragedies, and the life-philosophies with which each class met the crises peculiar to it." Booth's descriptions "made these studies a memorable and a permanent contribution to our knowledge of human nature and of society."[74] Such accurate and intimate data helped to demystify London slums; they made more realistic thinking about them possible.

Extensive participant observation, perceptive listening, and field-clinical experience in social action situations convinced the sociologist W. I. Thomas that he could not "believe in . . . comparisons between physics and sociology," in other words, in scientism; "you never have the same experimental control of a situation." The sociologist has to be satisfied with "high degrees of probability." Thomas's studies of intimate life-histories and of their contexts and his personal involvement in social struggles led him to that demystification of sociological research that lent such distinction to his career. To quote him again:

The case study method and the "natural history" method must not only precede the more scientifically acceptable method in order to produce realistic hypotheses and indicate what units should be defined and isolated; they must also be used as a general background of reference to the more limited statistical findings, which lead . . . to inferences which must be constantly checked for validity against the large mass of material not yet analyzable.[75]

Participant observation, perceptive listening, and experimental involvement in social action are old, somewhat recognized, but difficult procedures to employ in social exploration, critical re-valuation of social theory, and theory modification or reconstruction. Basically, their advocates counsel you to sit down and talk with people with quite different backgrounds from your own. Then, and above all, see how they actually behave in significantly challenging social action situations. Try to comprehend how the other persons sense their lives, thoughts, social worlds. This takes time, patience, and more than a little mind-stretching. Put aside as much as you can the common exercise of self-congratulation that you are not as your interviewees are—not so bound by tradition, so stupid, so gullible, so manipulated by the mass media, so inadequate, so "disturbed," so "pathological." Try gently to help informants forget their psychological barriers against self-revelation. This can take place concomitantly as you break down your own barriers against hearing and understanding—in *their* terms—what those interviewed have to tell you. Attempt to conceive as well as you can what it would be like to be living those other persons' lives—as it were, to be living within their skins. Sometimes this can be done—to the extent that it can be done—only by working and living with them as equals coping with mutually recognized social problems.

How many have had mind-stretching experiences such as the sociologist W. F. Whyte went through when he was working on his *Street Corner Society*[76] in South Boston? Recall what complicated procedures he planned at first for his study, the research team he thought he would need, all the rest, and then how instead he went into the field alone and began his field-clinical study of social behavior in which he came to participate. His head ached many times from culture shock, but he learned far more than he might have had he carried out his original *a priori* plan of research. His book vividly introduces its readers to the highly organized life of an Italo-American neighborhood.[77]

After such humanizing experiences, the stereotyped ideas with which sociologists "handle" a different sort of person start to crumble. The Black business operator or Chicano migrant worker or American Indian militant or even the academic colleague in a different specialty or status talks quite differently about many things than sociologists might, but the longer and more candidly we converse, the more sensible that talk becomes. Through an egalitarian search for common goals, males and females—whether sociologists or not—might open up new worlds of understanding of the other sex, but this does not often happen. Very few enter into such a relationship in an egalitarian manner, and thus only a few enter into a heterosexual association in other than stereotyped patterns of speaking and listening. We hold fast to our sex roles and sex stereotypes. A pimp or a thief or a drug pusher or a schizophrenic can reveal worlds of "reality" that make our own worlds take on a surprisingly altered character—social scientists though we might be. No wonder that a whole rash of new discussions of psychotherapy exploits the consequences of new levels of perceptive listening to individual problem-racked people.[78]

In consequence of a turning away by major disciplinary associations from humanist concerns in the social sciences, the mid-1970s are seeing the launching of an Association for Humanist Sociology, with a journal, *Humanity and Society,* and a Society on Anthropology and Humanism, with a journal, *Anthropology and Humanism.* In the first newsletter of the sociological organization, the organizing secretary, Charles P. C. Flynn, listed the principal concerns of those involved as the over-compartmentalization of the discipline, the limitations of empirical research, emphasis upon determinism to the exclusion of "choice and voluntary value-orientations," "disciplinary chauvinism," the "value neutrality question," and "paradigmatic pluralism and opposition to orthodoxy."[79]

What is so unusual about the humanizing experiences to be obtained through participant observation, perceptive listening, and the field-clinical study of social behavior? Are not at least the first two entrenched in the texts on social research methods? Are they not even something of a current fad in social problems research, in spite of propaganda by scientific positivists that those methods are more "journalistic" than "scientific"? Why are those methods so consistently opposed or defined into useless rigidity by proponents of scientism, commercialization, and academic bureaucratization? Have not realistic novelists, careful journalists, practical political analysts, and ethnologists given these procedures vivid exemplification and interpretative validation over a great many years?

The stress here is not just upon the usefulness of these procedures in an occasional research project. They are basic to the processes of humanizing and demystifying all social thought in a tradition that stretches back to the Greek sophists. This is not at all to suggest the rejection of such widely held scientific criteria as accuracy, representativeness, relevance, internal consistency, replicability, and clarity of statement. On the contrary, as the sociologist Glenn Jacobs points out, "Such a view presumes a radical empiricism in place of scientism, a disciplined skepticism about any substitute for man as his own measure."[80]

Perceptive involvement in social action, with its products of culture shock and intellectual marginality, is our basic humanizing and demystifying influence in social thought about people and society. Even specialists in ancient history or extinct languages see a new vibrancy in their subjects from expanding their experiences with a variety of living individuals and groups. Students of social affairs who return from searching field work to their libraries and computers are not the same people as those who went forth. Fortunately, the simplicity and the utter complexity of these humanizing procedures constantly press fresh views of changing humanity and society upon the attention of those engaged in perceiving and thinking with some freedom about the human lot. Extended experiences with a range of living individuals and groups cut through the reductionist spirit of so much of science which structures and controls in an *a priori* manner investigators' perceptions of human behavior.

After saying all this about demystifying theories of human life and living, after one does what one can to try to see other human beings fully and accurately, after searching as best one can for ways to make life more livable and more creative, nothing I have said is meant to dispel the sense sometimes of wonder and sometimes of loathing with which the human struggle fills any careful observer. As a philosopher, Baruch Spinoza took the remote intellectual stance of claiming: "I have been at great pains not to laugh at human actions, nor to grieve over them, nor to abominate them, but to understand them."[81] On the contrary, a humanist social scientist has to have sufficient sense of empathy and of participation to gain understanding through joining in the emotions and activities of those observed to the extent that that might be possible or practical. The social psychologist A. H. Maslow puts it this way:

If humanistic science may be said to have any goals beyond the sheer fascination with the human mystery and enjoyment of it, these would be to release the person from external controls and to make him less predictable to the observer (to make him freer, more creative, more inner-determined) even though perhaps more predictable to himself.

And to this he adds:

Science at its highest level is ultimately the organization of, the systematic pursuit of, and the enjoyment of wonder, awe, and mystery. . . . Science can be the religion of the nonreligious, the poetry of the nonpoet, the art of the man who cannot paint, the humor of the serious man, and the love-making of the inhibited and shy man. Not only does science begin in wonder; it also ends in wonder.[82]

notes

[1]George Simpson, *Science as Morality* (Yellow Springs, O.: Humanist Press, 1953), pp. 43–44.

[2]George Simpson, *Man in Society*, rev. ed. (New York: Random House, 1963), p. 59.

[3]B.A.G. Fuller, "Sophists," *Encyclopaedia of the Social Sciences*, vol. 14 (1934), pp. 259–61; p. 259 quoted.

[4]Protagoras of Abdera as quoted in *The Works of Plato*, Irwin Edman, ed. (New York: Simon & Schuster, 1928), p. 473.

[5]Socrates in ibid., p. 477.

[6]Ibid., p. 474.

[7]Gilbert Murray, *A History of Ancient Greek Literature*, 1897 (New York: Frederick Ungar Publ. Co., 1966), p. 163; cf. G. B. Kerferd, "Protagoras of Abdera," *Encyclopaedia of Philosophy*, Paul Edwards, ed. (New York: Macmillan Co., 1967), vol. 6, pp. 505–7.

[8]Murray, ibid., pp. 163–64.

[9]Havelock Ellis, *The Dance of Life* (Boston: Houghton Mifflin Co., 1923), p. 302.

[10]Protagoras as quoted by Moses Hadas, *A History of Greek Literature* (New York: Columbia University Press, 1950), p. 80.

[11]H. E. Barnes, *An Intellectual and Cultural History of the Western World*, 3rd ed. rev. (New York: Dover Publ., 1965), p. 131.

[12]Paul Blanshard, "Communication," *The Humanist*, vol. 33, no. 2 (March–April 1973), p. 36; A. McC. Lee, *Toward Humanist Sociology* (Englewood Cliffs, N.J.: Prentice-Hall, 1973), pp. ix–xii.

[13]Herbert Blumer, *Symbolic Interactionism* (Englewood Cliffs, N.J.: Prentice-Hall, 1969).

[14]*The Random House Dictionary of the English Language*, col. ed. (New York: Random House, 1968), p. 645; cf. *The Century Dictionary*, rev. ed. (New York: Century Co., 1914), p. 2913; *The Oxford English Dictionary*, rev. ed. (Oxford: Clarendon Press, 1933), vol. 1, p. 44.

[15]F. J. Turner, "The Significance of the Frontier in American History," 1894, in his *Frontier and Section*, R. A. Billington, ed. (Englewood Cliffs, N.J.: Prentice-Hall, 1961), chap. 3, p. 39.

[16]E. P. Cheyney, "Humanism," *Encyclopaedia of the Social Sciences*, vol. 7 (1932), pp. 537–42; p. 542 quoted; see also Cheyney, *The Dawn of a New Era: 1250–1453* (New York: Harper & Bros., 1936), pp. 268–71.

[17]H. J. Muller, *Science and Criticism* (New Haven: Yale University Press, 1943), esp. chap. 8.

[18] A. D. White, *A History of the Warfare of Science With Theology in Christendom*, 2 vols. (New York: D. Appleton and Co., 1896); W. G. Sumner and A. G. Keller, *The Science of Society* (New Haven: Yale University Press, 1927), vol. 2.

[19] W. H. Coates and others, *The Emergence of Liberal Humanism* (New York: McGraw-Hill Book Co., 1966), chap. 6.

[20] Corliss Lamont, "Highlights of the Humanist Movement," *The Humanist*, vol. 35, no. 1 (January–February 1975), pp. 52–53.

[21] B. F. Skinner, *Beyond Freedom and Dignity* (New York: Bantam Books, 1971), p. 191.

[22] The term "academic" is added because classicists and other specialists in "humane letters" have long been called "humanists." This is an inheritance from the fifteenth century Italian distinction between the study of the sacred (*studia divinitatis*) and of the humane (*studia humanitatis*), the humanities. P. O. Kristeller, *Renaissance Thought: The Classic, Scholastic and Humanistic Strains* (New York: Harper & Row, 1961).

[23] R. B. Fuller, *Operating Manual for Spaceship Earth* (Carbondale: Southern Illinois University Press, 1969), p. 36; cf. A. McC. Lee, "Garbage in, Garbage out," in his *Toward Humanist Sociology*, op. cit., pp. 21–23.

[24] Niccolò Machiavelli, "The Discourses," 1531, trans. by C. E. Detmold, in Machiavelli, *The Prince and the Discourses*, Max Lerner, ed. (New York: Modern Library, 1940), pp. 149–50.

[25] A. P. Stokes, *Church and State in the United States*, 3 vols. (New York: Harper & Bros., 1950).

[26] E. R. Clinchy, *All in the Name of God* (New York: John Day Co., 1934); A. J. Menendez, *The Bitter Harvest: Church and State in Northern Ireland* (New York: David McKay Co., 1974).

[27] Gilbert Murray, op. cit., p. 164.

[28] Moses Hadas, op. cit., chap. 13.

[29] G. E. von Grunebaum, *Medieval Islam* (Chicago: University of Chicago Press, 1946); Franz Rosenthal, "Ibn Khaldun's Life," in Ibn Khaldun, *The Muqaddimah*, trans. by Rosenthal (New York: Pantheon Books, 1958), vol. 1, pp. xxix–lxvii; C. A. O. van Nieuwenhuijze, *Sociology of the Middle East* (Leiden: E. J. Brill, 1971), chap. 3.

[30] Coates and others, op. cit., chap. 1.

[31] Reference here is not to a "clinic" in a medical sense, but to a similarly instructive, actual "field-clinical" social situation in which the social scientist is a participating observer in social action.

[32] A. H. Maslow, *The Psychology of Science* (New York: Harper & Row, 1966), p. 16.

[33] Jacques Maritain, *Existence and the Existent*, trans. by Louis Galantière (New York: Random House, 1949).

[34] Reinhold Niebuhr, *Nature and Destiny of Man*, 2 vols. (New York: Charles Scribner's Sons, 1949); Paul Tillich, *Courage to Be* (New Haven: Yale University Press, 1952).

[35] Glenn Jacobs, "Convergences of Artistic and Sociological Insight in the Paintings of Pieter Bruegel," *Sociological Abstracts*, vol. 20, no. 6 (October 1972), pp. xxv–xl.

[36] A. McC. Lee, *Multivalent Man* (New York: George Braziller, 1970), part 2.

[37] New York *Times*, August 26, 1973, pp. 1, 51; American Humanist Association, *Humanist Manifestos I and II* (Buffalo, N.Y.: Prometheus Books, 1973), pp. 24–31.

[38] Anatole France, quoted by Jacob Axelrad, *Anatole France* (New York: Harper & Bros., 1944), p. 427.

[39] F. J. Turner, op. cit., p. 62.

[40] Florian Znaniecki, *The Social Role of the Man of Knowledge* (New York: Columbia University Press, 1940), p. 165.

[41] Henri Peyre, "In Purgatory Still," New York *Times Book Review*, December 17, 1967, p. 4 (referring to Anatole France); Van Wyck Brooks, *The Ordeal of Mark Twain* (New York: E. P. Dutton & Co., 1933), esp. chap. 1; Lewis Leary, ed., *A Casebook of Mark Twain's Wound* (New York: Thomas Y. Crowell Co., 1962).

[42] Mark Twain, *The Mysterious Stranger*, W. M. Gibson, ed. (Berkeley: University of California Press, 1969). This is more authentic and complete than the original (1916) edition.

[43] *Mark Twain's Autobiography*, A. B. Paine, ed. (New York: Harper & Bros., 1924), 2 vols. (The expurgated edition of Charles Neider [New York: Harper & Bros., 1959] is far less interesting.)

[44] Maxwell Geismar, *Mark Twain: An American Prophet* (Boston: Houghton Mifflin Co., 1970), p. 536.

[45] F.C.S. Schiller, "Humanism," *Encyclopaedia of the Social Sciences*, vol. 7 (1932), pp. 537–42; pp. 542–43 quoted.

[46] Irving Babbitt, *On Being Creative* (Boston: Houghton Mifflin Co., 1932), esp. pp. xi–xliv.

[47] W. H. Coates and H. V. White, *The Ordeal of Liberal Humanism* (New York: McGraw-Hill Book Co., 1970), pp. 232–33.

[48] Karl Marx, *Early Writings (1844–1846)*, trans. and ed. by T. B. Bottomore (London: C. A. Watts & Co., 1963), pp. 155, 213.

[49] Karl Marx and Frederick Engels, *The German Ideology*, 1846, trans. and ed. by R. Pascal (London: Lawrence and Wishart, 1939).

[50] Karl Marx and Frederick Engels, *Basic Writings on Politics and Philosophy*, L. S. Feuer, ed. (Garden City, N.Y.: Doubleday & Co., 1959), p. 248.

[51] George Novack, *Humanism and Socialism* (New York: Pathfinder Press, 1973), pp. 108–9.

[52] Corliss Lamont, *The Philosophy of Humanism*, 5th ed. (New York: Frederick Ungar Publ. Co., 1965), pp. 26–27.

[53] Boris Nicolaievsky and Otto Maenchen-Helfen, *Karl Marx: Man and Fighter* (Philadelphia: Lippincott, 1936); Franz Mehring, *Karl Marx*, trans. by Edward Fitzgerald (New York: Covici, Friede, 1935); Isaiah Berlin, *Karl Marx*, 3rd ed. (London: Oxford University Press, 1963).

[54] Erich Fromm, ed., *Socialist Humanism: An International Symposium* (Garden City, N.Y.: Doubleday & Co., 1965), esp. pp. 117–35.

[55] Karl Marx and Frederick Engels, *Ireland and the Irish Question*, R. Dixon, ed. (New York: International Publishers, 1972), pp. 160–62.

[56] D. V. Glass, ed., *Social Mobility in Britain* (London: Routledge and Kegan Paul, 1954); W. L. Guttsman, *The British Political Elite* (London: MacGibben and Kee, 1963).

[57] Karl Marx, *A Contribution to the Critique of Political Economy*, 1873 (Chicago: Charles H. Kerr & Co., 1904), pp. 11–13.

[58] Italics added; Marx and Engels, 1959, op. cit., p. 146.

[59] Ethical Culture Societies are non-theistic, but they tend to have meetings on Sunday mornings programmed somewhat like those of Christian churches; American Humanist Association local units vary in program but usually have monthly speakers or discussion sessions plus the work of action committees on social concerns.

[60] C. W. Reese, *The Meaning of Humanism* (Buffalo, N.Y.: Prometheus Books, 1945), p. 34; see also Mason Olds, "John H. Dietrich: The Father of Religious Humanism," *Journal of the Liberal Ministry*, vol. 15, no. 1 (Winter 1975), pp. 46–52.

[61] Blanshard, op. cit.

[62]J. H. Randall, Jr., "Communication," *The Humanist*, vol. 3, no. 2 (March–April 1973), p. 36.

[63]Lloyd and Mary Morain, *Humanism as the Next Step* (Boston: Beacon Press, 1954); E. H. Wilson, "Liberal Religion's Unfinished Business," *Journal of the Liberal Ministry*, vol. 12, no. 3 (Fall 1972), pp. 3–15.

[64]Lamont, 1965, op. cit.; Paul Kurtz, ed., *Moral Problems in Contemporary Society*, 2nd ed. (Buffalo, N.Y.: Prometheus Books, 1973); Kurtz, *The Fullness of Life* (New York: Horizon Press, 1974).

[65]J. S. Huxley, *Essays of a Humanist* (New York: Harper & Row, 1964), p. 280; cf. George Simpson, 1953, op. cit.

[66]A. H. Maslow, *Toward a Psychology of Being*, 2nd ed. (Princeton: D. Van Nostrand, 1968), p. iii.

[67]Carl Rogers in B. F. Skinner and Rogers, "Some Issues Concerning the Control of Human Behavior: A Symposium," *Science*, vol. 124 (1956), pp. 1057–66; p. 1060 quoted.

[68]B. F. Skinner in ibid., pp. 1064–65.

[69]See also B. F. Skinner, *Beyond Freedom and Dignity* (New York: Bantam Books, 1971), and *Walden Two* (New York: Macmillan Co., 1948).

[70]Rogers, op. cit., pp. 1061, 1064.

[71]S. M. Jourard, "A Humanistic Revolution in Psychology," in Jourard, *Disclosing Man to Himself* (Princeton: Van Nostrand, 1968), pp. 3–8; pp. 8, 3–4; see also A. H. Maslow, *Motivation and Personality*, 2nd ed. (New York: Harper & Row, 1970), and *The Further Reaches of Human Nature* (New York: Viking Press, 1971).

[72]T. F. Fratto, "Toward an Anthropological Humanism," *Anthropology and Humanism Quarterly*, vol. 1, no. 1 (April 1976), pp. 1–2; p. 2 quoted.

[73]Charles Booth, *Life and Labour of the People of London*, 3rd ed. (London: MacMillan & Co., 1902–1903), 17 vols.

[74]R. E. Park, "The City as a Social Laboratory," in *Chicago: An Experiment in Social Science Research*, T. V. Smith and L. D. White, eds. (Chicago: University of Chicago Press, 1929), p. 46.

[75]W. I. Thomas, *Social Behavior and Personality*, E. H. Volkart, ed. (New York: Social Science Research Council, 1951), p. 89, footnote 3, pp. 93–94; see Michael Parenti, "Introduction to the Torchbook Edition," in Thomas, *The Unadjusted Girl* (New York: Harper & Row, 1967).

[76]W. F. Whyte, *Street Corner Society*, 2nd ed. (Chicago: University of Chicago Press, 1955), appendix.

[77]See also Charles Hampden-Turner, *Sane Asylum: Inside the Delancey Street Foundation* (San Francisco: San Francisco Book Co., 1976).

[78]T. S. Szasz, *Myth of Mental Illness* (New York: Dell, 1967), and *Ideology and Insanity* (Garden City, N.Y.: Doubleday & Co., 1970); R. D. Laing, *Self and Others*, rev. ed. (New York: Pantheon Books, 1970).

[79]C.P.C. Flynn, "Concerns and Working Principles for the Association of Humanist Sociology," *The Humanist Sociology Newsletter*, vol. 1, no. 1 (Summer 1976), p. 5.

[80]Glenn Jacobs, ed., *The Participant Observer* (New York: George Braziller, 1970), p. ix.

[81]Baruch Spinoza quoted by Moses Hadas, *The Living Tradition* (New York: New American Library, 1967), p. 155.

[82]A. H. Maslow, *The Psychology of Science* (New York: Harper & Row, 1966), pp. 40, 151. This chapter is expanded and adapted from the author's "Humanism as Demystification," *Sociological Analysis & Theory*, vol. 5 (1975), pp. 267–87; reproduced by permission of the editor, Arun Sahay, and the publishers, Victoria Publishing Co., 254 Deighton Road, Huddersfield HD2 1JJ, England.

three

---

*Feuds
between Sociologists
and Social Workers*

Both social workers and sociologists have been trying desperately for more than a century to live down their miscellaneous ancestry. Both are still embarrassed that their disciplines are rooted historically in the work of old-time clergy, police, utopian philosophers and reformers, apologists for the *status quo ante,* sentimentalists, reactionary manipulators, journalistic "muckrakers," civil libertarians and other practical reformers, and radical thinkers and agitators. It is true that both professions had more ancient philosophical as well as polemical and actionist progenitors. The two corps of modern professionals sprang more immediately, however, from nineteenth-century concerns, perceptions of social problems, efforts at social amelioration and reform or revolution, and intercult conflicts.

Both professions have sought to create modish images competitively useful in the evolving academic, political, and business worlds of the late nineteenth and the twentieth centuries. Both have tried to buttress these images with protective educational and accreditational procedures as well as the latest "scientific" fashions. Even though "preprofessional" social work and criminology are staples of most undergraduate sociology departments, both sociologists and social workers have strained to dissociate themselves from each other in order to build professions that would appear unique.

The principal image that sociologists project is that of being allegedly value-free scientists wedded to esoteric terminology, to impressive quantification, to statistical manipulation, and to theories of human relations and social structure based on what is claimed to be "hard data." Even the apparent scientific rigor of genetic determinism and sociobiology as well as that of behaviorism often tempts the scientistic sociologist. To be identified with commercialized specialists in marketing, mass communications, city and area planning, industrial procedures, military problems, medicine, and education is looked upon as useful in "image building." The humanizing experiences of social workers, journalists, labor organizers, and social reformers have contributed heavily to sociology, but "respectable," "establishment" sociologists know that identification with such folks often impairs an image calculated to attract foundation grants and contracts for research as well as academic employment and advancement within the sociological field.

The principal image offered by social case-work professionals was at first something that they hoped would resemble that of the physician or the psychiatrist. Then, as critics tarnished that image with characterizations of authoritarianism and of monopolistic and entrepreneurial practices, social workers strove to depend upon the more generalized prestige of professionalism within which to erect a more distinctive public image. Types of social worker other than caseworker partake of as much of the profession's changing image as they are able. Whether as caseworkers, group-workers, or community organization specialists, they all try to have themselves seen as practicing healing arts dramatized by suitable terminology, routines, professional accreditation, periodicals and other publications, professional associations, and dignity.

How different are these images from what sociological undergraduates and graduate students and social-work clients might tell legislators, institutional board members, and administrators! What would happen to a board member's conception of a caseworker's professional image if distraught welfare "cases" could invade a board room in person? What would happen to a university trustee's conception of a sociologist's professional image if resentful B.A.s and Ph.D.s could complain directly to them? Similarly, few legislators ever really see the human degradation with which social workers try to cope and how they cope with it. Nor do legislators want to become conscious of the degree to which they and their industrial sponsors contribute to that degradation. No one who really wants to obtain a Ph.D. speaks out during his or her comprehensive oral examination about experiences with personal dehumanization and exploitation suffered at the hands of the examiners or their colleagues. And so the public images of these professionals are preserved. The smothering depersonalization of bureaucracies in any field should be an old story to social workers and sociologists, but—they would insist—"we do all that we can" to prevent it from taking place or from having damaging consequences *here*!

A producer of TV "reality fiction" such as Frederick Wiseman[1] scarcely gives a statistically defensible cross section of a social-welfare center in one of his productions entitled "Welfare." Most of the "professionals" he deals with, too, are not fully accredited Masters of Social Work! His caricature, however, should unsettle the many professionals who now hearten themselves by thinking of the showpieces of their discipline and who shelter themselves from discomfort with ready rationalizations about the overwhelming tide of "unprofessional situations" for which personnel, finance, and facilities are lacking.

Showpiece social work is not commonly available, and, when available, it is often just that—a façade hopefully hiding deepset social inequities and other abuses. The professionalization of all social welfare policies and practices is a tremendously complicated challenge. It is a challenge social workers can scarcely avoid facing, but it is a challenge the ramifications of which go far beyond social work itself.

A *Newsweek* reviewer summarizes the "Welfare" TV film thus:

Everyone in Wiseman's study—welfare administrators as well as clients— emerges as a victim of the system's bureaucratic horrors. . . . A World War II veteran despairingly plucks cards and forms from each of his pockets. "Jesus, look at all these *places* I been," he pleads. "People keep sending me back here. And I still ain't got carfare." Caseworkers are robotized drones, their compassion deadened by frustration. . . . Downstairs in the records division, machines clack out a symphony of depersonalization; computers transform perforated tapes into digital readouts, lives are processed and filed. Upstairs, nothing works so neatly. "What you telling me 'bout technicalities?" a black man tells a social worker. "I'm talking 'bout eatin'."[2]

As another reviewer, an experienced and perceptive sociologist, S. M. Miller, adds: "Everyone is caught. Welfare workers have little discretion. They are torn between administrative responsibility to prevent deception and follow rules and the needs and illnesses of people. But greater discretionary power might mean that welfare workers would have too much power over clients." He was surprised, however, "by the number of welfare workers who were actively trying to help recipients."[3]

Wiseman has not yet produced a piece of his TV "reality fiction" about sociology teaching and research. I hope that he will. It might or might not be more difficult than with social work to present such efforts in dramatic form, but the parallels between his welfare portrayal and what actually happens in many research projects and teaching situations would become apparent. Too many tired, bureaucratized, and underworked senior faculty exploit non-tenured junior faculty and students. Overworked junior faculty buck for tenure of employment or an advancement by feeding their undergraduates slick and safe text materials, films, and lectures. Too many want their mobs of students to respond as required on examination forms that can be machine-graded. Too often their practice has little in common with idealistic educational notions teachers repeat so often about developing the individual student's curiosity and motivation to grow intellectually.

In all too many graduate schools, ridden by depersonalized scientism, students of sociology, social work, and other social sciences and their applications come to identify "research" with grantspersonship. They are led to look forward to profitable game-like relations with fund sources rather than to entering into the more perilous and useful "game" of doubting the accuracy of some aspect of traditional social knowledge or of questioning the human utility of some phase or all of the so-called "social system."[4]

Thus only a relatively few graduate students delve intimately and empathetically into the malfeasances and conspiracies so common among those who control professional, industrial, financial, and political power. Few examine the behavior patterns common to the masses of manipulated "normals" which make social change so difficult and social manipulations so easy. On the contrary, graduate students are led to concentrate on superficial aspects of the woes of "deviant" and oppressed groups. It may be financially more attractive and a lot easier to get an advanced degree by helping a graduate professor complete a bit of contract "research" (maybe "research and development" or "evaluation research" for a Federal agency, a corporation, a trade association, or a foundation) than it is to be so pretentious as to do independent research on a pressing social threat, crisis, or issue. Contract "research" typically aims at providing data with which to manipulate markets for consumer goods, to reduce pressures for the equalization of educational opportunities, to make workers less dissatisfied, to justify the technologizing of public education or the subsidization of private schools, to help the medical profession strengthen its monopolistic entrepreneurial practices, or to assist lawyers to select docile juries. Naturally all such projects are stated less bluntly. With the aid of scientistic jargon and "mature" methodology, they are alleged to have "scientific" as well as practical significance.

Fortunately, there have always been professors of sociology and social work who care more for the intellectual growth and independence of their students and for the health of their discipline in the service of society than for fitting themselves into a secure bureaucratic scenario. Fortunately also, there have always been students who ask unorthodox questions and try to find answers to them through personal investigation, reading, and having "rap" sessions with stimulating fellow students and others.

So much for the professional façades that social workers and sociologists try to develop and maintain. So much also for brief glances into the chambers of horrors behind too many of those façades. Invidious distinctions between the professions, and common backgrounds aside, just how should social workers and sociologists now try to picture themselves to themselves and to specific and relevant publics? How different should these images be from those described? How should those role conceptions permit them to deal with their truly overpowering constituencies (clients, students, sponsors) and with the highly controversial intellectual, professional, and social problems now confronting them? Are both social workers and sociologists now all too often merely parts of the symptoms of our society's malaise and/or tools of shortsighted and selfish social exploiters and oppressors? If so, do they have to be?

How should sociologists and social workers face up to such an accusation as that of the three Nobel prize-winning economists, Gunnar Myrdal of Sweden, Jan Tinbergen of The Netherlands, and Kenneth J. Arrow of Harvard University? They state:

The wastefulness of Western Economies—in energy, in food and in the despoiling of the environment—is not an oversight, but an inherent trend in a system which produces primarily for corporate profit. The economic crisis in industrial democracies raises serious questions about the very nature of the economic system of these societies.[5]

This crisis is not merely economic. It has deep-set ramifications that are political and also more broadly social, cultural, and psychological. This waste, these inconsistencies, this inadequacy of a mythological "system," these forces making for disintegration and for needed sweeping reorganization are crucial aspects of the scene in which social work and sociology professionals are presumably active. The principal problem of both professions is that far too few professionals consciously recognize these as problems with which they should try to cope. In shrinking from such recognition, they are left unaware of the nature of their real role.

War has been an integral part of our national life every year since the United States came into existence. It has long been the focal point of our Federal budget. Especially since we embarked on a series of thrusts toward international imperialism and even worldwide hegemony beginning with the Spanish-American War in particular, the United States has come to resemble more and more a latter day Roman Empire, adapted to the exigencies of our day's technology and world conditions. How can we discover steps of any sort that might be taken to reveal and assess the militarization and imperialization of our society?

We are so far from having an effective military-industrial peace program nationally and internationally that steps toward the goal appear to be in the realm of fantasy. To achieve an effective military-industrial peace program, some minimal needs would be

(1) the international control of international trade in order to dismantle the imperialistic exploitation of weaker nations; (2) the creation of a United Nations peace-keeping force of sufficient size and power to handle all international confrontations; (3) the placing of the vast resources under the oceans and in the polar regions in the possession and under the control of the United Nations; (4) the development of effective worldwide controls over population expansion; (5) the internationalization of access to technology and technologists through the systematic exchange of university personnel throughout the world; (6) the development of international negotiations for peaceful co-existence rather than—as now—for the maintenance of imperialistic advantages for multinational corporations and for the "have" nations, and other recourses that such points suggest.

The United States, as wealthy as it is, might well learn that a single nation can have both guns and butter only in the short run. The guns and what they control become progressively more costly and lead to the eventual loss of colonial and neo-colonial controls as well as to the eventual destruction of the nation's own internal morale. The British have had many lessons in this sort of thing from which they have not even yet learned anything. United States ventures in Korea and Vietnam have, for the time, taught a lot of rank-and-file Americans how costly such imperialistic efforts are, but our politicians do not appear to have ceased being tools of international adventurers. Given the nature of the present principal power centers of the world, it is highly unlikely that an equitable distribution of world resources can come about without recourse to war. Such a war would be of such destructive and revolutionary magnitude that it would achieve results far different—as is usual with wars—from those presumably sought. It would probably return humanity to a lower level of barbarism than the present one.

In terms of today's and tomorrow's needs, whether sociologists or social workers shall strive to lead creatively or be content with mere walk-on roles depends upon the extent to which they insist upon rewriting outmoded scenarios and then standing firm in their efforts to perform such rewritten ways of working and living. Social workers can do this through probing critically into the consequences of their own activities and more generally of those of their agency and other agencies. They can look into alternative and more basic procedures. Sociologists can do this through learning to know much more intimately how a variety of people actually cope with life and living. And they, too, can look into alternative and even radically different ways of making life more livable for more people. With the great wealth of examples available in historical documents and cultural anthropological research publications as well as in the experiences of living social actionists, such a quest for alternatives can result in syntheses or adaptations of previously tried life styles rather than in speculative efforts.

The crisis of our times thus raises this question: Since sociology is an instrument of social competition and conflict, since there are so many kinds of sociology vying for pre-eminence in credibility or legitimacy, what kind of sociology relates best to the professional concerns and needs of those involved in actual human problems, in social casework, group work, and community organization as well as in other social welfare activities on whatever level? Stated a bit differently: Since the various types of sociology appear to serve interests of diverse groups and social classes, *whose* sociology is likely to be most helpful to those involved in mass concerns?

In replying to these questions, I should like to insist first that the alleged gap between social work and sociology is both an invidiously artificial one and one damaging to the two disciplines. For sociologists, the gap reflects their long struggle—mentioned at the outset of this chapter—to disown their own reformist and polemical origins. For social workers, the gap is symptomatic of their anxiety to be recognized as autonomous and identifiable professionals and not just stepchildren of an *omnium-gatherum* college category such as they long saw sociology to be.

It is true that social work can be defined as an application of sociology and psychology to individual, group, and community problems, but this makes the relationship look like a one-way linkage. That conception presumes that sociologists and psychologists develop the methods, perspectives, theories, and even techniques of application—that is, the remedial measures—and that social workers learn from those specialists what may be useful in their profession and then go forth to apply the memorized formulas and procedures. But this leaves out of consideration the highly significant contribution of praxis, of the field-clinical study of actual human behavior in social situations, to sociology and psychology not only in their application to human problems— individually and socially and societally—but also in their development as theoretical disciplines.

Dedicated social workers use their experiences to test and to modify not only traditional social wisdom but also to test and to modify psychological and sociological theories they may have learned. Individuals and groups moving back and forth between practical social welfare activities and critical theoretical efforts in the social sciences have thus made crucial contributions in both areas.

How should social workers and sociologists now try to have themselves perceived? As I see it, both groups should discard their artificial façades and, along with those façades, their concern about fighting for status within the outworn hierarchy of older professions. Both that hierarchy and the basic definition of professionalism have long needed reorganization and redefinition to relate them more intimately to popular needs. The mystiques of science and of health practice are wearing thin with growing popular awareness of the human fallibility behind professional masques.

Social workers and sociologists should willingly have themselves seen clearly for what they are: trained people who are seeking to understand and to cope with human problems in an outworn organizational setting that requires drastic revision. They should relate to their clients and students not as priestly authoritarians but as fellow seekers after helpful knowledge and solutions, not as co-participants in a game of bluff or of scrounging but as co-workers in the struggle to reorganize society. That's a tall order, one from which the entrenched in any calling or institution typically shrink, but society is being reorganized and will continue to be reorganized—sometimes radically—again and again. The question is not whether or not to reorganize but whether well-informed instruments of democratic policymaking or charismatic opportunists for selfish interests will provide the leadership.

Can these professionals deal with their clients, students, sponsors, and more general publics in a more democratic manner? Both social workers and sociologists are commonly routinized, co-opted, and even robotized by an overload of clients, students, and other types of problems. Great pressures develop to treat each client or student or human problem situation as a depersonalized unit to be handled as part of a bulk or to be subjected to handy formulas. A former caseworker, the sociologist Glenn Jacobs, generalizes about the situation in a manner that fits a great many in either social work or sociology: In response to a comment that a given person was "young and idealistic and wants to help people," a supervisor asserted, "Well, please tell him what the story is!" And what is that "story"? Jacobs says it

means one must perform the everyday function, whether legitimate or otherwise, in a manner that is no secret to anyone who keeps his eyes open. Witness the myth of services. . . . [The] worker . . . receives an elaborate code of instructions for recording services he never really performs. The deception has grown out of the need [among others] to fulfill the terms of the reimbursement procedure of the federal and state agencies.[6]

Forms must be filled out whether the symbols noted down stand for behavior or for nothing. Just as certain routines have to be performed to make college credits appear to mean what they are claimed to mean, so the welfare agency officials have to be able to "document" their claim that the prescribed services were performed.

How else can social workers and sociologists deal with their constituencies? They can unionize and fight for adequate facilities and resources, for professional freedom, and for enough colleagues to do a defensible job. To some extent, these goals are now being sought through existing trade unions of teachers, social workers, and governmental employees. The struggle includes the keeping of unions democratically representative of their membership.

How far can such efforts now be taken within our society as it is now organized? The task is difficult and complicated but certainly not impossible. The problems of social workers and of sociologists do not differ greatly in this respect from those of other people-serving professionals in our society. To work for the reorganization of society so that social workers and sociologists, among others, can do the tasks they can learn need to be done is a conception that shocks and even terrifies many middle-class citizens. The time is passing, however, when we can hide such a sweeping need by talking about such myths as a self-perpetuating social stratum hopelessly dominated by a "subculture of poverty."[7] We also have other subculture problems which similarly are not necessarily unchangeable—those of smug professionals and of conspiratorial managers of businesses, undemocratic labor unions, government agencies, and crime syndicates. Changed life conditions and changed social controls can modify any human group or class and its subculture. Such organizations as unions and political pressure groups can provide leverage to work for such goals.

There are hazards to one's employment when one tries to respond to such a radical challenge. I would certainly urge confronting that challenge rather than "copping out," but I have also advised my students of the wisdom of providing themselves with the security and employment flexibility to be found in acquiring a second calling upon which they might fall back in an emergency. Some of my more daring students have also been the more imaginative, and they have found that such an alternative strengthens their determination to be constructive citizens and specialists.

As the Nobel prize-winners quoted above have put it, we are faced with "serious questions about the very nature of the economic system" of our society. The sociologist W. G. Sumner foresaw this in 1898 when he asserted that the struggle against plutocracy "is to be the social war of the twentieth century." In that war, he said, "militarism, expansion and imperialism will all favor plutocracy . . . the returns for which will not go into the treasury, but into the hands of a few schemers."[8] Our depression of the 1930s ended only in the vast destruction of World War II. That war is estimated to have cost 60 million lives, and six-sevenths of those killed were on the so-called "winning side." Only one-seventh died on the "losing" Axis side.[9] Most of us are sheltered from realistically perceiving the basically ongoing and expanding crisis created by the still-continuing series of wars and threats of wars and by the fact that the United States military-industrial complex has become the arms manufacturer, power broker, and dispute arbiter of much of the world. Will the current economic sogginess end in World War III, with a human cost even greater than that of World War II, a cost that could conceivably mean human extermination?

To continue the discussion, how should these two professions deal with highly controversial intellectual and social problems? Briefly I would say: forthrightly and radically. The human situation today is so grave that only such an approach to our problems can be justified. Only thus can these and related professions cease being symptoms of social malaise, sops to distract people from being aware of widespread social disintegration. In middle-class circles, these are hard lines. They are lines somehow to be brushed aside or rationalized. Such a recourse cannot, however, be avoided much longer. The profligate waste of our so-called economic "system" is making radical social reorganization more pressing.

Now to the basic question to which I am devoting myself in this chapter: Among the many schools of sociology—functionalist, neo-positivist, ethnomethodological, Marxist, cultural, ethological, sociobiological, symbolic interactionist, humanist, and all the rest—what sort is most useful to social work and thus to human welfare? I take the position that it is the kind of sociology—roughly called "humanist"—that will make a lot of social work as currently practiced a thing of the past. It is the kind of sociology that can so help to restructure society as to make social work not only much different but much more important in the service of human goals.

In spite of the notable role in social science down through the years of concern to find humane solutions to social problems, by the late 1940s sociology was under a cloud of repressive Joseph-McCarthyism[10] and another cloud of abstract, functionalist, and scientistic Talcott-Parsonianism.[11] McCarthyism's red-baiting excesses stimulated a nervous dread of the socially critical and controversial, of any basic or radical approach to human affairs. The teachings of the Harvard sociologist Talcott Parsons were dogmatic and elitist, useful both to the obscurantist and the managerial. He tried to erect *the* universal sociology out of terms vague enough to avoid being contradicted by direct observation of human behavior. The pressing social problems of that period concerned social workers, daring journalists, radical trade unionists, and political agitators. On the contrary, sociologists were then more likely to be dealing with ideas and symbols that they looked upon as subtle and profound, the problems not of society but of sociological theory and method, or to be spending their time accumulating survey data for those in power.

The highlights of previous sociological history were quite different from what one saw commonly in the 1940s. For example, even though W. G. Sumner's greatest contibution to sociology was his library based cross-cultural work, *Folkways* (1906),[12] his challenging essays[13] written from the 1870s onward reflect his intimate involvement in the municipal affairs of New Haven and in Connecicut's public educational facilities and his concern about the growth of plutocracy and especially of plutocratic imperialism.[14] Without that practical background, *Folkways* would have lacked the sense of life and living that it contains. Similarly, such publications as Charles Booth's *Life and Labour of the People of London* (1892–1897, 1902),[15] Paul U. Kellogg and associates' *The Pittsburgh Survey* (1909–1914),[16] Shelby M. Harrison and associates' *The Springfield Survey* (1918–1920),[17] W. I. Thomas and Florian Znaniecki's *The Polish Peasant in Europe and America* (1918),[18] and studies inspired by the famous "Chicago school" of sociologists surrounding Robert E. Park and Ernest W. Burgess,[19] especially during the 1920s and 1930s, reflect intimacy of observation and dedication to humane goals. The indebtedness of all these and many other contemporary sociological writers to professional social workers is quite evident and is fully acknowledged.

Park and Burgess directed sociological research not toward the erection of a chimerical structure of abstract theory but toward "the diagnosis and control of social problems"[20] in the service of humanity. Maurice R. Davie of Yale similarly stated his sociological preoccupation and that which he tried to impart to his students as one with "the successes and failures which societies have had in attempting to meet their great group needs."[21] On the other hand, subsidies for the solution of managerial and other manipulative problems during the depression of the 1930s and especially during World War II turned the center of many sociologists' research concerns away from humanist or people-serving projects towards efforts useful primarily to the powerful, towards work at special-interest problem solving for a fee. Neo-functionalism and its variants provided "value-free" scientistic rationales for such an amoral and sometimes immoral reorientation of the so-called "science" of sociology.

Then, in 1950–1951, after increasing rumblings of dissatisfaction from those concerned with sociology's growing dehumanization and technocratization, the Society for the Study of Social Problems entered the professional sociological and social work scene.[22] It represented outspoken evidence by many of its participants of strong concern for more humane values, for more of a turn toward humanist sociology. Its appearance was greeted with cries of outrage from those then in control of the American Sociological Society (now called the American Sociological Association). As a member of that ASA group, Peter M. Blau, recently put it, "I have been concerned with the anti-systematic, anti-theoretical and anti-quantitative biases that seem to characterize many members of the SSSP."[23]

That statement might have been written at any time during the first quarter century of SSSP's life by any of the scientistic. It is the cry of persons who cannot assimilate the cumulative wisdom to be derived from the field-clinical study of actual human behavior *in situ* whether of individuals or groups. It is the moan of those who need a precise structure of ideas in which to believe, however fanciful that structure might be so long as it appears to them to be "scientific." Once that so-called "basic" intellectual fabrication has become part of them, accepted as given, they can tolerate their intellectual insecurities, their suspicion of the unbridged gaps between their abstractions and what actually takes place in human society. It is a desperate grasp for what looks so tenable, so secure, in the physical and biological sciences: "hard" and quantified data. They do not appear to realize how elusive the "hardness" of data may be even in the physical and biological fields. No matter how contrived the "hardness" of social data might be, they think its "hardness" substantiates their conclusions, provides a platform for their elitist pronouncements, and boosts the marketability of their products to grantors and contractors.[24]

The philosopher Morris R. Cohen discusses the similar habit of physicists and chemists

to distrust naked observation and to resort to various mechanisms, repetitions and mathematical calculations to establish their facts; for biologists to use controls to check their experiments; for philologists to verify their quotations and references. . . . These cautions are organized so that no one can omit them and maintain his professional standing. Sometimes indeed these habits become mechanical. We forget their rationality and oppose any extensions or improvements of them which men of genius discover.[25]

In other words, they become barriers as well as gates to scientific discovery. Little wonder that it is the great investigators who are puzzled by what others take to be obvious. As John Dewey puts it: "Every great advance in science has issued from a new audacity of imagination."[26] Both Cohen and Dewey looked upon science of any kind as a way of exploring constantly changing realities, not as a way of building a rigid representation of "reality" and of its "laws" or of finding plausible techniques attractive as merchandise for the market place.

Members of the Society for the Study of Social Problems who are humanist sociologists do not throw out the triplet babies—system, theory, and quantification—with their intellectual bath water. To humanist sociologists, system, theory, and quantification are useful tools, but they are not a "holy trinity" that should be permitted to dominate sociological research and thinking. Systematization of social observations must be done with care and with an intimate awareness of the nature of the firsthand observations discovered to possess some systematic relationship. Theories and methods exist in abundance. They can be quite useful when employed with discrimination, with respect for social context, with an understanding of the continuous nature of social processes, with adequate attention to the cultural background of the people studied, and above all with painstaking regard for the observer-subject relationship.[27]

The Society for the Study of Social Problems consists of a mixture of social scientists, social workers, and other concerned students and professionals. As an affiliate of the American and of the International Sociological Associations, SSSP has given the sociological discipline as a whole a substantial push toward rapprochement both with social workers and with the more serious and less routine journalists, belletrists, and others involved in public affairs. It promotes a significant move toward scientific realism and away from the traditional scientistic image sociologists once constructed for themselves in order to obtain legitimacy for their profession in university and in intellectual, political, and business circles. It also facilitated the subsequent organization of Sociologists for Women in Society, the Black and Radical Caucuses within the various sociological associations, the Association of Black Sociologists, the Section on Marxist Sociology of the American Sociological Association, the Association for Humanist Sociology, and other highly stimulating but less visible organizational and policy developments.

This series of organizational changes continuing from the 1950s represents a cooperative movement toward making sociology and social work both meet a little more adequately the frightening crisis of our times. Please note that it was achieved by forthright organizational innovation and not by the kind of "boring from within" glorified in liberal professional circles and often so delusory and ineffective—so often just rhetorical refurbishing rather than social change.

Social work has traveled far from the poor-relief philosophy of some three centuries ago that was modified little up to the middle of the nineteenth century. Its problems are no longer capsulized as centering about the character weaknesses of the shiftless and irresponsible. Elitist and racist hereditarian theories are still put forward, but sound scientific findings have undercut more and more of their policy-making influence.[28] In the words of the social work researcher, Philip Klein, and his associates, "In so far as specific modes of action for the betterment of social and political life are gradually crystallized, social work as a practical art gains a more clear-cut foothold."[29]

Sociology, too, is no longer tied so closely to the mystical positivism of an Auguste Comte,[30] the simplistic evolutionism of a Herbert Spencer,[31] the pedantic functionalism of a Talcott Parsons,[32] or the caricaturing statistical manipulations of a Paul F. Lazarsfeld.[33] It is now much more open to intercult competition. Concerns with the humane no longer need to be disguised with jargon or with needless statistics—even though such practices do persist.

A generation ago both fields looked upon the possibility of working for the reorganization of society as heretical, as an allegation damaging to the public image of either discipline. Today few social workers or sociologists are utopians, but many realize that working for basic social change is not any longer a matter of choice. That is what they must do—as effectively as they can—in order to accept the responsibilities of their professions.[34]

notes

[1]Frederick Wiseman, "Welfare" (film). Boston: Zipporah Films, 1975.
[2]H. F. Waters, "Wiseman on Welfare," *Newsweek*, September 25, 1975, pp. 62–63; p. 62 quoted.
[3]S. M. Miller, "Fred Wiseman's 'Welfare,'" *Focal Points* (Boston University), no. 5 (October 10, 1975), p. 2.

[4]A. McC. Lee, *Multivalent Man*, rev. ed. (New York: George Braziller, 1970), chap. 14.

[5]Gunnar Myrdal, Jan Tinbergen, and K. J. Arrow quoted in Tristam Coffin, ed., "The American Economy, Looking Ahead," *Washington Spectator*, special report, Fall 1975, 2 pp.; at p. 1.

[6]Glenn Jacobs, "Life in the Colonies: Welfare Workers and Clients," in *The Participant Observer*, Jacobs, ed. (New York: George Braziller, 1970), chap. 11; pp. 253-54.

[7]E. B. Leacock, ed., *The Culture of Poverty: A Critique* (New York: Simon and Schuster, 1971), esp. Hylan Lewis, "Culture of Poverty? What Does it Matter?" pp. 345-63.

[8]W. G. Sumner, "The Conquest of the United States by Spain," in Sumner, *Essays*, A. G. Keller, ed., vol. 1 (New Haven: Yale University Press, 1911), pp. 297-334; p. 325.

[9]Quincy Wright, *A Study of War*, 2nd ed. (Chicago: University of Chicago Press, 1965), pp. 1542-43.

[10]Dennis Wrong, "Theories of McCarthyism—A Survey," *Dissent*, vol. 1 (1955-1956), pp. 385-92; Martin Trow, "Small Businessmen, Political Intolerance, and Support for McCarthy," *American Journal of Sociology*, vol. 64 (1958-1959), pp. 270-81; R. H. Rovere, *Senator Joe McCarthy* (New York: Harcourt, Brace, 1959).

[11]W. C. Mitchell, *Sociological Analysis and Politics: The Theories of Talcott Parsons* (Englewood Cliffs, N.J.: Prentice-Hall, 1967); H. J. Bershady, *Ideology and Social Knowledge* (New York: John Wiley & Sons, 1973); Guy Rocher, *Talcott Parsons and American Sociology* (New York: Barnes & Noble, 1975).

[12]W. G. Sumner, *Folkways* (Boston: Ginn & Co., 1906).

[13]W. G. Sumner, *Essays*, A. G. Keller, ed. (New Haven: Yale University Press, 1911, 1913, 1914, 1919), 4 vols.

[14]H. E. Starr, *William Graham Sumner* (New York: Henry Holt and Co., 1925), esp. chaps. 1-2, 9-12; for a caricature of Sumner that ignores his intellectual growth and his adaptation to changed life conditions, see Richard Hofstadter, *Social Darwinism in American Thought*, rev. ed. (Boston: Beacon Press, 1955), chap. 3.

[15]Charles Booth, *Life and Labour of the People of London*, 3rd ed., 17 vols. (London: MacMillan & Co., 1902-1903); T. S. Simey and M. B. Simey, *Charles Booth: Social Scientist* (New York: Oxford University Press, 1960).

[16]P. U. Kellogg, ed., *The Pittsburgh Survey*, 6 vols. (New York: Russell Sage Foundation, 1909-1914).

[17]S. M. Harrison, ed., *The Springfield Survey*, 3 vols. (New York: Russell Sage Foundation, 1918).

[18]W. I. Thomas and Florian Znaniecki, *The Polish Peasant in Europe and America*, 5 vols. (Boston: Badger, 1918-1920).

[19]R. E. Park and E. W. Burgess, *Introduction to the Science of Sociology*, 2nd ed. (Chicago: University of Chicago Press, 1924).

[20]Ibid., p. 210.

[21]M. R. Davie, *Problems of City Life* (New York: John Wiley & Sons, 1932), p. 3.

[22]E. B. and A. McC. Lee, "The Society for the Study of Social Problems: Visions of Its Founders," *SSSP Newsletter*, vol. 5, no. 1 (1973-1974), pp. 2-5, and "The Society for the Study of Social Problems: Parental Recollections and Hopes," *Social Problems*, vol. 24 (1976-1977), pp. 4-14.

[23]P. M. Blau, "Reflections on the Future of Social Problems Theory," *SSSP Social Problems Theory Division Newsletter*, no. 4 (Summer 1975), p. 3.

[24]Irwin Deutscher, *Why Do They Say One Thing, Do Another?* (Morristown, N.J.: General Learning Press, 1973).

Feuds between Sociologists and Social Workers 85

[25] M. R. Cohen, "Method, Scientific," *Encyclopaedia of the Social Sciences* (New York: Macmillan Co., 1933), vol. 10, p. 394.

[26] John Dewey, *The Quest for Certainty* (New York: G. P. Putnam's Sons, 1929), p. 310.

[27] S. T. Bruyn, *The Human Perspective in Sociology: The Methodology of Participant Observation* (Englewood Cliffs, N.J.: Prentice-Hall, 1966).

[28] L. J. Kamin, *The Science and Politics of I.Q.* (New York: John Wiley & Sons, 1974); Marshall Sahlins, *The Use and Abuse of Biology* (Ann Arbor: University of Michigan Press, 1976).

[29] Philip Klein and others, *A Social Study of Pittsburgh* (New York: Columbia University Press, 1938), p. 7.

[30] Gertrud Lenzer, "Introduction," in *Auguste Comte and Positivism: The Essential Writings*, Lenzer, ed. (New York: Harper Torchbooks, 1975), pp. xvii–lxviii.

[31] Judah Rumney, *Herbert Spencer's Sociology* (London: Williams and Norgate, 1934).

[32] See footnote 11.

[33] J. S. Coleman, "Paul F. Lazarsfeld (1901–1976)," *ASA Footnotes*, vol. 4, no. 9 (December 1976), p. 7.

[34] This chapter adapts and expands the author's Louis Goldstein Memorial Lecture, School of Social Work, University of Connecticut, Hartford, "What Kind of Sociology Is Useful to Social Workers?" published in *Journal of Sociology and Social Welfare*, vol. 4 (1976–1977), pp. 4–13.

four

Key Issues in Sociologies as Weapons

In his most influential book, the sociologist Robert S. Lynd discusses "Knowledge for what?" He is speaking especially of knowledge of society, and his question is thus as perennially significant and controversial as the closely related one, "Sociology for whom?" He concerns himself with social science as "an organized part of the culture which exists to help man in continually understanding and rebuilding his culture."[1]

Lynd holds the position that scientific observation, verification, and generalization can furnish data and theories transcending biasing influences. This is a general view of social science shared by both positivists and humanists, also by the "established" and the "oppositional," by the elitist or managerial and the egalitarian or participatory. Lynd realizes, however, how far short social science is now and is likely to be in the foreseeable future of an ideal application of the scientific ethic. He warns, for example:

Social science cannot perform its function if the culture constrains it at certain points in ways foreign to the spirit of science; and at all points where such constraints limit the free use of intelligence to pose problems, to analyze all relevant aspects of them, or to draw conclusions, it is necessary for social science to work directly to remove the causes of these obstacles.[2]

Lynd thus sees social science as a very human enterprise, caught up in striving and combat. He does not share the scientism of those who hope to build social science into an idealized fantasy of the physical and biological sciences.

Many sociologists, early and more recent, attempt to use social science findings to construct a static model of symbols reflective of the characteristics and tendencies they think they see in nature. They assume that, to the extent that social science is adequately and dependably developed, it provides uncontrovertible information and theories upon which to base policy-making. Since its terms, in this view, are dictated by nature, evolving social science "must" surely transcend human interests and prejudices. It can report that natural order of human affairs in just as credible a manner as scientific procedures are said to uncover what exists and evolves in the physical and biological worlds.

The founders of sociology were entranced by the accomplishments and especially by the claims to social power for intellectuals made by physical and biological scientists. Throughout the ages intellectuals have sought such supportive sanctions for their views. When the utility of supernaturalism and of traditional academic philosophies began to wane, they flocked to "nature" via "science" as the sanction for their endeavors. Sociology's founders thus tried to help germinate a prestigious and authoritative natural social science, one presumably formed with a compendium of wisdom uninfluenced by political, economic, racial, class, ethnic, or sexist biases. As viewed from the vantage point of later generations, those founders were scarcely aware of many of the biases of the separate worlds within which they themselves operated.[3]

In reacting against metaphysical abstractions of traditional philosophy and ethical mandates transmitted by theologians, many of sociology's founders did not take into consideration the fact that social science is not only a creature of culture and embedded in it; it is also caught up in social processes. It is itself an aspect of social competition and conflict. On the ethical obligations of the scientist, Robert S. Lynd joined other social scientists in breaking with those who claimed with the economist Wesley Mitchell that "science is concerned to show only what is true and what is false," that "science itself does not pronounce practical or esthetic or moral judgments."[4] Lynd contends that if scientists fail to make such judgments, "in this world in which the gap between sophisticated knowledge and folk-thinking is so wide, they but aggravate the limitations on the utility of science to man."[5]

Lynd thus perceives clearly that sociology raises a question more pressing than "Knowledge for what?" It asks a question that many social scientists look upon as demeaning, as impugning their motives, or as just irrelevant. That question implies the principal theme of this book: "knowledge for whom?" It is demeaning to a social scientist if one expects an answer more specific than: Society in general. The usual position is that, as the social scientists R. A. Scott and Arnold Shore have it, "any significant addition to our stock of social scientific knowledge, as long as it is based on solid research, will ultimately be useful to policymakers in enabling them to understand their alternatives more clearly, to formulate better or more rational policies, and to evaluate consequences of their decisions more clearly."[6] But a "significant addition" created by whom? With what biases? For what purposes? For which policy-makers? Working for whom? Judging alternatives in what ethical or practical context? Such questions concerned Lynd deeply, but it is not clear how far he would have pushed their implications. They open doors to broader degrees of relativism than he might have been willing to accept. When put specifically, such queries recognize that the scientist who is trying to mirror the character and tendencies of human society is also a person who is individually involved in social processes, in fact that whole "schools" of social scientists are caught up in quite similar and similarly distorting social processes.

Consciously or unconsciously, sociologists gather, organize, and apply knowledge for conscious or unconscious participants in competition and conflict. It is crucial in evaluating any sociological effort to find out for what kind of individual or organization, social clique or social class the work was consciously or unconsciously put together. All sociologists study or write within one or more group-cultural contexts based upon their respective social class, ethnic background, career interests, and other influences. Their writings are thus to be seen as significantly autobiographical, regardless of their subject. They are also written for an audience and with one or more social and individual purposes. In other words, probing questions about any sociological work should include: Knowledge by whom? for what? and for whom?

"Knowledge for whom?" is often brushed aside in academic

sociological circles as a nasty or perhaps a boorish question except when it is applied to the "non-scientific." Many sociologists assert that that question in its specific sense is asked principally by those who have contracted an alleged social disorder, "alienation,"[7] a catchword pathology recently popular among some sociologists as a convenient and profitable research ploy. To be "scientific," modish sociological operators claim that it is only necessary to figure out what sort of research topic might induce a research grant from a foundation controlled by business men and their professionals and politicians. They have ready rationalizations for such efforts at serving or at least at pleasing powerful interests. Only the "alienated" or "oppositional" would carry objectivity or accuracy or human service to the point of mandating disengagement for social scientists from the *status quo*—even though it is more often the disengaged who appear to make important contributions to our knowledge of human society and social relations. "Alienated" social scientists are said by the sociologist Edward Shils to "overestimate . . . the role of deception, manipulation, and coercion, and the degree of deliberate concerting action by the elites against the rest of society."[8] Only in the immediate and undimmed shadow of such a scandal as "Watergate" is the reactionary character of such a statement apparent without further argument.

While it might embarrass a "proper" social scientist to have to admit that a subsidy came from an embattled trade union or a minority political party or a "cause" organization fighting for some oppressed group, the thin disguise of special interest afforded by foundation names or government agency labels permits relations with such entities to be used as badges of honor rather than as suggestions of bias. At the same time, a sociologist giving expertise to a civil-libertarian crusade, to a fight for sexual equality, or to a struggle against racist behavior by a powerful organization is "unscientific," a "reformer," a "radical," perhaps even a "dilettante bourgeois liberal." Since such a sociologist is working for a "whom" at odds with—"alienated" from—the existing structure and values of legitimated social controls, the respectable social scientists feel that they can raise the question in this instance of "Knowledge [specifically] for whom?" And it is clearly meant to impugn the actionist-scientist's scientific integrity.[9]

The suggestion is this: Let us confront the currently "normal" sociology from a broadly humanist, existential, radical viewpoint. That is to say, let us try to see what sense "normal" sociology makes in terms of fundamental social-democratic concerns and norms. From the stance of sociology for people, what does the currently "established" sociology appear to be, with its pretenses of objectivity and of positivist authority? For whom is that sociology developed, entrenched, and promulgated?

At the same time, in order to have a balanced perspective, let us see how humanist sociology is confronted by positivists who are typically elitists or managerial in their orientation. That is to say, let us try to see what sense humanist sociology makes in terms of the methods and theories utilized by positivists. From the standpoint of an elitist sociology for management, what does humanist sociology appear to be, with its pretenses of egalitarian human service? For whom is humanist sociology developed, given some degree of institutional acceptance, and promulgated in educational and consultative channels?

"Normal" or "establishment" sociology changes slightly from time to time, especially as one controlling power clique succeeds another.[10] It has been identified with such terms as positivism, neo-positivism, social or cultural evolution, social surveys, structural-functionalism, systemic analysis, and operant conditioning. These terms represent chiefly modifications in stance and rhetoric, method, and emphasis but not in orientation toward the ongoing structure of legitimated social controls. Each formulation typically commits itself to "orderly change," to the maintenance or restoration of "equilibrium" or "consensus" or perhaps a "moving equilibrium," to "adaptation to changed conditions," to "change from within" (in other words, by those in control, not by outsiders), and to the protection of "society" (i.e., their social class) from "pathological" or "disruptive" or "deviant" influences.

All of these commitments, including the one dealing with the "pathological" or "disruptive" or "deviant" as defined, reveal the identification of the "normal" discipline's ideology with the *status quo* as seen through professional class eyes, not with some autonomous and unbiased intellectual power structure. In other words, positivist sociology typically contributes its share in the brainwashing of future functionaries for business, the professions, and government as they are socialized in our schools and colleges. Its practitioners also make sure that their offerings of data and views to policy-makers will be taken to be "constructive"—in other words to be supportive of the existing "social order," as they like to call it.

But normal positivistic sociology is something more than a social sedative and a body of techniques and theories with which to create plausible documentation for managerial decision-making. It also helps to define a substitute, an almost anthropomorphic stand-in, for the authority of divine revelation. Positivistic sociology is the discipline that cannot help but transmit "nature's" dependable knowledge—if not actually "the truth"—and thus the basis for finding "the way" toward social peace, tranquility, and equilibrium. All that is needed is enough research funds—regardless of their sources. Through sociology and allied bodies of knowledge, we can learn, in the words of Buckminster Fuller, the "rules that evolution is employing and trying to make clear to us. They are not man-made laws. They are the infinitely accommodative laws of the intellectual integrity governing the universe," to quote one of his positivistic passages.[11]

To a humanist sociologist this passage is overwrought anthropomorphism if not deism, not far from the metaphysical extremes to which Auguste Comte[12] pushed his sociological positivism in the mid-nineteenth century. It is still another example of elitist effort to sanction the power of social scientists and at the same time to strip individuals of their sense of personal control and responsibility. To a positivist, Fuller's is probably a fairly sound position, subject only to some quibbles about terminology and his lack of formal sociological credentials. Where medieval scholars sought power through fantasizing the nature and wishes of deity and plotting ways to manipulate him or her, positivists see similar opportunities in discovering the "laws of nature" so far as society is concerned. They try to find ways to exploit such "laws" whether or not that may imply some anthropomorphic explanatory device as well.

From the foregoing, some of the challenges between humanist sociologists and the positivistic are clear. Let me next list some points not at issue between the two groups and then set forth some issues on which there appear to be sharp contrasts. This effort is from my own view of humanist sociology's stance[13] and from my own studies of positivism as an ideology. In an earlier chapter, I relate humanist influences upon social thought to social-historical frontiers, to migration, and to other marginalizing pressures that have pushed thoughtful people toward more people-centered and people-responsible orientations.

Many of the words used to describe humanist sociology recur in discussions of other emphases in sociology. All types of sociology are put forward as ways to understand the nature of social groups, of society, and of their impacts upon human lives. They all assume or specify applications of such knowledge. They all have access to the wealth of research methods, of basic research data, and of hypotheses which social scientists have developed. They all try to coordinate their findings and their applications with those of other social sciences that they accept as comparable and compatible.

Humanist sociology differs from other types in its emphasis upon the aspects of social structures and of arrangements among people and within social institutions which are conducive to individual freedom and dignity, survival, and the enjoyment of living. As I see it, it is intended to serve people, not their manipulators. Like humanistic psychology but starting with the whole social context rather than with the whole person, humanist sociology tries to cope with problems of people in all their humanity. It accepts the implications of the ancient adage of Protagoras that everything in life is to be measured in terms of people, in terms of popular needs and desires, limitations and opportunities. It is frankly existential and relative, not to be diverted into searches for such will-o'-the-wisps as universals, absolutes, and essences. It deals especially with what has been happening, is happening, and is likely to happen. It tries to understand and find ways to cope with ongoing social processes and change. It leaves speculation about ultimate causes and ultimate consequences to those who busy themselves with untestable and unverifiable hypotheses.

People appear to be only accidental parasites on an insignificant planet when one takes a cosmic viewpoint, but the business of a humanist scientist is not to be befogged by such a mystifying perspective. People we are. People are our primary business. We do well to get on with what we can accomplish to help prolong, make more tolerable, and even beautify and glorify our days upon this planet.

To sum up positivist-humanist contrasts, here are seven broad considerations that appear to me to be very much at issue in the uses of such sociologies as weapons in social struggles:

In many positive views, sociology should be:	*In a humanist view, sociology should be:*
1. Nature-centered	People-centered
2. Elitist	Egalitarian and broadly representative
3. Ethically neutral	Ethical
4. A responsibility of impersonal methods and machines	A human responsibility
5. Supportive and interpretive of existing knowledge and social organization	"Oppositional," critical of existing knowledge and social organization
6. Dedicated to the maintenance or restoration of a presumed equilibrium or moving equilibrium in society	Dedicated to an acceptance of the persistence of social change
7. A product of professionals carefully trained to be technicians of method and theory	A product of carefully trained scientists who value intimate observation and creative intellectual ferment

These points are to be examined in more detail. As it is clear from their statement, they are as much challenges of positivist sociologists to humanists as they are of humanist sociologists to positivists. Which column is the more acceptable depends upon one's viewpoint, upon one's group-cultural embedments, upon one's perception of one's desired roles in interpersonal relations.

1. Nature-centered *versus* people-centered: Positivists ask: Aren't people part of nature? Doesn't nature control all things? Isn't it the better part of wisdom to look to the apparently dominating and basic tendencies of nature for guidance? Aren't there natural environmental, biological, and societal determinants that transcend the rough-and-tumble randomness of individual behavior and of social processes?

While many supernaturalists and nature-determinists claim to be "humanists," to be concerned chiefly with human welfare, their search for a substitute for human responsibility is usually clear enough in their writings. And with that shift in responsibility goes a belittling of the worth and dignity of humanity.

As the humanist social scientist sees it, only people can develop the knowledge and foresight with which to meet the challenges of climatic change, disease, starvation, imperialistic oppression, elitism, ethnocentrism, and all the rest of the problems to which humanity is heir. Merely to try to explain away any or all such problems as their being "natural" is childlike, an exhibition of a need to have a parent-substitute on whom to be dependent. It is quite possible that human ingenuity, given a chance, can solve any or all of them. A great many people are fortunately past the evasion, "God's will be done!" But "normal" social-scientific literature often contains that statement's rough equivalent, "It's just natural! We can't do anything about it!" Instead of "God," the determinant has become our biological nature or custom (culture) or environment or all three combined.

2. Elitist *versus* egalitarian: Intellectualism typically develops as a pathway to social distinction and power both for the intellectual and for those served by intellectuals. Since only those initiated into some type of intellectualism can fully comprehend the competence of initiates, ingroup members become the gatekeepers and certifiers of new members of an intellectual cult. They recognize themselves as members of an elite to whom society can entrust educational or medical or legal or some other kind of specialized decision-making. Even when governmental bodies give added sanction to such elites through certification, that certification is still typically controlled by people drawn from the self-perpetuating cult. Not only positivists but intellectuals in many other traditions and specialties look upon themselves as, justifiably, members of a prestigious elite. Bureaucratization being what it is, success in being prepared for certification in such an elite is often identified with high scholastic grades achieved in the academic initiating process rather than with criteria more accurately and specifically predictive of subsequent career accomplishments.

Humanist sociologists are aware both of the elitist traditions of intellectuals and of society generally and also of the way in which the bureaucratization of intellectual cults introduces rigidifying and distorting influences. They perceive the bountiful evidence of elitism's rewards in terms of status and preferment. They also realize that it blocks adequate appreciation of the dynamic multivalence of individual lives and of society. Elitist I.Q. tests screen out members of ethnic (including "racial") minorities and members of economically deprived groups from educational and career opportunities.[14] Similarly, vested elites erect defenses of certification—sometimes in terms of irrelevant criteria—to protect themselves from aggressive "outside" competitors.

What any educated person might learn through egalitarian association with people of different backgrounds—including those with little formal education—is clear to those who have undergone such experience in depth. Humanist social scientists know that a keen and fresh awareness is a cue to their penetration of new areas of understanding. This awareness is their sharp but significant reaction as new perceptions of human relations become apparent and meaningful to them. They realize that barriers of social pretentiousness and of social distance associated with elitism are as disabling intellectually to the person and especially to the social scientist as elitist ethnocentrism is disabling politically and economically to society.

3. Ethically neutral *versus* ethical: This bald statement requires modification and specification. Ethics is concerned with truth and with moral, esthetic, and practical values. Positivists do not pretend to be neutral with regard to what they perceive to be criteria for the accuracy of data and the verifiability of generalizations—in other words, with regard to their criteria for "truth." At the same time, they say that they do not wish to permit traditional moral or esthetic or practical considerations to influence or be confused with their conclusions or predictions as scientists. They claim that they can present objective alternatives for decision and action. They can set forth data suggesting the probable consequences of each alternative. Then the specialists in values of a practical sort—the business and political policymakers—can use this information to reach an informed decision—if they wish to. But the decision, with its moral or immoral, esthetic or practical implications, is entirely the responsibility of the policy-makers, not of the social scientists.

This type of "ethical neutrality" presumably helps to make the social-scientific processes of investigation and generalization as impersonal and thus as unbiased as possible. It helps to free positivist sociologists to erect a scientistic fabric of symbols which presumably reflects "reality." Their search is guided only by an evolving social-scientific (actually rather neo-scholastic) body of method and theory that involves so-called "hard data," i.e., quantified findings. In sociology the method is usually some adaptation of sample surveying, with its emphasis upon limited and structured observation and upon statistical summations, correlations, and other manipulations. That this limited ethic is adaptable to a management-serving orientation appears in the fact that it usually focuses on alternatives in public interest (such as political candidates or issues) or felt needs (such as automobiles or food products) that can be influenced.[15] Such a choice of variables rarely takes place without reference to the interests served. The choice thus can imply social responsibility through posing popular choices of socially significant alternatives. It can also imply a high degree of social irresponsibility through posing choices so chosen and arranged as to be significant only to an antisocial manipulator.

Humanist sociologists are similarly committed to the ethics of "truth," as they see it, but they are also of the opinion that an ethical neutrality with regard to moral and practical values is neither possible psychologically nor desirable socially and scientifically. They recognize social-scientific knowledge to be a human construction, an art form, that should reflect social realities as accurately as possible. Instead of leaving policy decisions entirely to political and business leaders, however, they believe that the ethical implications of possible decisions should be spelled out and discussed. Humanist sociologists themselves, as servants of humanity rather than of ruling elites, are responsible for interpreting and promulgating their field-clinical and participant-observation findings as widely as they can. They recognize that significant changes in public policy can come from popular education, organization, and agitation.

Even though he confuses humanist sociology with a distrust of reason, the sociologist Reinhard Bendix admits that "the cultivation of judgment and moral sensibility . . . provides a bulwark against the dangers of scientism, against the preoccupation with techniques for their own sake, and against the unthinking denigration of contextual understanding." Bendix should have recognized as well that science as a whole and not just humanist science, as he says, "takes the distrust of reason as its model."[16] Science shackles reason with the imperative of observational bases and where possible with experimental recourses or tests of praxis and verification.

4. Responsibility of impersonal methods and of machines *versus* human responsibility: Positivists give the impression that they would like to be the expert tenders of a system for developing knowledge that is somehow wholly exterior to themselves and for whose products they themselves have no responsibility. Facts they develop about poverty or sexism that might disquiet sources of subsidies would thus be the uncontrolled and uncontrollable products of *a priori* methods or procedures, not of their own abilities or judgments.

Positivists have to grant that members of the social-scientific professions invented the population-sampling methods selected and used, developed the interview schedules, instructed the interviewers, devised ways to code and process interview reports, and made what sense they could of the resulting summaries and statistical manipulations. But the whole series of steps, positivists contend, is controlled by predetermined and standardized rules used in many similar situations and bearing the aura of professional sanction. Other than the professions' collective responsibility for the development of methods, the human beings working in a research bureau do not feel themselves responsible for the results. No wonder that the results are often so trivial. No wonder that so many probing questions are left unasked. No wonder that routinized interviewing rather than fundamental studies of actual human behavior in problem situations is too often the procedure followed.

Humanist sociologists realize that the buck of responsibility in a social-scientific investigation cannot be passed on to a set of methods or a computing machine. They are not satisfied with mere replications of the research of others, with the use of routine methods, with superficial surveys. They see the virtues of C. Wright Mills's precepts:

Avoid any rigid set of procedures. Above all, seek to develop and to use the sociological imagination. Avoid the fetishism of method and technique. Urge the rehabilitation of the unpretentious intellectual craftsman, and try to become such a craftsman yourself. Let every man be his own methodologist; let every man be his own theorist; let theory and method again become part of the practice of a craft. Stand for the primacy of the individual scholar; stand opposed to the ascendancy of research teams of technicians. Be one mind that is on its own confronting the problems of man and society.[17]

After a study is published, others can take up the responsibility through offering criticism, but the original investigator has the primary responsibility for what is reported and analyzed.

5. Supportive and interpretive *versus* "oppositional" and critical: These opposing views arise from fundamental conceptions of the current role of sociology in existing societies. Let's assume that one believes our current class, racist, sexist, and manipulative excesses, our persistent tensions and recurrent wars, depressions, famines, and dislocations are all to be faced as either manageable or necessarily continuing problems of society. Within a so-called evolving "social order," positivists contend that some of these problems can be somewhat mitigated. Others can perhaps be kept from getting worse. With such a view, what is needed is supportive understanding for those involved in making that "order" work better. Its objectives and policies need to be interpreted or "clarified" and adequately "communicated" to its constituencies in order to achieve as broad a favorable consensus as possible.

Sociologists viewing themselves as dissenters from this view, as oppositionally critical of existing elites, their technicians, and their policies, are spoken of as being "not constructive." As the sociologist Edward Shils puts it, such people have not gotten over the "original association of sociological research with poverty and the miseries of the poor."[18] Shils's point is that sociologists should realize that they can be upwardly mobile and that the upwardly mobile should leave behind them concern for as well as involvement in human misery!

Humanist sociologists do not knowingly permit themselves to be co-opted directly or indirectly by those in powerful positions in ongoing society. To the extent that they are able to achieve a free-ranging critical stance, they try to understand social structures and to empathize with people in their predicaments in as many different segments of society as possible. In doing so, they may come up with either "constructive" criticisms that may be useful to those currently in positions of power or "oppositional" or even "destructive" criticisms of that which exists and of its probable tendencies. Many times their findings will correctly appear to be those of investigators who are not engaged in established social organizations. Only from such a free-ranging stance can one achieve a sufficiently unenchanted (not co-opted) orientation to see clearly existing power relationships and their probable social consequences.

6. "System" maintenance *versus* social change: Currently the rhetoric of managerial operators and of positivist sociologists embraces social change as an everyday fact of life. Their actual attitudes toward substantial social change, however, and especially change toward a greater distribution of social power and opportunity resemble more the traditional one of whites who talk about upgrading the status of blacks but caution that it can only take place gradually over a long period of time, "fifty to a hundred years"! In other words, let us have "peace" (that is to say, changelessness) in our time. The highly sophisticated public relations practitioners for business enterprises faced with pressures for equal employment opportunities for women and minorities have devoted themselves to such doubletalk, and they have at times had sociological helpmates.

Humanist sociologists recognize that social change is constantly taking place. They also understand the manners in which those in positions of control are able to cope with the probable directions of change and to exploit such possibilities for their own ends. To the extent to which more democratically oriented groups or organizations are ready to exploit social change as it comes or as it can be stimulated or facilitated, humanist sociological findings can help push for participatory social arrangements, even to the extent of sweeping revolutionary changes. In a society in which those with vested interests in stability have extensive resources to fight against influences and organizations which seek needed change, humanist scientists can nevertheless develop pertinent information that might become very useful in popular struggles to achieve a more egalitarian and participatory society.

7. Technicians of method and theory *versus* intimate and creative observers: This contrast appears to pit those who are trained in the carefully developed methods and theories of sociology against naïve observers and inspired idea people, and that is just what is

intended. In the present context, the problem with positivist sociologists is not that they are poorly trained but that they are typically too content with what they have learned, too inflexible in applying their knowledge, too routine, and too prone not to ask searching questions of themselves and of their subjects. Their familiarity with a variety of methods that have been used can be helpful as a fund of suggestions but only so. All too often such familiarity is stifling and inhibiting and leads to uncritical imitation.

At the same time, sensitive observers approach their subjects with as little preconception as possible and thus, so to speak, naïvely. They are not satisfied with statements of opinions tailored to the formal context of a questionnaire. They want to see how people of a given sex, social stratum, age level, and ethnic background actually cope with each other and with significant challenges to their ways of life. When they come to studying their observational notes and to assessing what significance they may have, the creative ferment of comparing findings with those of others can be quite useful. It may send the observer back for more experience with the people being studied. It may help to suggest the need to probe into broader societal and historical contexts. It can thus open many doors.

The struggles outlined briefly here for the use of sociologies as weapons is no novelty in human affairs. It is at least as old as the classical conflict between Protagoras and Plato. Every effort to "negotiate" a settlement of this tension in social philosophy and in sociology has failed, and this is just as well. Out of this tension, this struggle over the thoughtways and for the loyalties of intellectuals and of society, have come some of our most fruitful theorizing and substantial contributions to social action.[19]

Let us turn now to a discussion of the stakes in the struggle for which sociologies are becoming significant weapons. These stakes are the control of the "manipulable normal" members of society.

notes

[1] R. S. Lynd, *Knowledge for What?* (Princeton: Princeton University Press, 1939), p. ix.
[2] Ibid., p. 249.
[3] Herman and J. R. Schwendinger, *The Sociologists of the Chair* (New York: Basic Books, 1974).

[4]Wesley Mitchell, "Science and the State of Mind," *Science*, vol. 69 (1939), pp. 1–4; p. 3 quoted.

[5]Lynd, op. cit., p. 242.

[6]R. A. Scott and Arnold Shore, "Sociology and Policy Analysis," *American Sociologist*, vol. 9 (1974), pp. 51–59; p. 52 quoted.

[7]L. S. Feuer, "What Is Alienation? The Career of a Concept," *Marx and the Intellectuals* (Garden City, N.Y.: Doubleday & Co., 1969), pp. 70–99; Edward Shils, "The Calling of Sociology," in Talcott Parsons *et al.*, eds., *Theories of Society* (New York: Free Press, 1961), pp. 1405–48; P. L. Berger, *Invitation to Sociology* (Garden City, N.Y.: Doubleday & Co., 1963), pp. 162–63; R. W. Friedrichs, *A Sociology of Sociology* (New York: Free Press, 1970), pp. 63–64; M. Petrosyan, *Humanism* (Moscow, U.S.S.R.: Progress Publishers, 1972), chap. 2; A. McC. Lee, "An Obituary for 'Alienation,'" *Social Problems*, vol. 20 (1972–1973), pp. 121–27.

[8]Shils, op. cit., p. 1423.

[9]A. McC. Lee, "The Nyden Case: An Alumnus Revisits Pitt," *Insurgent Sociologists*, vol. 7, no. 1 (Winter 1977), pp. 70–73.

[10]See R. W. Friedrichs, "The Potential Impact of B. F. Skinner Upon American Sociology," *American Sociologist*, vol. 9 (1974), pp. 3–8; M. D. Rosenthal, "Sociobiology: Laying the Foundations for a Racist Synthesis," *Harvard Crimson*, February 8, 1977, p. 3; Irwin Sperber, *Fashions in Science* (Ph.D. dissertation, University of California at Berkeley, 1975).

[11]R. B. Fuller, *Operating Manual for Spaceship Earth* (Carbondale: Southern Illinois University Press, 1969), p. 133.

[12]Auguste Comte, "The Religion of Humanity," *A General View of Positivism*, trans. by J. H. Bridges (Stanford, California: Academic Reprints, n.d., re-issue of 1848 ed.), chap. 6.

[13]A. McC. Lee, *Toward Humanist Sociology* (Englewood Cliffs, N.J.: Prentice-Hall, 1973).

[14]L. J. Kamin, *The Science and Politics of I.Q.* (New York: John Wiley & Sons, 1974), esp. chap. 2.

[15]Amitai Etzioni, "Policy Research," *American Sociologist*, vol. 6 (1971), pp. 8–12 in special supplement; p. 11 quoted.

[16]Reinhard Bendix, "Sociology and the Distrust of Reason," *American Sociological Review*, vol. 35 (1970), pp. 831–43; p. 841 quoted.

[17]C. W. Mills, *The Sociological Imagination* (New York: Oxford University Press, 1959), p. 224.

[18]Shils, op. cit., p. 1422.

[19]Chapter adapted and expanded from the author's "Humanist Challenges to Positivists," *Insurgent Sociologist*, vol. 6, no. 1 (Fall 1975), pp. 41–49.

five

The Stakes:
The "Manipulable Normals"

They crowd the supermarkets. The mass media and the sports world fill their lives with personalities and sensations. They accept trivial and inconsistent news reports as credible portrayals of the world around them. They do not revolt against the Tweedledum and Tweedledee of two-party politics. So many are consenting consumers, willing voters, docile employees, non-objecting draftees or willing volunteers for the armed forces, and self-sacrificing workers on wartime "home fronts" or in peacetime daily struggles.

With all their superficial similarities, they are highly varied. Yet in all their diversity they do not want to be identified as "deviant" or "strange," "difficult" or "common," "radical" or "queer." In other words, they are society's self-proclaimed "normals" who form themselves into invidiously distinct groups, believe in established current ideologies and fads, accept the so-called "social system" as given, and try to "get by" or perhaps even to "hit it lucky" in a "safe" manner.

That is what passes as a superficial view of the stable members of society, the backbone of our social "order." Even though closer investigation reveals it to be still another stereotype, a caricature, it serves as a starting point: Who are the so-called "normals" whom power brokers appear to be able to manipulate or some say to "orchestrate" so readily? To what extent can and do sociologists aid or subvert the efforts of such brokers?

A great deal of sociological literature deals with "deviants," with people noticeably different mentally or behaviorally or physically from others, and with the underprivileged. Except for superficial "public opinion" surveys, sociologists give little attention to the consequences of there being so many docile "normals" in society who provide power brokers with their most dependable materiel. Why are these "normals" taken so much for granted by so many social scientists?

"Affirmative action" legislation and its implementation have done much to question who is "normal" and thus who should be treated equally. Who is in some way different and thus to be subject to special consideration or treatment? This legislation presumably assures—at least it promises—equal opportunities in employment, education, housing, and other social activities for women and for members of various minorities.

"Affirmative action" re-focuses attention on explanations for ethnic, racial, class, and sex differences in aptitudes, intelligence, and emotions. It stimulates a resurgence of the nature-nurture controversy. It provides renewed support for the contentions of both genetic and environmental determinists. To the extent that it becomes effective in actual social practice, "affirmative action" means an invasion of the seats of power and of the customary and comfortable "togetherness" controlled by and consisting largely of white, assimilated, upper- and middle-class males and reinforced by white, assimilated lower-class males.

To comprehend more fully and accurately the network of "old boy" conspiracies the "affirmative action" advocates confront, we need to understand much more precisely than we often do the crucial roles in socialization played by autonomous male and female peer groups in various social classes. Reference is not to such sibling-substitute peer groups as *supervised* play and class-room groups. It is to the more or less egalitarian, unsupervised, voluntary play and identity groups (clubs, gangs, cliques, social fraternities, athletic teams) of boys and young men and to their successors among older men. It is also to the similar groups of girls and young women and to their successors among older women. Such groups compete strongly—many times successfully—with home and school in the molding of significant patterns of maleness and femaleness and methods for "getting along" and "getting ahead."[1] Organized sibling-substitute peer groups are often available for study by supervisers and other outsiders.[2] Autonomous male or female peer groups are difficult to observe without altering their character.[3]

Since children's and youth's activities are so often studied only in supervised situations, the multi-faceted character of their life experiences and thus of their developing personalities tends to escape us. We may not know enough about individuals' group experiences to understand fully the significance of the psychologist William James's conclusion that a person "has as many different social selves as there are distinct *groups* of persons about whose opinions he cares. He generally shows a different side of himself to each of these different groups." James then illustrates his point: "Many a youth who is demure enough before his parents and teachers, swears and swaggers like a pirate among his 'tough' young friends. We do not show ourselves to our children as to our club-companions, to our customers as to the laborers we employ, to our own masters and employers as to our intimate friends."[4]

Whether or not this division of the person into several social selves is a discordant splitting or not depends upon the degree to which social distance separates the groups involved, and the degree to which the individual has acquired an ability to move about readily as an accepted member of groups (family, school, autonomous peer, other) with contrasting values and behavior patterns.

The sociologist Willard Waller further illustrates this characteristic multivalence of people by referring to the "determination of youngsters to stick to the standards of their own group, and their willingness to suffer any injustice from that group rather than betray it." He concludes that this puzzles adults only "because they do not realize how mighty is the force of opinion in the play group or understand that status in that group does not depend upon adult standards." Sometimes children do not find it easy to resolve or otherwise deal with conflicting loyalties; in Waller's words, "the stool-pigeon is trustworthy from the adult's point of view but not from that of the [child group's] insider. And what is humiliation in one group is honor in another." One of Waller's students described the situation thus:

I received my first licking at school, of which I was alternatively very proud and very ashamed, depending upon the group in which I found myself. Among my classmates I was proud of having weathered the storm of a licking. Among my elders I was caused to feel ashamed, because, I suppose, I had violated some educational convention or taboo.[5]

Autonomous peer groups are seldom studied by fully and empathetically participating observers. When such studies are attempted, they usually leave much to be asked especially on the younger age levels. They are thus ordinarily the work of adults who do not comprehend the existence of "several social selves" in themselves and in others. Often such adults in their own childhood and youth did not fully experience autonomous peer-group activity typical of their own social class and ethnic group. In other words, they were not assimilated into as contrasting a variety of groups as were their less academically involved peers.[6] As the political scientist C. J. Friedrich notes, frequently this type of person is one who has been a teacher's pet or a social reject among his or her peers, one who was "ridiculed and even persecuted by his more normal schoolmates," or one who uses intellectualism as an avenue of escape. He adds that "that kind of childhood begets a sense of frustration and a disposition to frown upon the common crowd. . . . Whether as historians or sociologists, philosophers or poets, such men [and he should have added women] have helped to build and perpetuate the idea of the elite."[7]

An educational sociologist, Patricia C. Sexton, contends that "boys who rise to the top in school often resemble girls in many important ways. . . . Scholastic honor and masculinity, in other words, too often seem incompatible."[8] She would have been more accurate had she said that boys and girls "who rise to the top in school" tend to be introverted. Efforts to attain scholastic honor and its attainment tend to be socially de-sexing. Both girls and boys feel this sense of an elite-apartness. Both know that their intellectuality sets them outside the usual peer play groups. To go in for academic achievement means less time and energy for fun and games; it is something to be very quiet about or to accept as others' criterion for avoidance or rejection.

Developmental psychologists, novelists, and participant-observing social scientists help us to sense how autonomous peer groups function among girls and boys of various social strata. They point out how those groups and their roles and subcultures serve as prototypes in male and female minds and actions for significant subsequent group participations. The gossip of such groups in childhood and youth examines the nature of sexuality and explores rumors and facts about the other sex. They speculate about and then later discuss the actual character of sexual experiences along with news of their world and ways of coping with parents, teachers, and other adults. As Sexton points out, members of such groups are "the source of massive apathy and passive resistance to academic learning." Thus the "gang is a basic feature of boy life, one viewed with as much disapproval by adults as devotion by boys."[9] The girls' play and identity groups are often not as visibly conspiratorial as the boys' gang, but they share a similarly defensive nature.

Such autonomous male group experiences become habitual prototypes for later behavior. To those experiences are traceable more than a little of the uneasy and surreptitious sexism, the recourses to brutality and violence, the contempt for moral preachments as sentimentality, and the extreme clannishness of certain types of adult male group—exemplified by poker clubs, groups of salesmen, military or football squads, college social clubs, gatherings of college alumni or army veterans, or even political strategy groups in unions, in the White House, at Westminster, or in a multinational corporation board room. These characteristics contribute the readiness and the sense of security to the members of a group enabling them to make "hard decisions" that apparently serve the group members' self-interests at least in the short run. The "hardness" of such decisions often means the degree to which they dehumanize outsiders and subject them to inconsiderate or even violent and destructive measures. Foreseeable possibilities of long-term disasters that could arise from such "hard decisions" tend to be rejected as speculative or irrelevant or just sentimental.

Beneath the romantic appeal of such accounts of boyhood gangs (autonomous peer groups) as those set forth in Mark Twain's *Tom Sawyer* (1876) and *Huckleberry Finn* (1885) are clear indications of the prevalence of casual juvenile brutality, "delinquency," and stereotyped masculine "virtues" on the several social levels mentioned. Such works as Booth Tarkington's *Penrod* (1914) and *Seventeen* (1916), Eugene O'Neill's *Ah, Wilderness* (1933), W. G.

Golding's *Lord of the Flies* (1954), and John Knowles's *A Separate Peace* (1960) portray the rebelliousness against female domination and femininity, the struggles toward self-realization in terms of sexual knowledge and of popular masculine symbolism typical of male play-and-identity groups in our culture.

Participation in autonomous peer groups begins very early in life for most children and has continuous and profound influence, but the significance of these groups as vehicles for rebelliousness during adolescence focuses greater attention on that age level. In many traditional cultures and also in parts of our own, the anthropologist Rosalie H. Wax points out that "boys are encouraged to be virile adolescents and become 'real men.'" Such "virility" is typically identified with competitive physical prowess and ability and willingness to inflict violence. That emphasis contrasts sharply with most home and classroom efforts among the British and Americans. In effect, as Wax continues, we seek "to deprive youth of adolescence— . . . [to] demand that high school students behave like 'mature people'—which, in our culture often seems to mean in a pretty dull, conformist fashion."[10]

Traditionally females have had fewer opportunities for autonomous peer group activities than did males, but economic and social changes in women's roles are modifying the patterns of their upbringing. This goes beyond the wearing of slacks, shorts, and overalls. As the sociologist Mirra Komarovsky notes, "Little girls are increasingly asked, 'And what are you going to be when you grow up?' 'Don't be a sissy' may be addressed to Sis no less than to Buddy." More than a little confusion results from the persistence of traditional feminine upbringing and role patterns alongside the more recent ones. As Komarovsky continues,

When men received superior schooling, enjoyed legal advantages and wider economic opportunities, had the exclusive right of political participation and the like, they could *in fact* excel in the "masculine" sphere. Today, under the influence of old attitudes, men continue to expect too much of themselves in a world which no longer gives them the former advantages. Only mischief can come from such a discrepancy.[11]

Thus the cohesiveness of the adult male successors to childhood and youth autonomous peer groups still remain a problem for feminine and minority egalitarian aspirations.

More recent short stories and novels suggest that female play-and-identity groups of an autonomous sort are tending to masculinize their experiences as they join the movement toward "women's lib," but this movement does not yet appear to have had much influence on the character of the groups of boys and young men and their adult successors. Margaret Mead asserts: "The boys' gang . . . is a desperate defensive measure against being sissies . . . but the girls are also busy not being sissies."[12] Since the male offensive and defensive alliances against women and the feminine persist, girls and women tend to form more and more effective offensive and defensive alliances of their own with which to penetrate the male bastions of power and control. If one looks at the Northern Irish developments especially since 1968, one sees that this tendency—slower to arrive there than in the United States—is helping to assimilate women into violent activities and thus to spread the social base for guerrilla combat as well as for aggressive nonviolent efforts.[13]

Thus autonomous play-and-identity peer groups tend to be nurturers of aggressiveness and deviance among males and among females. They exhibit pressures toward conformities of their own, but in doing so they provide some resistance to the homogenizing pressures of parents and teachers. To the extent that mothers and teachers succeed in replicating their own stylized adult values, they help to place males in a similar sort of cultural "box" as the one which has traditionally limited the originality, opportunities, and aggressiveness of females. The bait for males in that cultural box is made enticing by career advantages which are presumably more available to the male conformist in many professional, technical, and administrative roles than to the female. At the same time, the many males and females who reject the feminized cultural box include those whom autonomous peer groups have coached in the amoral or immoral procedures of "wheeling and dealing," of being "practical," of "playing the game" in the "real world" as the "fellows" understand it, and thus of making quickly and forcefully the "hard decisions" that are said to assure "success." They include those who come to dominate trade and industry, politics and government, academic and professional institutions, and also the secret haunts of organized crime.

These two broad types of socialization in our society—the feminized bureaucratic and the amoral "wheeler-dealer"—are major colorations of both male and female personalities. They help to characterize myths and theories by which people live and work.

Like all generalizations about the nature of personalities, these are broad and idealized typifications. They suggest tendencies. Only a few human beings illustrate one or the other in a complete manner. At the same time, the two types of elitism correspond to two distorted conceptions about the "common people" which strongly influence official policy decisions reflecting notions about the nature of our society's rank-and-file "normals." Such popular conceptions have significant social consequences. Let us therefore compare the two distorted conceptions with a third one based upon statements of participant observers who have experienced society more broadly during their early socialization years and later.

These three conceptions of the "common people"—the "manipulable normals"—are labeled somewhat in this fashion: (1) "the masses," by members of the cultish self-reproducing intellectual elites, (2) "social materiel," by intellectuals who serve actionist elitists, and (3) "human beings," by humanist intellectuals with broad social experience. Although, as the terms suggest, the first two tend to overlap, it is useful to discuss them separately.

1. *The masses:* Intellectuals trained in bureaucratized educational patterns typically glorify an elite based upon those patterns and look down upon the common people who have not been so initiated. That traditional viewpoint is an old one but one constantly updated. Plato quotes Socrates as pleading for philosophers—a self-defined and self-selected elite—to be made kings, "or the kings and princes of this world [to] have the spirit and power of philosophy." Thus "political greatness and wisdom [would] meet in one." For the public weal, he would also have "commoner natures . . . [be] compelled to stand aside."[14] Criteria and justifications for this intellectual elitism have included being privy to divine revelations and at least to the teachings of charismatic thinkers. Now they tend more to range from the genetic to the environmental determinist extreme. Sometimes they are couched merely in terms of being products of customary social arrangements, thus of being parts of the "natural" social "order."

Until scientific scrutiny revealed the ethnocentric and classcentric character of I.Q. and many other psychological tests, geneticists utilized them to provide scientistic support for the differential treatment of members of ethnic, racial, and class groups in

110   Sociology for Whom?

immigration, in education, in employment, and in housing. "Affirmative action" legislation is bringing about a resurgence of such geneticism as a means for denying more equal opportunities to women and to minority groups. Those who look upon intellectual and emotional differences as due more to environmental conditioning sometimes come to similar conclusions about differential treatment. They base their policy rationalizations on the time and resources required to overcome environmental influences. They do recognize, however, the possibility that persons and groups may react favorably to better life conditions, including education and opportunities for improvement. Except when such elitist intellectuals are so fearful of change as to rationalize opposition to any social modification as a possible threat to "the social equilibrium" (the fancied basis of their personal security), they may support an extension of education as a way of obtaining conforming compliance among the otherwise undependable masses.

2. *Social materiel:* Intellectuals who seek personal glory or social improvement through serving actionist elitists include such disparate thinkers as Vilfredo Pareto and W. G. Sumner on the one hand and Karl Marx, Friedrich Engels, and V. I. Lenin on the other. They are all sufficiently accurate observers and sufficiently candid analysts of society and the human condition to reach some common conclusions. They recognizably talk about the same society. Because of their dissimilar backgrounds and concerns, however, their emphases contrast sharply.

Pareto and Sumner preoccupy themselves with the problems, including the shortcomings, of currently dominant elites and with the characteristics of social materiel, especially with those which are somewhat stable. Pareto's psychological "residues" vary among individuals and groups both of the elites and of those he calls the "plebeians." These psychological characteristics appear to be partly genetic and partly habitual determinants of thought and behavior. Sumner's "folkways" and more tenaciously held "mores" are customs or popular culture patterns that also vary from group to group and tend to dominate habitual thought and behavior.

On the other hand, Marx, Engels, and Lenin preoccupy themselves with ways in which currently dominant elites can be replaced. Encouraged by relatively culture-free popular actions in support of violent efforts at change in revolutionary situations, they do not pay as much attention as do Pareto and Sumner to the cultural boxes into which people grow and which so limit their willingness to "shake the applecart" except under extreme provocation, as a result of "consciousness-raising" experiences. They assume that events and agitation can demonstrate to people the need for violent revolt at times when social conditions are ripe for such an effort.

Pareto concludes that a "subject class" can develop leadership and is thus dangerous to a governing class only when the latter is "inspired by humanitarian sentiments primarily." Governing classes protect themselves through "the shrewd use of chicanery, fraud, corruption" and through assimilating "most of the individuals in the subject class who show those same talents, are adept in those same arts, and might therefore become the leaders of such plebeians as are disposed to use violence." When the masses are thus deprived of organizers, "the subject class is almost always powerless to set up any lasting regime."[15] Pareto sees the possibility of elites replacing one another, but the masses of society on the whole remain the elites' materiel.

Sumner places his faith for leadership and other valuable social contributions in people "of talent, practical sense, industry, perseverance, and moral principle." This viewpoint is likely a reflection in part at least of his Protestant theological school training. He had his doubts about the "genius, who is not morally responsible, or not industrious." The great mass of those whom he called the mediocre carry a society's cultural patterns. They hold some of these patterns in common but many vary from group to group. They modify the patterns in unplanned and rather automatic ways in response to changed life conditions, and thus they provide the current definitions of the materiel to be dealt with by those in dominating positions.

As Sumner says,

What is the limit to the possibilities of fanaticism and frenzy which might be produced in any society by agitation skillfully addressed to the fallacies and passions of the masses? The answer lies in the mores [in core popular-culture patterns], which determine the degree of reserved common sense, and the habit of observing measure and method, to which the masses have been accustomed.[16]

Thus for Sumner, a change in society that would amount to establishing a different social contract among society's members is a remote possibility. The recrystallization of bureaucracy and of social strata in the Soviet Union would not have surprised him. As he predicted for such developments, the Russian revolution could bring forth new elites and replace certain social structures, but the mores of all significant groups would modify but slowly. The mores would change only to the extent persistently expedient to the people in the light of changed social conditions.

In contrast, Marx and Engels visualize the replacement "of the old bourgeois society, with its classes and class antagonisms," by a society "in which the free development of each is the condition for the free development of all." This utopian vision would be the final outcome of struggles between the now dominant bourgeoisie and the rising proletariat. Marx and Engels foresee their utopian outcome as an inevitable result of historical processes. Like its feudal predecessor, bourgeois society nurtures within itself the instruments of its own destruction. To facilitate this revolutionary change, communists "as the most advanced and resolute section of the working-class parties of every country"—the elite—would lead and thus make possible the "conquest of political power by the proletariat," the overthrow of "bourgeois supremacy."[17] Then, presumably, the need for political parties would disappear, and social classes would hopefully wither away.

Lenin sketches international aspects of proletarian class struggles in the currently "parasitic or decaying capitalism" in his essay, *Imperialism, the Highest Stage of Capitalism* (1917). He explains the lack of proletarian class-consciousness and rebelliousness in imperialist capitalistic countries by pointing out how the

receipt of high monopoly profits by the capitalists . . . makes it economically possible for them to bribe certain sections of the workers . . . and win them to the side of the bourgeoisie of a given industry or given nation against all the others. The intensification of antagonisms between imperialist nations for the division of the world increases this urge. And so there is created that bond between imperialism and [proletarian] opportunism.[18]

Thus the workers' revolution Marx[19] predicted for nineteenth century Britain failed to materialize. The imperialists could buy off enough of the British proletariat to keep them docile and controlled, undisturbed in their cultural boxes.

For the purposes of policy guidance toward a more egalitarian society, it is becoming clear to some analysts at least that a more eclectic conception of society and of social action than that of Marx, Engels, and Lenin is necessary. I say this even though I realize that the volume of their written works is so great and so contradictory that it can be used to support many divergent strategies. As one socialist analyst, Paul M. Sweezy, concludes from post-revolutionary developments in the Soviet Union and from post-Maoist China, the "notion that abolition of private property in the means of production ushers in an essentially classless society . . . is exploded once and for all." He sees rather "a conception of socialism as a class-divided society like all that have preceded it, and one which has the potential to move forward or backward depending on the fortunes of a class struggle through which alone the human race can aspire to leave behind the horrors and miseries of the past and lay the foundations for a future worthy of its capabilities." In other words, an exploiting class can establish its power "on control of an all-encompassing repressive state apparatus" as well as "on private property in the means of production."20

These writers deal with grand scenarios for the influencing of social materiel. Much of the concern of those employing social technicians is with far less sweeping efforts—with image-building or image-maintenance for individuals or groups of politicians, business people, or artists; with changing product priorities in the markets; with preparing public acceptance for war, peace, or compromise moves; and with rationalizing the lowering of living standards through inflationary devices.

Under any ruler's conception of the common people, struggles to influence their thoughts and actions play crucial roles in the processes of policy-making, morale maintenance, and agitation for change. A question to be carefully examined then is what kind of an arena exists for struggles among the proponents for ideas for and against changes in the social power structure. In the United States as in other modern countries, the control of all major media of mass communications by a relatively small group of entrepreneurs limits access to them not only by dissidents and minorities but also by representatives of the common people more generally. Often only such spectacular events as the Watergate break-in, riots, bombings, foreign military actions, and natural catastrophes can force their way into the entertainment-prone mass media. Even those events are either made to serve special interests or are given a sense of melodramatic unreality.

3. *Human beings:* In looking so briefly at the snobbery of intellectual elitists and at the complicated tasks of intellectuals working for actionist elites, the case for dependence upon one or another elite as trustees of social welfare or as midwives of social change appears to leave no substantial alternative. At the same time, the undependability of single individuals and of elite groups with unchecked social power—what Lord Acton called "the tendency or the certainty of corruption by authority"[21]—is notorious in human history. Many have come to the conclusion that people can only make the best of their lot by trying to assure themselves of a representative or fair or generous controlling elite.

As human history becomes more vast and more interrelated and its problems more complex and technical, few intellectuals or actionists feel that they can make a case for broadly participatory democracy. Thomas Jefferson observed in 1824 that people "are naturally divided into two parties: 1. Those who fear and distrust the people, and wish to draw all powers from them into the hands of the higher classes. 2. Those who wish to identify themselves with the people, have confidence in them, cherish and consider them as the most honest and safe, although not the most wise depository of the public interests."[22] Is the latter merely political rhetoric? How much substance can it or does it have?

Society needs specialists of many types. Even though education might be made more available and improved, every person can have but limited knowledge of most aspects of the social and physical problems and opportunities to be met in her or his daily routines and glimpsed in the broader world beyond. Nevertheless, a person from any social stratum, ethnic or racial group, age level, degree of competence, or emotional configuration has useful contributions to make to discussions of the broader aspects of social policy and of decision-making. Whether such a person's ideas appear to others to be rational or irrational, they may well reflect significant aspects of human concerns in our society. Now that more social scientists are more intimately studying wide ranges of social groups, they are bringing back conceptions of non-academic wisdom and surprising products of non-academic experiences. They tell us more and more about our society's rank and file "normals" in all their rich variety. Even our psychiatrists, as they empathize with their disturbed patients, get perspectives on so-called "sane" society's problems that we need to understand and use.

The political scientist Carl J. Friedrich recognizes that social scientific knowledge and industrial technology have made society's policy-making seem to be far beyond the ken of any person. At the same time, he holds that "belief in the common man is not only vital to the democratic creed but quite tenable." In saying this, he avoids the spell of "the visionary prophets of the democratic age. Naught but ill results from the thoughtless repetition of outworn formulas. The almost incredible faith in the omnicompetence and rationality of the common man, of you and me, must be replaced by a tempered yet firm conviction of the common man's *political* capacity." He thus grants the "*limited* competence, indeed . . . the fallibility of every man, be he ever so uncommon."

In view of the fact that humanity surely lacks absolute standards of right and wrong, of good and bad, Friedrich contends that our "communal policies depend upon calculations of probability. The common man . . . perceives more readily than the expert the general impact [upon himself, his family, his community] of proposed policies." Friedrich is not talking about highly technical matters that require special training or experience. "The common man is trustworthy because he is, in the aggregate, a man of character rather than of intellect—consistent, and averse to high-falutin deviations. He is 'safer' than the uncommon man." As Friedrich sums up his position, "What we need is a balanced confidence in our power to operate a community of common men by common judgments upon matters of common concern."[23]

What can we learn from these disparate views of society's "normals"? Do they have any common focus? Must we accept Pareto's assurance that elite will succeed elite in the control of society, a view apparently shared by some socialists? How stable are Sumner's mores when he perceives that they change slowly or rapidly in response to changed social conditions? As a conservative, he stresses their stability and thus provides support for opponents of change, as for example in interracial educational, employment, and housing arrangements.[24] Many reformers and revolutionaries, on the other hand, would unrealistically brush aside or minimize considerations of culture and of its entrenchment in personal attitudes and habits. Rather than facing and attempting to deal with culture's reality, they look upon it as an ideological ploy of the opposition. In contrast, Sumner in effect agrees with the assertion of Mao Tsetung, shared by many other Marxists, that "Man's social being determines his consciousness," a statement I interpret as a recognition of culture's role in human affairs. Consciousness raising then means breaking out of an habitual cultural mold. Mao adds that the Chinese "are living in a period of great social change. . . . Changes of such magnitude are of course reflected in people's minds. . . . People of different classes, strata and social groups react differently to the great changes in our social system." Mao thus points out that he and his followers have to cope with people's "social being," with their habitual way of living, in other words with their culture patterns, and he advocates a drastic manner of doing so,[25] a manner Sumner sought to avoid.

The characteristic of human beings in society that appears to underly whether or not people and their social arrangements will change readily or reluctantly is the degree of pervasiveness of fear. For the creation of a more livable society, we might well ponder Ralph Waldo Emerson's statement, "We are afraid of truth, afraid of fortune, afraid of death, and afraid of each other."[26] Truth is so often heresy, a threat to myths fondly cherished. According to *Newsweek* reporters, the "whistle blowings" by individuals to expose malfeasance in business and government are threats to such myths; such revelations "almost always result in blighted careers or worse for the idealists."[27] The exposers do have the satisfaction, nevertheless, of making a humanitarian impact on social policies, sometimes of considerable significance. Fortune, whether good or bad, calls for new ways of life, and new ways of life are speculative, unsettling, perhaps even disastrous. Many an immigrant pines for the old, deprived way of life in spite of a gadget-filled American home. In spite of efforts by physicians and clergy, few are not haunted by the thoughts of their own death and by that of those close to them. And who can tell about the way relations with other people will work out? Even the closest friendships can turn sour, and it is all too easy to have fearful fantasies about strange and different people.

A great many of us find what we take to be security in the familiar and customary, in conformity, in accepting the apparent assurances of continuity in the world we experience. In consequence we are sooner or later disillusioned with changes in and manipulations of our customs, with the ease with which conformists are exploited or degraded, and with the lack of dependable continuity in employment, in neighborhood life, and in the character of our associations and institutions.

Fear of change and the frequent suggestion of change's fearsome consequences by associates and by public spokesmen constantly help crystallize society's groups, classes, bureaucracies, myths, and policies. Any current situation may be far from attractive, but, as the Irish folk saying has it, "Better the divil ye know!" Thus we try to protect ourselves from fearful possibilities by trusting dependable routines that are usually broken only by an occasional holiday or vacation. When we are thrust into the dislocations of a war or natural catastrophe, all the old pillars of our security seem to be swept away or at least held in suspense. Curiously, then, a short-sighted delusion of tribal egalitarianism can convert panic or at least disorientation into a hedonistic catharsis. This catharsis helps to account for the enthusiasm with which otherwise sane people can throw themselves into the destructive futilities of war.

Changing life conditions demand social adaptation, an avoidance of rigidification. A more responsive society, with greater opportunities for individual expression as well as for institutional adaptation would make the catharsis of war less enticing. It was in the interests of stimulating a more responsive and responsible type of society that Thomas Jefferson, among other sagacious social analysts of broad experience, asserted that a "little rebellion, now and then, is a good thing, and as necessary in the political world as storms in the physical. . . . It is a medicine necessary for the sound health of government."[28] Such frequent rebellions would keep society sufficiently responsive to popular needs to avoid rigidification.

As we shall see in the next chapter, a strategic grasp of the pervasiveness of fear equips social manipulators with the means to influence and exploit us. The changes they advocate might be socially constructive, destructive, or futile. A knowledge of ourselves, of those who would preserve or change or merely exploit us or our society, and of our society's nature can help us to control our own fears more readily and thus to keep them from being used for antisocial purposes.[29]

notes

[1]Willard Waller, *The Sociology of Teaching* (New York: John Wiley & Sons, 1932), chap. 13.

[2]Kenneth Keniston, *Youth and Dissent* (New York: Harcourt, Brace & World, 1971).

[3]H. A. Bloch and Arthur Niederhoffer, *The Gang* (New York: Philosophical Library, 1958), chap. 1.

[4]William James, *Psychology* (New York: Collier Books, 1962), p. 192.

[5]Waller, op. cit., p. 185.

[6]A. McC. Lee, *Fraternities Without Brotherhood* (Boston: Beacon Press, 1955), chap. 6.

[7]C. J. Friedrich, *The New Image of the Common Man* (Boston: Beacon Press, 1950), pp. 247-48.

[8]P. C. Sexton, *The Feminized Male* (New York: Random House, 1969), p. 13.

[9]Ibid., pp. 13, 7.

[10]R. H. Wax, "The Warrior Dropouts," *Trans-Action*, vol. 4 (1967), pp. 40-46; p. 41 quoted. See also Kenneth Polk, "Class, Strain and Rebellion Among Adolescents," *Social Problems*, vol. 17 (1969-1970), pp. 214-24; I. J. Silverman and Simon Dinitz, "Compulsive Masculinity and Delinquency," *Criminology*, vol. 11 (1973-1974), pp. 498-515.

[11]Mirra Komarovsky, *Women in the Modern World* (Boston: Little, Brown, 1953), pp. 62-63, 299-300.

[12]Margaret Mead, *Male and Female* (New York: William Morrow & Co., 1949), p. 270.

[13]Bernadette Devlin, *The Price of My Soul* (London: Andre Deutsch, 1969); Lil Conlon, *Cumann na mBan and the Women of Ireland* (Kilkenny, Ireland: Kilkenny People, 1969).

[14]Socrates quoted in *The Works of Plato*, Irwin Edman, ed. (New York: Simon & Schuster, 1928), p. 410.

[15]Vilfredo Pareto, *The Mind and Society* (New York: Harcourt, Brace and Co., 1935), vol. 4, pp. 1516-17.

[16]W. G. Sumner, *Folkways* (Boston: Ginn & Co., 1906), pp. 41, 52.

[17]Karl Marx and Friedrich Engels, "Manifesto of the Communist Party," *Basic Writings on Politics and Philosophy*, L. S. Feuer, ed. (Garden City, N.Y.: Doubleday & Co., 1959), pp. 1-41; pp. 29, 20 quoted.

[18]V. I. Lenin, *Imperialism*, 1917 (Moscow: Progress Publishers, 1970), pp. 119-20.

[19]Karl Marx (1855) in Marx and Frederick Engels, *Articles on Britain* (Moscow: Progress Publishers, 1971), pp. 225-26, and Marx and Engels (1870), *Ireland and the Irish Question*, R. Dixon, ed. (New York: International Publishers, 1972), pp. 292-95.

[20]P. M. Sweezy, "Theory and Practice in the Mao Period," *Monthly Review*, vol. 28, no. 9 (February 1977), pp. 1-12; pp. 11-12 quoted.

[21]J.E.E. Dalberg-Acton, letter to Mandell Creighton, April 5, 1887, in *Essays on Freedom and Power*, Gertrude Himmelfarb, ed. (Boston: Beacon Press, 1948), pp. 358-67; p. 364 quoted.

[22]Thomas Jefferson, letter to Henry Lee, August 10, 1824, in *The Life and Selected Writings*, Adrienne Koch and William Peden, eds. (New York: Modern Library, 1944), pp. 714–15; p. 715 quoted.

[23]C. J. Friedrich, op. cit., pp. 40–42.

[24]Gunnar Myrdal with Richard Sterner and Arnold Rose, *An American Dilemma* (New York: Harper & Bros., 1944), appendix 2.

[25]Mao Tsetung, *Selected Readings* (Peking: Foreign Language Press, 1971), p. 480.

[26]R. W. Emerson, "Self-Reliance" (1841), *The Complete Writings* (New York: W. H. Wise & Co., 1929), vol. 1, pp.138–52; p. 148 quoted.

[27]Tom Nicholson and others, "The High Cost of Whistling," *Newsweek*, February 14, 1977, pp. 75, 77.

[28]Thomas Jefferson, letter to James Madison, January 30, 1787, op. cit., pp. 412–14; p. 413 quoted.

[29]Passages in this chapter are adapted from the author's "Northern Irish Socialization in Conflict Patterns," *International Review of Modern Sociology*, vol. 5 (1975), pp. 127–34, by permission of Man Singh Das, Editor.

six

Strategies for Social Change

Efforts to change society are encapsulated in stirring formulas. In relation to the existing social forms of a given country, these doctrines often appear revolutionary. They call for such freedoms as those of speech, assembly, the press, and worship. They ask for an end to self-incrimination and to arbitrary search and seizure. They claim the right of people to change their government peacefully or by force, to abolish private control of the means of production, to have a "dictatorship of the proletariat" rather than feudalism or a plutocratic democracy, and to let social classes and other obstacles to egalitarianism wither away.

And then, after a popular upheaval has at least nominally achieved some of such goals, what happens? That eighteenth century revolutionary, Thomas Jefferson, reported consequences of one revolution in these terms:

The generation which commences a revolution rarely completes it. Habituated from their infancy to passive submission of body and mind to their kings and priests, they are not qualified when called on to think and provide for themselves, and their inexperience, their ignorance and bigotry make them instruments often, in the hands of the Bonapartes, . . . to defeat their own rights and purposes.[1]

Similar concerns are echoed in the statements of many another revolutionary actionist and theorist. They learn how quickly and with what powerful assets reactionary forces can erode popular gains.

Jefferson perceived the strong anti-democratic reaction of his contemporary "merchants, priests, and lawyers." He saw abundant evidence of their "adherence to England and monarchy, in preference to their own country and Constitution." On the one hand, according to Jefferson, "merchants have no country. The mere spot they stand on does not constitute so strong an attachment as that from which they draw their gains." On the other hand, he did not fear "the assaults of force; but," as he noted, "I have seen and felt much, and fear more from English books, English prejudices, English manners, and the apes, the dupes, and designs among our professional crafts." He placed his faith "for security against these seductions" in the common people of his day, "our agricultural citizens, in . . . their independence and their power."[2] These people were not in any percentage agribusiness entrepreneurs; they were the eighteenth century equivalent of our rank-and-file "normals."

Such concerns with reactionary groups and influences have often been cited to discourage those who would work for any type of social change, for example to counteract the prejudiced and exploitative treatment of women, blacks and others minorities, sexual deviants, delinquents and criminals, the unemployed, and mental patients or to humanize society in a more general manner. Instead of prejudice, propaganda, and traditional alliances being looked upon as insuperable barriers, intimidating anyone who might work for change; realistic strategists for change look upon them as challenges to be met. At the same time, realistic strategists *against* social change take those blocks and procedures as part of their assets, to be exercised and strengthened as effectively and decisively as possible.

Social scientists, novelists, and journalists talk about how often people ask in effect to be robbed by professional gamblers, by confidence experts, and even by muggers and second-story operators. They conclude that many people are, in one way or another, victim-prone. They point out that victimizers trade on needs, including especially fear and greed, embedded and awaiting them in their victims' minds.

122 *Sociology for Whom?*

In a sense, strategists of propaganda and action operate similarly to those victimizers whether they are working for or against change. People's minds provide ready-made opportunities for the manipulators of attitudes and actions—to the extent that such opportunities exist. Those opportunities are popular interests, concerns, needs, and prejudices, especially popular fears and greed.

Whether "winning" or "losing" at a given time, no experienced strategist of social action ever regards any event in a social struggle as evidence of a final victory. For instance, both the winning and the losing political parties start the next campaign the day after an election. Struggles to abate sexism or racism may have gains or setbacks in some arena such as a court trial or a legislative action, but their proponents immediately move on to another arena—or many other arenas.

To the extent that strategists and those who implement strategies provide leadership for a popular movement, the temporary consolidation of gains for a time at least may not appear to them to be difficult. If they are really experienced strategists, however, they will not permit apparent success to diminish their efforts. To the extent that actionists are able to obtain gains that run beyond or contrary to a basic social movement, they face an even sharper struggle to achieve social acceptance. In any effort to support egalitarian gains, we need to remember the roles of the basically conservative "professional crafts" so distrusted by Jefferson, the roles of persons practiced in medicine, law, education, and theology. Those crafts perform crucial roles in social legitimation, in intellectual rationalization, in education, and in opinion formation.

Propaganda consists of so many things that it is difficult to define. It takes the form of policy statements, textbooks, editorials, news stories, television debates, soap operas on television or radio, Presidential press conferences, televised Congressional hearings, parades, kidnappings, hijackings, riots, biographies, and autobiographies. Propaganda refers to the many ways we have of disseminating ideas rapidly and effectively to many people. More formally, it is the expression of a contention overtly set forth or covertly implied in order to influence the attitudes, and through attitudes, the opinions and actions of a public.[3]

All propaganda can best be understood as the communications aspect of social competition and conflict. It often expresses some individual's or group's own aspirations or a contention about one or more of the great social issues of our day. In either case, the propagandist tries to relate the message to an audience's personal concerns. Propaganda can thus be visualized as a bridge of symbols from the special interest of a person or an agency to a related special interest in our minds. Or it can be thought of as a lariat with which a propagandist tries to rope in our support for or against some project.

The great social issues provide the symbolic banners under which our warring partisans in propaganda go forth. It is usually in terms of those banners that propagandists presume to fight or compete, not in terms of their more specific goals. Two candidates for a local office may contend against each other to gain a position involving complex imponderables (as well as an attractive salary and perquisites), but they each select one or more relevant or irrelevant issues on which to base their fight. Thus an expressed viewpoint on an international issue may decide a local election. Current debates center around such controversial issues as sexism, racism, human survival, elitism, exploitation, taxation, unemployment, militarism, poverty, classism, imperialism, plutocracy, democracy, ecology, and consumerism.

Let me suggest with a few brief illustrations how propagandists work:

Richard Nixon did not avowedly try to save just his own hide, as it were. On the contrary, he talked about preserving "the integrity of the Presidency," "the welfare of the nation," and "peace in our time." The latter expression was popularized in the 1930s by England's then prime minister, Ramsay MacDonald, a source with pro-Nazi overtones that suggests a nasty possible parallel.

Out of millions upon millions of Americans—not to mention other people around the globe—ill fed, ill clothed, and ill housed as well as uneducated or poorly so, propagandists with powerful support focus our attention on token fragments of the world's problems rather than upon the general situation. The fragments are usually defined in terms of a specific health problem, type of ethnicity, or religious affiliation, and the victims are "proved" to be the "cause" of their own sorry state. As the Black writer, Ralph Ellison, points out, "In our society it is not unusual for a Negro to experience a sensation that he does not exist in a real world at all."[4]

A third instance of propagandistic work is seen in the publicity of the multinational oil corporations. They do not attempt to justify steadily rising oil company profits as profits or to explain the relation between such profits and the dismantling of legislation which protects the human environment, or to admit the degree to which they control our politicians and thus our governing processes through campaign contributions, bribes, and favors. On the contrary, oil propagandists orate about national security, about citizen needs and comforts, and about how oil companies desperately require fresh capital in order to develop a greater American energy potential in order to make the United States self-sufficient in energy. As M. F. Granville, board chairman of Texaco, states the matter, "All domestic price controls should be removed as quickly as possible. This will clear the way for increased domestic oil and gas production, and will permit the petroleum industry to make the long-range plans and commitments that are so necessary in this business." He also insists that the "U.S. must accept further reasonable accommodations between environmental objectives and energy imperatives."[5] It is appropriate to place next to these remarks the cynical statement by R. J. Ringer, the author of a popular "success" book, *Winning Through Intimidation:* "Ambitious people should see the world as it is—overpopulated, polluted, headed for the worst depression of all time—and get to the well before it dries up forever."[6] Ringer's formula is no novelty. Let us hope that we can learn how to cope with such destructive people and with the general situation they help to create before it is too late.

In the 1930s, during the Depression on the eve of World War II, two fascinating waves of enthusiasm swept this country. One resulted in a serious drive to take the corporate profits out of munitions manufacturing and thus out of warmaking. Many were wishfully crying: "Next time we will conscript wealth as well as men. Next time there will be no war profits."[7] That drive had the backing, for a while, of even the American Legion, but not for long.[8]

The other wave of enthusiam had a related goal. It sought to offset the tendency of people to get caught up in notions that would make it easy for warmakers to exploit and thus to lead them into another disastrous international holocaust. This second wave was called propaganda analysis. Hitler's holocaust cut this wave short.

By the beginning of the 1940s, both these efforts had failed. Congress had again made it profitable for major corporations to participate lucratively in war. And propaganda analysis—the imperative art for a healthy democracy—was put away in moth balls. It became unpatriotic for people to question American or even Allied wartime propaganda. As our high schools and colleges continued to turn toward the training of technicians for industry and government, education in the liberal arts and sciences for intelligent living continued largely as the responsibility of dedicated "old-fashioned" teachers. Thus, propaganda analysis as a crucial part of that education is still too much in moth balls. But then, ever since the United States embarked on its program of expanding industrial and military imperialism in 1898, we have been deeply involved both in our own international conflicts and in those carried on in behalf of our entrepreneurs by dependent or "client" nations.

Propaganda analysis became quite an educational movement in the late 1930s. It spread quickly through the programs of adult study groups and the curricula of high schools and colleges especially from 1937. On October 7, 1937, the editor of the *San Francisco News* asserted that propaganda analysis "is one more weapon for democracy in the ceaseless battle against obfuscation and special interest." The *Hartford Courant's* editor added on November 8, 1937: "The less gullible the public becomes through understanding, the less danger there is of action, political, economic or social, being based on emotion." He called propaganda analysis "commendable and worthy of encouragement."

These editors were responding to the launching of the Institute for Propaganda Analysis, which (it was hoped) would give added impetus and educational focus to the wave of interest in propaganda analysis on the eve of World War II. That Institute had highly prestigious officers and board members drawn from leading universities and colleges. The late Boston merchant, Edward A. Filene, initiated the venture with funds. Columbia University Professor Clyde R. Miller became its first executive relinquishing his previous responsibility as Teachers' College's successful publicist. On April 3, 1939, *Newsweek* hailed propaganda analysis as "one of the newest and fastest growing ideas in American education" and credited the Institute for Propaganda Analysis with its development and dissemination.

The Institute worked with the American Association of University Women, the League of Women Voters, trade unions, peace groups, religious organizations, YM and WCAs, YM and WHAs, settlement houses, and other voluntary groups, as well as with high schools and colleges. Its staff published some fifty analytical bulletins, a teacher's guide, and several other books, and participated in a great many conferences. Shortly after the Pearl Harbor attack in 1941, the Institute issued a bulletin entitled "We Say Au Revoir." The Institute's reasons for "dying" were as notable and as symptomatic of the social situation as were the reasons for its enthusiastic welcome and acceptance only a little more than four years earlier. As the Institute's last bulletin announced, its board of directors decided that the "publication of dispassionate analyses of all kinds of propaganda, 'good' and 'bad,' is easily misunderstood during a war emergency, and more important, the analyses could be misused for undesirable purposes by persons opposing the government's efforts." An alternative would have been for the Institute to cease being objective in its analyses, but, as the Institute's final statement continued, "for the Institute, as an institute, to propagandize or even to appear to do so would cast doubt on its integrity as a scientific body. If it were to continue it would have to analyze all propaganda—of this country and of Britain and Russia as well as of Germany, Italy and Japan."[9] Since many of the Institute's board members had already become propaganda counselors to branches of the Federal government, the only action on which the board could agree was to suspend the Institute's operations. That is what they did.

The Institute's publications and especially the many works inspired by those publications continue nevertheless to make stimulating contributions to education and public discussion in textbooks and other media not only in this country but throughout the world. In opposition to that and related influences, however, the managerial-technical bias has gained increasing strength in high schools and colleges which had been dedicated to liberal arts and sciences. This bias tends to propagate and strengthen courses for propaganda producers rather than for the protection of propaganda consumers. These producer-oriented courses are typically labeled public relations, publicity, mass communications, public opinion polling or surveying, and related topics. Such courses might well be given but not at the expense of or in place of courses in propaganda analysis for the protection of students as propaganda "consumers."

In the sense of preparing people for active roles in a democratic society, propaganda analysis can well be seen as an essential art or instrument that is useful in many liberal arts disciplines. Whether it is a live part of a course in history, social psychology, literature, education, or philosophy depends upon both students and teachers. It is unfortunate that current terms of academic competition often tempt a variety of teaching specialists to avoid any approach with such controversial or consumer-oriented implications as propaganda analysis. Many academicians are tempted either to be bland or to serve the established manipulators of motivations and of social events. The colorless but profitable games of complex methodologies are quite seductive. It is fortunate that there are teachers who do view themselves primarily as literate persons—regardless of their discipline—who are involved professionally in observing, analyzing, and interpreting human behavior and other phenomena for the benefit of student and popular audiences. It is these teachers who most effectively weave propaganda analysis into their courses as a dependable and useful art.

In the four years of its existence, the Institute for Propaganda Analysis granted 231 requests for the reprinting of its materials in textbooks, general works, encyclopaedias, articles, lectures, and sermons.[10] These were extensive word-for-word quotations; short quotations and paraphrases did not require such permission. Since 1942, the executive trustee of the Institute's materials has granted an uncounted but continuing series of such permissions.[11] The social historian Harry Elmer Barnes recognized the usefulness of the Institute's work when in the late 1930s he cited its staff's work as "the most important single educational enterprise in the United States today so far as preparation for the democratic way of life is concerned."[12] Many other pro-democratic teaching procedures were available then and others have since been added, but propaganda analysis remains a significant part of pro-democratic education and guidance to the extent that it is made available and is used.

How do we go about analyzing propaganda struggles taking place today? How do we penetrate the glittering generalities, the name-calling terms, the obfuscations, and the delusory inferences that are such overwhelming parts of our day's public competitions and controversies? To what extent and with what techniques can those disenchanted with policies of established media of social action gain hearings and push for their goals?

Recent writings on the subject focus too often on these three superficial approaches: (1) the kind of logic or illogic used by a propagandist, (2) the contents of propaganda messages, and (3) the notion that a medium defines the character of a propaganda message—in other words, as the writer Marshall McLuhan asserts, that the "medium is the message."[13]

About formal analyses of the logicality or illogicality of a given propagandist's statements, I would raise this question: So what? How far have we gone toward assessing the significance of a propagandist's behavior when we determine whether or not he is obeying the traditional canons of logic? What do we learn when we know that a propagandist is using an *ad hominem* argument? What if he or she is discussing an issue in terms of a personality or of personal relations rather than in terms of accuracy or of the relevance of an issue to our interests and concerns? Saying that an argument is presented illogically does not get us far enough. It does not face up to the practice as a procedure common in human communication. It does not weigh the effectiveness of an illogical statement as a rhetorical device. For example, how can we consider discussions of the Watergate scandals separately from the personalities involved?

As much can also be said of the other classical fallacies of logic employed by analysts who do not probe further. Bad logic they are, but propaganda analysts need to understand living social thought and behavior whether it is logical or illogical. We have to go beyond the technical question of whether or not a propagandist is playing the game according to a given set of rules. The most logical propagandist could still be a destructive influence in society.

Similarly, many social scientists have been interested in analyzing the contents of propaganda messages.[14] They can thus work out how politicians or industrial publicists build their cases out of facts, imageries, and positive and negative vagaries. They perceive how propagandists employ polarized terms as the main props for their messages. Things are good or bad, American or communist, Christian or atheist, for or against the national interest, and all the rest. Content analysts can also go beyond those glittering generalities and see the techniques of association and identification with which propagandists try to tie glittering generalities to what we want on the one hand and to what they are trying to sell on the other. These are bridging devices such as testimonials, bandwagon and plain-folks appeals, and efforts to transfer the prestige or disrepute of one thing onto something else.[15]

But propaganda is not just a message. It loses meaning when it is taken out of its context of competition or struggle.

In spite of the popularity of the writings of Marshall McLuhan, propaganda is also not just what the media permit it to be. He claims that, "in operational and practical fact, the medium is the message."[16] Thus he titillates advertising men anxious for a new sales gimmick and merchandisers grasping for instruments with which to achieve greater power in the world's markets. Actually, he has added nothing but a caricaturing formula to the search for ways to participate in and to cope with the modern flood of propaganda.

Any careful student of newspaper readership who has done firsthand interviewing knows how greatly the behavior of readers varies—not alone from page to page but also within pages. The variations are due to many influences. Position of an item on a page and of the page in the newspaper, typographical effects, and pictures influence reader attention. A front-page story is more likely to be seen than one on an inner page, but the results of reportorial footwork, perceptiveness, and writing ability can attract reader attention on almost any page. Such factors also can help determine whether the reader gets beyond the headlines or perhaps the first paragraph. The presence or absence of reportorial hard work, personal courage, and brilliance in expression does much to define the message in a newspaper or on radio or television and thus to determine its effectiveness in influencing opinions and actions as it travels through those media.

Let us briefly consider the daily press further. It evolved as an integral part of American plutocracy and, especially since the 1890s, of plutocratic imperialism. Its reportorial and editorial heroes who defy some aspect of the "system" were and are exceptions to journalistic practice, sometimes at their own personal and professional cost. Such heroes often serve highly useful social purposes, but at the same time, they also provide a glamorous façade for a fairly typical business operation with policies far more attuned to commercial than to general popular interests and concerns. Even William Randolph Hearst, a capitalist who owned a large chain of newspapers and other enterprises, had in 1924 a startling answer to the question: "Is the political influence of the American press, in general, declining or increasing, and why?" He answered:

I rather think that the influence of the American press is on the whole declining. This, I believe, is because so many newspapers are owned or influenced by reactionary interests and predatory corporations, and are used selfishly, to promote the welfare of these reactionary interests, rather than the welfare of the public. This tends to weaken the confidence of the public in all newspapers more or less.[17]

The role of the press is seen dramatically in the correlation and lack of correlation between press support for Presidential candidates and election results. The list of Presidents elected with majority opposition of the press (in terms of circulation) includes Jefferson, Madison, Lincoln (first candidacy), Wilson, F. D. Roosevelt, Truman, Kennedy, and Carter. Those supported by a majority of the press include Grant, Cleveland, McKinley, Theodore Roosevelt, Taft, Harding, Coolidge, Hoover, and Nixon.[18] According to the newspaper owner, Marshall Field, these lists suggest that "the majority of the newspapers have supported our greatest presidential protectors of vested privilege and have opposed our greatest liberal presidents!"[19] Viewed slightly differently, it might be stated that when there has been an apparent issue between candidates of vested privilege and those fighting for human rights, the press opted for the former, and the public, for the latter. Many a newspaper publisher would probably agree with the novelist Samuel Butler's viewpoint: "The older I grow, the more convinced I become of the folly and credulity of the public; but at the same time the harder do I see it is to impose oneself upon that folly and credulity." Many a democratic theorist and actionist has faith in the future of our society based on that alleged "folly and credulity."[20] Society offers no better alternative.

As any newspaper circulation promoter is aware, newspapers are frequently bought *in spite of* their editorial page and their general editorial policies on politico-economic matters and *because of* their comics, sports, and other features and their non-controversial announcements and advertisements. This has been increasingly the case as daily newspaper competition has disappeared from all but a few centers. As of 1977, the twelve largest daily newspaper chains control nearly two-fifths of all daily newspaper circulation, and three-fifths of all dailies belong to chains.[21] As independently owned papers get bought up, "the press of America is losing its independent voices, one by one. If the trend continues, the music may end up resembling the slick, superficial harmonies of a barbershop quartet. And that is bad,"[22] as one newspaper columnist, C. B. Seib, sees it. With less competition than in this country, the large London papers have carried the conception of circulation based upon reports of the politically and economically irrelevant much further than have our papers, but the American are moving in the direction of the English.

Thus current newspapers glow with melodramatic struggles between political candidates who parade under different major party labels but with only slightly different actual policies; with Congressional investigations inspired or controlled by selfish interests; with sensational court trials of little social significance; with political bunglers and scapegoats thrown—sometimes oh so gently—into prison or oblivion; with sports and more sports; and with whatever else exciting and harmless may be available. Little of a constructive nature is told of the continuing struggles of women against "old boy" male conspiracies and of the miseries of Blacks, Chicanos, American Indians, and poor whites. How lightly do newspapers touch upon the irresponsibilities of the American-centered international military-industrial complex and of multinational corporate imperialism. How they distort or obscure the current destruction of liberal education in our public colleges and universities and its replacement with narrow trade-schoolism. How they ignore the diversion of public funds to religious and elitist private schools and the plutocratic nourishment of unrepresentative trade-union hierarchies with their "sweetheart contracts" and their lack of concern for the class-oriented political needs of their membership. These are just a few of the pressing matters newspapers neglect or distort.

I am certainly not opposed to sports and to sports coverage in our mass media, but I am pointing out that now as in ancient Rome's Coliseum sports are not only a means of expression and entertainment but also an effective way to distract popular attention from political and economic manipulations. Only occasionally does a demonstration against war or imperialism or racism or sexism, a race riot or a wildcat strike get sufficiently out of control to be reported accurately. Such events are seldom given such sensitive and adequate reportage as to tear a hole in our media pall of orthodoxy.[23] It is little wonder that managerial pundits in their think-tanks are often asked to determine whether Americans are subtly becoming more politicized or can hopefully be thought to be so involved in personal problems, in sports, in interpersonal crime and violence, in drugs, and in other cop-outs as to remain relatively apathetic socially.

Radio and television, for all their vast audiences, have modified but not at all replaced in influence the daily and weekly press and other periodicals. They have taken over from gossippers and the press as the first to report news of a sensational nature. Newspaper extras are now rare. Voices of actual participants in great events permit radio to bring a new dimension of "reality," a very believable dimension, that printed media cannot duplicate. Television brings an even greater sense of immediacy, intimacy, "reality." Newspapers have pictures, but television's pictures move and talk, and they can come directly from the scene of action. People do not comprehend how selective and even faked television's "reality" can be.

Both radio and television news broadcasts tend to consist chiefly of brief items, so far as any one topic other than a spectacular event is concerned. Radio and television also cater unidimensionally to a broad audience. They address through any one station one generalized public at a time.

Newspaper readers, on the other hand, do not have to start reading at the top of the first column of page one and then proceed through to the bottom of the last page's last column, but in effect that is what radio and television listeners and viewers during a single broadcast are expected to do. Only newspapers can offer a rich variety of items simultaneously that attracts many reading publics. Newspapers can, with one edition, furnish materials for many specialized publics simultaneously—race track enthusiasts, stamp collectors, a wide range of shoppers, financiers, outdoor people, bridge players, children, old folks, and many more.

Perhaps the chief contribution of radio and television is to substitute a theatrical sense of community for the actual disappearance of community life in our more urban and more private world. Familiar voices and tube personalities diminish the urge to find actual community experiences. Thus the folksy Jimmy Carter, mindful of the impact of F. D. Roosevelt's "intimate fireside chats," launches his own series of talks so that he can be influential in the people's TV community.

In order to understand propaganda and its social action setting satisfactorily, analysts have to work with a seven-point approach which covers the various means or factors that propagandists utilize. Those factors are (1) personnel, (2) organizations, (3) messages, (4) media of communication, (5) ideas already existing in the minds of the people they want to reach, (6) the changing social scene of events, conditions, and developments, and (7) the *key* factor, strategy. This is the factor that involves wisdom, imagination, timing, adroitness, and luck.

If a person chooses to focus on only one aspect of a struggle making for or against social change, most will be learned by his trying to figure out the strategies being used by the competitors or the conflicting partisans. It is what working action analysts always try especially to get at. Just what is a given propagandist's game plan? How is it likely to be carried out? What are its chances of success? Why?

Central in any social action strategy are the selection and definition of the point or points at issue. This really means selecting the place and terms of a struggle. Skilled propagandists consider selecting and specifying (or obfuscating) issues to be the primary and most urgent business in a campaign. It is a matter to which they give constant and continuing attention. They have to. Shifts in the fields of conflict or competition must constantly be prepared for, attempted, and guarded against.

One of the problems faced by strategists is the jerry-built character of most public opinion surveying efforts by commercial pollsters. What data such surveyors can yield about basic materiel, the ideas already existing in the minds of the people they want to reach, often consist of oversimplifications, the significance of which is easier to assume than to determine. Opinion surveyors have long tried to cope with problems of prejudice, honesty, and accuracy upon the part of their relatively untrained and underpaid interviewers, but they largely ignore the fact that respondents will give different opinions in different group contexts. And what relation does any expressed opinion have to the manner in which an individual will speak or otherwise behave in some action situation? The interviewer, with her/his introductory remarks, gives clues to the interviewee as to what sort of person the interviewer might be. Those clues suggest what customary or habitual criteria the interviewee will think appropriate to use in this particular interpersonal situation.

An interviewer may be able to talk with an interviewee as a depersonalized professional might talk with a depersonalized respondent, or they may speak to one another as fellow schoolteachers, secretaries, townspersons, housewives, armed forces veterans, church members, or even old friends. The interpersonal relation in terms of which rapport is thus established—as any experienced participant observer early learns—colors the interviewee's response to significant questions, especially to those dealing with matters of value and opinion rather than of routine information.

At some point in a depersonalized interview, the interviewer may drop a cue which makes the interviewer appear to be someone other than an impersonal instrument recording responses like a machine. The respondent may then immediately "freeze" and try to reinterpret previous statements or at least to hedge on additional ones. A highly permissive type of rapport may thus give way at that juncture to the usual formal and perhaps wary relation between two unacquainted people or between two group members in terms of the common group's interaction patterns they have now identified. The interviewee might later tell a friend, "If I had known that that interviewer was the police chief's niece, I'd never have said such things!" "Who'd have ever guessed that that interviewer is a brother of little Bill's schoolteacher!"[24] Even if we ignore the personal shortcomings of interviewers, which are indeterminate enough, the polls in effect add together responses from such a variety of social contexts that their results might be compared—with a little exaggeration—to a population census counting people, hogs, cows, rabbits, and dogs as comparable units![25]

While social action strategists do use public opinion surveys, the wiser ones often supplement them or depend more directly upon what might be called "political scout surveys." These are efforts locally, in a state or region, or nationally to tap the reactions perceived by trusted key observers of gossip and behavior to a given issue or situation. Assessments arising out of such a survey made through channels that are available to a political or commercial organization often provide useful estimates upon which to base strategies.

Go back over Richard Nixon's propaganda strategies. What stands out in his plans and methods of procedure? In his case, it is both his selection of issues and his success in redefining them to suit his opportunistic purposes. Some of the propaganda monster issues of our century furnished Nixon with his major materiel. He used especially the Communist Menace during the period between our World War II alliance with the Soviets and our Nixon-made 1970s détente with the Communists and China. For Nixon, American Communists have only been a threat when he could use them to put red tar and feathers on an opponent. Other monster issues that Nixon found useful were those of National Security, the Integrity of the Presidency, and Peace in Our Time.

When problems developed in connection with his 1972 election campaign and Watergate became a national catchword for conspiracy and corruption, Nixon presumably offered all sorts of cooperation to officials of the Department of Justice, the Federal courts, and the House of Representatives. He also urged them to get on with the investigation. Hurry, hurry! But he hoped that the investigation would be on his own terms. He was being maligned, he contended, and the whole process of investigation was handicapping him in his international efforts. He had his attorneys define the limits within which his cooperation had to be confined in order to protect the Integrity of the Presidency and National Security. This included the narrowest possible definition of a basis for impeachment, trial, and removal from office. Through well stage-managed press conferences, Nixon made an amazing number of favorable points for himself with the uncritical or prejudiced in his audiences through his adroit redefinition of issues.

Pat examples of issue-selection-and-definition are furnished perennially by politicians and political parties, spokesmen for management and for labor, fomenters of intergroup tensions and dissensions, manipulators of international relations, and product advertisers. In a political campaign, the propagandist's art and procedure are thought by many propaganda analysts to triumph when the propagandist avoids being a jot more specific than is necessary, and when he forces his opposition to become specific. The issues of a campaign, in the practice of professional politicians, are kept sufficiently vague so that they can hope to claim the support of "all good and decent people, all true Americans." Then, following each election, we have the recurrent American routine of the winning candidate attempting to justify his failures to live up to his promises. Before an election, politicians typically exploit our fears and thus give life to monster slogans. After an election they do what they can to convince us that while we still must live with the fear of threats to our status, to our future and that of our children, their "wise" decisions represent the least of evils. Thus, inflation and unemployment could be worse. Energy will cost more but not as much as it might. International tensions excuse skyrocketing "defense" spending and hence taxation and the curtailment of spending for education, for the oppressed and exploited, for the handicapped, and for other humane purposes. But it all could be worse!

Investigative journalists who inject authenticity into the news media—sometimes having to use minority and radical media to do so—and teachers of the fine art of propaganda analysis in our classrooms and in adult study groups exist in greater numbers than may be apparent. These two groups may be able to help move our society toward a more democratic, a more participatory form of organization. They at least are doing what they can, many times under great handicaps, to strengthen our faith and confidence in ourselves and in our country's and the world's future.[26]

As the social psychologist Alex Carey told an Australian national radio audience, "Nothing in American, post-war foreign policy or domestic politics can be understood unless the role of domestic propaganda is understood." Being aware of the growing role of social scientists in guiding that propaganda, Carey added:

But no matter how deceitful the propaganda, there has never been any shortage of social scientists willing to explore and develop new ways of making it more effective. Since Watergate there are stirrings that could promise an eventual rebirth of democracy in the United States. But that is still a long way off. And if it is ever to come it will have to be over the dead careers of a horde of social scientists.[27]

Strategies for Social Change   137

notes

[1]Thomas Jefferson, letter to John Adams, September 4, 1823, *The Writings of Thomas Jefferson*, A. A. Lipscomb, ed. (Washington, D.C.: Thomas Jefferson Memorial Association, 1903), vol. 15, pp. 464–67; p. 464 quoted.

[2]Ibid., letter to H. G. Spafford, March 17, 1814, vol. 14, pp. 118–120; pp. 119–20 quoted.

[3]A. McC. Lee, *How to Understand Propaganda* (New York: Rinehart & Co., 1952), pp. 2, 6–7.

[4]Ralph Ellison, "An American Dilemma: A Review," in J. A. Ladner, ed., *The Death of White Sociology* (New York: Random House, 1973), pp. 81–95; p. 82 quoted.

[5]M. F. Granville, chairman of the board, Texaco, Inc., quoted in Texaco advertisement, *Newsweek*, April 18, 1977, p. 87.

[6]R. J. Ringer quoted in "The Power Boys: Push Pays Off," *Time*, January 19, 1976, pp. 60–61; p. 61 quoted; see Ringer, *Winning Through Intimidation*, 2nd ed. (New York: Funk & Wagnalls, 1974).

[7]Popular statements quoted by Institute for Propaganda Analysis, "Strikes, Profits, and Defense," *Propaganda Analysis*, vol. 4, no. 6 (April 29, 1941), p. 1.

[8]C. A. and M. R. Beard, *America in Midpassage*, vol. 1 (New York: Macmillan Co., 1939), p. 406.

[9]Institute for Propaganda Analysis, "We Say au Revoir," *Propaganda Analysis*, vol. 4, no. 13 (January 9, 1942), p. 1.

[10]Especially from A. McC. and E. B. Lee, *The Fine Art of Propaganda* (New York: Institute for Propaganda Analysis and Harcourt, Brace and Co., 1939; Octagon Books, 1972).

[11]The author was formerly executive director of the Institute for Propaganda Analysis and has served as its executive trustee since 1942.

[12]Institute for Propaganda Analysis, op. cit., p. 2.

[13]Marshall McLuhan, *Understanding Media* (New York: McGraw-Hill Book Co., 1964), p. 7.

[14]O. R. Holsti, "Content Analysis," *The Handbook of Social Psychology*, 2nd. ed., Gardner Lindzey and Elliot Aronson, eds. (Reading, Mass.: Addison-Wesley Publishing Co., 1968), vol. 2, chap. 16; H. D. Lasswell, Daniel Lerner, and I. de S. Pool, *The Comparative Study of Symbols* (Stanford: Stanford University Press, 1952).

[15]Lee and Lee, op. cit.; A. McC. Lee, *How to Understand Propaganda* (New York: Rinehart & Co., 1952).

[16]Marshall McLuhan, op. cit.

[17]W. R. Hearst quoted in *Editor & Publisher*, vol. 57, no. 3 (June 14, 1924), p. 3.

[18]Based in part on lists in F. L. Mott, "Newspapers in Presidential Campaigns," *Public Opinion Quarterly*, vol. 8 (1944), pp. 348–67.

[19]Marshall Field, *Freedom Is More Than a Word* (Chicago: University of Chicago Press, 1945), p. 83.

[20]Samuel Butler, *The Way of All Flesh*, 1903 (New York: Macmillan Co., 1925), p. 393.

[21]"The Big Money Hunts for Independent Newspapers," *Business Week*, February 21, 1977, pp. 56–60, 62.

[22]C. B. Seib, "Who Owns the Press?" *Washington Post*, March 25, 1977.

[23]A. McC. Lee, *Multivalent Man*, 2nd ed. (New York: George Braziller, 1970), chaps. 3 and 14.

[24]Summarized from ibid., p. 127.

[25]A. McC. Lee, *Toward Humanist Sociology* (Englewood Cliffs, N.J.: Prentice-Hall, 1973), pp. 154–56.

[26]Parts of this chapter were adapted from Tom Reilly, "A Conversation With Alfred McClung Lee," *Journalism History*, vol. 4 (1977), pp. 2–7.

[27]Alex Carey, "Ideology and Science," Australian National Radio Broadcast, June 9, 1976, 9 pp. ms., p. 3.

seven

A Sociological View
of Human Survival

Many a cocktail party and business luncheon hummed happily at the enthusiasm generated among the young in connection with the celebration of the first Earth Day, April 22, 1970. The elderly and the financially entrenched and others dedicated to the *status quo ante* asserted that now perhaps we all had really turned another corner, this time "for the better." Hopefully, youngsters would now forget about confronting the "establishment" over war, educational irrelevance, drugs, and all the rest as they had done so frequently and disturbingly during the 1960s. Now they would turn to something "really sensible."[1]

The entrenched who so reacted, as presumptive owners and managers of the earth, often did not realize at the time all the ramifications of "ecology." Many of them would shortly learn more about those ramifications. They would also be told, and would find it hard to believe, that human survival is involved in "ecology" and is far from certain.

There were also voices of dissent—from the left and also from the right—to Earth Day. Some who were fighting against war or for rights for Blacks or for women's rights asserted that antipollution agitation is a cheap and easy diversion, a cop-out. It is inoffensive and thus would syphon off energies better used in more pressing and more controversial struggles. Almost by reflex, the Daughters of the American Revolution also questioned Earth Day—but for a different reason: They said they suspected it would awaken an irresponsible interest in the destruction of our planet's resources. Such a concern might lead anywhere. They therefore called Earth Day "subversive" and asserted that reports on an environmental crisis are "distorted and exaggerated." They even discovered that Earth Day fell on Lenin's birthday![2]

As others have recognized, the revolution in which ancestors of the D.A.R. participated was an incident in social processes which still continue.[3] If the D.A.R. members meant by "subversive" the radicalizing of intellectual circles and of popular thought, they were more nearly correct than they may have guessed. Even D.A.R. dowagers might pause at the authoritative assertion by Paul and Anne Ehrlich that mothers' milk in the United States today "contains so much DDT that it would be declared illegal in interstate commerce if it were sold as cow's milk." For that matter, infants around the whole world now are said to ingest "about twice the daily allowable maximum [of DDT] in standards recommended by the World Health Organization."[4]

Existing threats to human survival overshadow even the brutalization and prodigal waste of recent and current examples of genocidal neglect and exploitation, of riots, and of wars. Such threats stimulate many thoughtful social scientists to fundamental rethinkings of every aspect of people's relations with other people, with social institutions, with the physical environment, and with nation states.

In terms of our present technology, resources, distribution arrangements, and social organization, our planet is already greatly overpopulated.[5] Excessive population and population growth-rates distract attention from all sorts of other frightening human problems. They also increase the possibility of a world-wide disaster—even human extinction—by disease, starvation, pollution, or thermonuclear war.

"Overkill" is apparently the military "preparedness" slogan of the day. As the interdenominational Fellowship of Reconciliation summarizes the situation:

The U.S. and the U.S.S.R. have about 66,000 nuclear bombs between them [as of 1976]—enough to kill everyone on earth sixteen times over. They are making more. Many other countries have nuclear capability. Each weapon makes the possibility of war by miscalculation, misunderstanding, accident or design more certain. In addition, many weapons are potential targets for theft and use by terrorist groups.

The United States itself has on hand enough nuclear weapons "to destroy every major city in the world."[6] The political scientist Mulford Q. Sibley concludes,

The only hope against nuclear annihilation is the destruction of this mythology [of the efficacy of military violence] and reliance solely on non-violent means of "defense." Non-violent means—the promotion of justice and the organization of non-violent resistance—cannot guarantee security, to be sure, but they are far more compatible with it than threat of military violence.[7]

The mass media readily permit the multinational banker-contrived unemployment, inflation, and energy crisis of the 1970s to distract attention from other threats to human survival. The need for jobs and for some degree of job security diverts attention from too many other projects protective of human health and welfare, from the exploitation of women and minorities, and even from human survival. Regressive steps become easy.

Physical and biological innovators provide us not only with such environmentally blighting agents as autombiles, pesticides, and inorganic nitrogen fertilizers but also with procedures through which we might stretch or recycle the world's resources. What blocks the use of such procedures is a lack of social ingenuity and especially of social determination and of participant control. Physical and biological developments in themselves do not now appear to include any panacea for human survival. At best, the physicists, chemists, and biologists can furnish humanity with more time in which to develop effective and acceptable innovations in human interrelations and in social organization. Social innovations, especially those leading to better health and education, need to be made operative. Social opportunities need to be made more nearly equal. Without those steps joined with the control of population growth, of resource waste, and of human greed, the undernourished will shortly include far more than the one-half of humanity now so afflicted. A great many more than the present ten to twenty millions will die each year of malnutrition.[8]

Until we have substantial and convincing evidence that humanity can not only survive but also thrive, threats of declining facilities for living and even of extinction are going to continue to promote radicalization, especially of the young, as well as cynicism and dull resignation among a great many older people. For the present, the increasingly realistic and pressing threat of extinction to the human species would provide a powerful leverage—if it were accepted widely enough as credible and were so used—for the overturn of complacent assumptions. It could help launch a realistic campaign to save "our endangered human species."[9] It is all too easy for a resident rationalizer in one of the think-tanks for entrenched plutocrats, R. Bruce-Briggs of Hudson Institute, to assert: "Somehow this inefficient and predatory system keeps tottering on, eroding feudal societies, corrupting socialist regimes, providing a higher living standard for workers and peasants, and confounding the nihilist fantasies of so many intellectuals."[10]

When the woe saying about environmental pollution and destruction came to be followed by specific repair programs with price tags affixed thereto, the enthusiasm of the entrenched for the "new cause" of "the children" changed to concern and even to backlash. If college students and their fellow travelers had only stuck to "panty raids" and goldfish-swallowing contests as they had in the "good old days"—or even to "streaking" naked across campuses and through common room. :! "Antipollution efforts are progressing, with varied success, in a great part of the world," a New York *Times* writer, Brendan Jones, optimistically reported, "but this development is also beginning to cause anxieties for business in many countries." There is fear "in some countries [that it] will make it harder for them to compete in exporting with rival nations that follow lax or less-costly environmental standards." Even in such countries as Italy, Japan, and the Union of South Africa, however, where the rush to expand industry had been especially heedless and rapid, "extreme pollution conditions have been recognized and remedial measures started."[11]

In other words, from the early 1970s, it began seeping into the skulls of some preoccupied business people and politicians that the "open earth of the past" is no longer with us; the "closed earth of the future requires economic principles which are somewhat different from those . . . of the past."[12]

But what to do about it all? Business as usual? That is the almost overwhelming temptation to those who fear to think in other terms. They distrust "speculative," "untested" paths suggested by "idealists" or "academic theorists." Above all, they would not support any planning that might shackle somehow what is still romantically and inaccurately labeled "free enterprise" or "private initiative" and is really plutocratic manipulation. "Practical" leaders often ask, isn't the theorists' warning of still another Armageddon—people against people in a struggle to survive on nature's spent and ruined resources—contrived, overdrawn? How can humanity be an endangered species? People are adaptable animals!

Let us examine some concomitants in human behavior of current developments in pollution, resource exhaustion, ecological tampering, and contrived unemployment, inflation, and diminution of social services. Let us look at those concomitants in terms of the following questions: What changes are taking place now in culture and social organization that appear to be influencing people's chances of survival? Can they be modified? Do they need to be modified? If analysis should point to the wisdom of such a course, can they be reversed? Are they symptomatic of the working out of some long-term and inexorable law—ecological, biological, psychological, cultural, and/or organizational—of human degradation and/or extinction? Or are alternatives available to present tendencies in crucial aspects of society? And to whom are they available and on what terms? To what extent might control of change become both democratic and rational? Can a complex of programs for terrestrial renewal now become workable rapidly enough to save the human race as we know it?

The making of some contribution to the discussion of these overwhelming questions from a social-scientific point of view depends upon the kind of social science in terms of which one treats them. As we saw in connection with the discussion of *Sociology for Whom?* in the first chapter, prevalent social-scientific orientations lead to a variety of ways of handling our questions and thus to rather different data and analyses. The extent to which each of these orientations may enter into future social diagnoses for policy-making purposes has a significant bearing upon whether or not control of change can become rational, effective and democratic. We must therefore take another look at these orientations and their social implications before turning more directly to our questions.

Social science has as yet had no dominant traditions comparable in acceptance to Ptolemaic or Copernican astronomy or Aristotelian or Newtonian or Einsteinian dynamics. What are ordinarily called "schools" in social science do not have clear-cut paradigms such as those which have figured so prominently in the physical and biological sciences.[13] Schools of economists have included the physiocratic, classical, marginal utility, mathematical, historical, socialist, Marxian, socio-ethical, romantic, universalist, institutional, Keynesian, and many more. Political science schools, to name a few, have been labeled legalistic, institutional, functional, historical, ethical, social psychological, socialist, and behavioral. As we have seen, the range of sociological schools is suggested by the terms, institutional, ethical, evolutionary, cultural, comparative, social psychological, symbolic interactionist, structural-functionalist, sociometric, ethnomethodological, Marxian, macrosociological, and existential-humanist.

When one turns from the pretentious jargons and the overlapping theoretical formulations of the sociological "schools" to the social roles their members hold or anticipate holding, clearer-cut and more practical orientations become apparent. These orientations are role commitments for which school theories and jargons serve in part at least as embellishments or disguises. These role commitments are not ideologically precise enough to be thought of as being centered in scientific paradigms, but two of them are somewhat crystallized and ideologically dominant. Two other major ones are more speculative and controversial.

Among social scientists, as among other types of intellectuals, people commonly attach themselves to one of four role commitments, to one of four types of status-ladders—the bureaucratic, technical, entrepreneurial, or innovative.[14] In Western society today, the vast majority seek recognition, security, and expression either as bureaucrats or as technicians. These two role types have sprouted our two principal social science orientations. Those who take a more speculative and adventuresome course—either the entrepreneurial or the innovative—provide us with most of our flexibility, most of our ability to adapt to changed life conditions. The entrepreneurs bring selected products of creative social scientists into the marketplace. Through their research bureaus and think-tanks, they facilitate the application of social scientific findings to the needs and aspirations of sources of finance or of other

146   Sociology for Whom?

types of power. The free-floating innovators in social science, to the extent that we have some who can eschew the rewards of bureaucracy and of consulting fees and find their "calling" in scientific discovery, have given us the fourth principal orientation of which we shall speak further.

Bureaucratic social scientists find their career opportunities in courtier-like service within a hierarchy. Often, in spite of differences in "school" background, bureaucrats-called-social-scientists discover they share much in common in terms of managerial-bureaucratic ideology. They find this view of life expedient to use as a way of integrating their facts, theories, and recommendations.

The managerial-bureaucratic orientation might also be called a scientistic one, but then that characterization would fit the second orientation—the problematic-technical one—almost as well. They both lean heavily on methods, symbols, and conceptions—jargon—borrowed from the physical and biological sciences. Managerial-bureaucratic persons typically visualize society as a "system" or a "social order" in some sort of "equilibrium." This systemic structure, with congeries of subsystems nested within it, is usually subjected to what is called "functional analysis." This conservative and largely ahistorical type of analysis assumes that the "system's" parts do or can be made to satisfy the needs of the "system" and of its members. Somehow the "system" will more or less automatically maintain integration and balance, or it can be made to do so. These bureaucratic technicians typically look upon accurate historical considerations as irrelevant, weightless, or at least unnecessary.[15]

Social-scientific technicians find their career opportunities through publicizing their possession of a "kit" of vendable research methods, experience, and plausible theory. Rather than placing faith in a single organizational hierarchy, they depend upon their desirability and mobility in the employment market. Their rewards in good times are thus higher than those of the bureaucrats. Their problematic-technical orientation is not necessarily wed to the maintenance of an organization or of societal equilibrium. Like the bureaucrats, they usually have modish techniques, ostensibly objective and nonmanipulable (often statistical), with which to furnish data for guidance and/or for propaganda purposes to paying clients.

Like the bureaucrats, a group of technicians may derive from diverse "schools," but they often discover that their problematic-technical orientation becomes an adequate basis for understanding and procedure. For them the current assignment is the focus, whether it be a prestigious research grant in a university setting or a policy-research contract from a corporation, trade association, trade union, or government agency. They try to determine the probable effectiveness of a promotional campaign for a product or a candidate. They look into whether or not employees will strike or can be kept from striking. They chart investment possibilities upon the basis of available evidence. They rarely concern themselves, except as a private hobby or as an academic disguise, in the broader ramifications of their assignments or in the application of sophisticated social theory. Perhaps even more so than the bureaucrats, they tend to let themselves become depersonalized tools in a society they see as dehumanized.[16]

Social scientists who are primarily innovation-motivated may play with managerial-bureaucratic or problematic-technical problems, but they tend to concern themselves more often with problems associated with a general humanist-existential-democratic concern with society. They are the "impractical" ones who are not bound by organizational exigencies and loyalties or by the need to peddle a technical kit. Regardless of how they might finance themselves (for this the professorship-on-tenure can be most helpful), they refuse to function as though they had financial obligations or as though they were wearing someone's collar of servitude.

This role commitment is roughly that of those who are either on or trying to get on the high road of social science; for that matter, it is the high road of social thought in our society. In relating themselves to this role, social scientists need to relate themselves to the work of social philosophers, historians, and belletrists as well as of other humanist and even non-humanist social scientists.

This orientation calls for a people-centered social science that serves human needs and goals. Since these social scientists are typically not elitist and manipulative in their social values, their viewpoint and working stance are not attractive to power-seekers as emulators even though the latter stand ever ready to exploit the innovators' products. To the extent that innovators can gain support for their work, it is in consequence of their production of attractive solutions to specific problems seen out of long range context or due to a vague social notion justifying and rewarding research activity as an allocation of human energies that may somehow guide and enrich life in society. In other words, innovators find their rewards through contributing to popular education (formal and informal) and to constructive popular movements rather than through providing services to managers and entrepreneurs in special-interest groups.[17]

This is not to take the impossible position that the highroad to social thought is a straight or narrow one. That road is apparently as varied and as persistent as the Ho Chi Minh Trail in Indo-China, the blocking or destruction of which the United States military so often announced. One complex problem is that, like all other terms in social thought, "humanist" and "existential" as well as "democratic" are subject to a wide variety of definitions. Some of the definitions are far from applicable, given the intent of the present discussion. "Existential humanism" is here taken to mean an intellectual focus on what exists and upon what is relevant to human welfare. Such doctrinaire existentialism as that of Jean-Paul Sartre and such doctrinaire humanism as that attributed to Karl Marx distort what we regard as a tenable—probably the most tenable—orientation for a person dedicated to the scientific study of human relations.[18]

To characterize this definition problem by a comparable example of delusory rhetoric, as plutocratic socialist policies and practices are introduced into the United States, their sponsors in Democratic and/or Republican "establishment" circles hail them as "traditionally democratic" or "soundly American." Thus imperialistic adventures on behalf of industrial interests, attacks upon democratic safeguards in the Federal Constitution, special privileges and subsidies for individual corporations and for whole industries, and repressive drives with so-called "law and order" methods against peaceful Black and other "disturbing" demonstrators are frequently wrapped in patriotic red-white-and-blue symbols. Similarly, publicists for managerial or "contented cow" social scientists often interpret their findings and recommendations as "humanist" or "humanitarian" and "scientific."[19] To label as "existential" the updated restatement of old supernatural social control dogma, as exemplified by Roman Catholic philosopher Jacques Maritain's effort,[20] is also assumed to make its mandates acceptable to those outside the bonds of that dogma's cult.

Both managerial-bureaucratic and problematic-technical social scientists have quick verbal escape hatches ready for themselves when evidence becomes recalcitrant or an evolving situation makes findings appear banal or absurd. They both can retreat into lofty and abstract systems theory. They both can conveniently refer to what they define as the limitations of "scientific" (actually many times scientistic) research methods and of a precisely preconceived "scientific" problem. For the research technician, any mischance due to a changed social situation or to shortcomings in research findings can provide a possible opening to obtain a new or broadened "research" grant or contract. Both bureaucrats and technicians give as little offense as possible to the current "establishment's" sense of propriety. In other words, they cooperate with operators in tune with the currently respectable "climate of opinion."

Spirits yearning to be free perforce get cast many times in managerial or technical roles in our highly commercialized society. Occasionally one of them is a social-science researcher like Daniel Ellsberg who shared in developing a comprehensive Pentagon study of the Indo-Chinese War. As writers for *Newsweek* report, quoting a friend of Ellsberg, he arrived in Saigon in 1965 "'as a roaring hawk and left two years later as a fighting dove.' . . . [He] became increasingly bitter with the official optimism that contradicted everything he saw himself on his many trips around the country."

Ellsberg contends that he "leaked" the 47-volume manuscript to the press in 1971 from his post at Massachusetts Institute of Technology's Center for International Studies only after he had failed to convince top Washington officials that they should read at least summaries of what he called "the U.S. equivalent of the Nuremberg war crimes documents."[21]

What society has gained and can still gain from social scientists yearning to be free can rarely be documented. Nor can we document adequately how much society loses from those in secure positions who do not use their freedom to tackle pressing human problems and thus perhaps to find answers (albeit tentative ones) we all so sorely need. Possibly for both the bureaucratic and the technical groups, understanding and emotional identification with the revolts of their children against restrictive or outworn policies help at times to stimulate parental regression to more idealistic and less defensive attitudes and thus to more creative efforts.

Here then are elements of the crisis in social science concomitant with the darkening environmental crisis facing mankind. Dedicated humanist-existential-democratic social scientists of the world, granted opportunities to work and to express themselves, would come up with a variety of analyses and prescriptions, with ways out of the environmental crisis so far as this crisis can be resolved through social reorganization. Even though they would be likely not to agree, their dependence on similar data and their relatively similar dedication to humanity would yield significant convergences. From them, in relatively free discussion, could emerge the guidance mankind requires in this period.

At the same time, the widespread infiltration of academia and of the "scientific" (now chiefly "professional" or even "trade") societies by persons managerially and manipulatively minded places humanist-existential-democratic social scientists at an overwhelming disadvantage—even within the citadels alleged to be those of learning.[22] Humanists in social science are the "naïve ones," the "organizationally irresponsible," the "impractical." This commercialization of social science is scarcely a new tendency in American and in world life, but it has become more inclusive and more pervasive during and since World War II.[23]

The previous chapter notes that many social scientists no longer concern themselves with propaganda analysis as an aid to citizens—with the service of popular concerns. They now develop and test manipulative procedures for those in power under such labels as "publicity," "mass communications," "public relations," and "survey research." In doing the biddings of organizational hierarchies or clients, these social scientists aid in the main those with the greatest stakes in plutocratic control-centralization, in polluting industrial operations, in resource consumption or destruction of a heedless sort, and in the perpetuation of a cheap labor market through the overproduction of human beings. In brief, many social scientists neglect propaganda analysis for consumers in order to devote themselves to mass communications and market research for manipulators. Others have found refuge from controversy or commerce in the more bland abstractions of something they call the "sociology of knowledge."[24]

All this is not to gainsay the fact that applied social scientists or "social engineers" are a significant medium through which social-scientific findings are often brought to bear upon specific social problems. But as engineering becomes the overwhelming preoccupation of social science discourse, more accurate, dispassionate, creative, and people-centered work is neglected.[25]

When social scientists remain in academic positions beyond graduate-school days, it is often to have a stable and prestigious base from which to sally forth to sell their wares—or because they can "only" teach. Fortunately for society, despite growing odds to the contrary, there continue to be free spirits in social science, as well as in other academic disciplines, who find stimulation in the company of students, who dedicate their spare time to fundamental investigations, reasonings, teachings, and writings, and who inspire their students to do likewise. An occasional wave of excitement and even of rebellion in our universities owes much to those fine and free spirits.

In view of the overemphasis on special interests, what can we anticipate learning from social scientists to guide us through what the sociologist Read Bain calls the "still crudely theological and mythic" fogs of "social thought" and of "mature social policies" in our society today[26]? Our public relations practitioners, many of whom acquired their trade during war years working for war agencies in and out of the Federal government, find it easy to trivialize the impact of popular impulses to "do something about the environmental crisis" through providing such devices as wastepaper collection campaigns. They had seen how such a procedure had harmlessly—and to little practical point—kept anxious spirits happily preoccupied and out from under the feet of those managing affairs during wartime.

The adequate recycling of paper, iron, tin, aluminum, and other useful resources is a pressing need, but it would require changes in government and industry that would stimulate both popular involvement and probably also popular radicalization. Little attention is given to the even more pressing need for the recycling of human body wastes rather than using them to pollute our rivers, lakes, and oceans. That would interfere with the sale of mineral and synthetic fertilizers of questionable value and of decreasing availability. Employers of public relations specialists would rather risk the consequences of resource waste than to risk deliberate promotion of unforeseeable social consequences.

To return to an earlier question: What changes are now taking place in culture and social organization that appear to be influencing man's chances of survival? In terms of that question, we can find clues to these possible changes through analyzing popular mythologies and through counteracting facile and antisocial manipulators thereof in the existing social smog.

If we were dealing with the environmental crisis within a biological frame of reference, we could delve into such matters as how chemicals used as growth stimulants for beef cattle and other food animals are helping to make the old people's disease, cancer, an increasing disaster for the young.[27] Or we might examine the shortening of man's tenure on earth in consequence of unwise diet, the increase in radioactive materials and of carbon dioxide in the atmosphere, uncontrolled pesticides, polluting fertilizers, food preservatives and other food additives, noise, and so on.[28] But cultural patterns and social organization join integrally with physical and biological measures to define our future. Taking a social-scientific approach, let us restrict ourselves to more specifically social—personal, group, societal—considerations.

Social-scientific literature and other possibly relevant data suggest negative as well as positive cultural and organizational developments that bear upon our ability to cope with the environmental crisis. We shall limit ourselves to six negative and six positive items:

First the negative developments: (1) the dehumanizing tendencies (already mentioned) in social science itself; (2) powerful pressures to reduce people to atomized worker-consumer-voter units, at times to be militarized and then demilitarized efficiently and harmlessly; (3) encouragement of divisive and destructive popular movements; (4) federative unification and "scientific sharpening" of mass-manipulative media; (5) continued growth of plutocratic imperialism in the hands of increasingly international or supranational corporations; and (6) warfare in a plutocratically imperialistic world.

The positive developments: (1) the potentialities (already mentioned) of humanist-existential-democratic social science; (2) the expansion of the power of the people and the vertical invasion of the seats of power by their representatives during the past five centuries; (3) the revolt of the young against exploitation, complacency, and irrelevant education; (4) increasing individual autonomy; (5) the inefficiencies and inconsistencies of huge organizations; and (6) pressures to achieve a more rational and tenable basis for a participatory community. If positive tendencies and resources—those named and others—can operate powerfully and rapidly enough, humanity may have a chance.

As for the negative developments, the dehumanizing tendencies in social science have already been discussed, and we will therefore begin with the second item. Thus:

2. Powerful social pressures toward the "one-dimensional man" of Herbert Marcuse[29] exist, but their success is scarcely as possible as that philosopher and some likeminded psychologists contend in their confused elitism.[30] One need not be a very acute observer or reader of social data to understand that most United States[31] and Soviet Russian[32] labor unions function to buy off workers in return for political ineffectuality. Except for the spectacular but limited efforts of such as Ralph Nader,[33] the number of consumer protection organizations and agencies lags far behind the need. On the other hand, advertising and other merchandising efforts directed at consumers achieve frightening effectiveness.[34] The much vaunted exposé in the purloined Pentagon papers having to do with Federal administrative duplicity in the Indo-Chinese War points to stygian corruption in both major political parties, corruption further underscored by the Watergate revelations and subsequent tidyings up. Few doubt that both parties will attempt to continue with only cosmetic changes. The revealed subservience of their present and past leaders to campaign contributors led to blunders and/or crimes of such enormity as to leave the relevant publics stunned and cynical—to the extent that they were at all informed.

Only those who were cheated out of years of life, who lost health, and who saw "buddies" mutilated and killed in Indo-China, and those others—black and white, male and female—who lived under the draft's influence at home, in the armed forces, or in exile, feel strongly about the callous manipulation of the military-industrial complex. Many of them are now trying to break out of what they see as a squeeze toward one-dimensionality.

But pressures toward one-dimensionality cannot really function to homogenize Americans or mankind. That is possible only in the tightly reasoned fantasies of a Herbert Marcuse or of a biologically-determinist psychologist or of a science-fiction writer. Even in such an allegedly efficient and perfect "machine" as the Nazi *Wehrmacht*, there were critical incidents of sabotage and revolt.[35] Whether as worker or consumer, voter or soldier, few human beings yield all their autonomy—even under coercion or enticement. In addition to the rare Henry David Thoreau or Aleksandr Isayevich Solzhenitzyn (controversial Soviet Russian Nobel prize-winner in literature) or César Chavez (the effective and nonviolent leader of American farm workers), uncounted others say "no" to power more unobtrusively in a multitude of ways.[36]

Think of the dignity and self-control of the rebel convicts in Attica (New York) Correctional Facility (prison) in September, 1971, as they held thirty-nine guards and civilians hostage in an extreme effort to have their lot humanized. Contrast their self-control with the indiscriminate bloodshed—including the slaughter of twelve of the hostages—by the state troopers and sheriff's deputies who carelessly supressed the insurrection. Even brutalized prisoners in a high-security prison can exhibit human qualities.[37]

This is not to belittle the powerful pressures throughout the world upon families and upon schools to provide uncomplicated bureaucrats and technicians with whom to staff the farflung networks of neo-feudal, suprastate corporate conglomerates. Entrepreneurs and groups of financiers coordinate and manipulate these networks of industries, distributors, mass-communications media, puppet governments, controlled governmental and voluntary agencies, politicians, and agents. They exert pressure to supplement their strategies through trying to specify how their future employees shall be trained, through obtaining the election or appointment of "cooperative" officials, and through developing "desirable" mass media policies and behavior. The company transfer of administrative and technical employees from corporate unit to corporate unit helps strip functionaries of all other binding "roots" except those put down within the corporation's "community." Little wonder that this and related "human engineering" problems of bureaucracies now attract massive research grants, and that managerial-bureaucratic and technical social scientists are so often preoccupied with ramifications of such internal organizational problems.[38]

3. Divisive and destructive popular organizations are rarely conceived and constructed—as was the American Legion[39]—by

manipulative social engineers. They do not need to be. They constantly come into existence. Those which have "news" qualities and do not appear threatening to basic advertiser interests receive the nurturing social fertilizer of effusive free publicity. Those which appear threatening also get publicity but of a negative sort. Organizations which trade upon popular frustrations and insecurities—especially if they appear useful in controlling or directing popular concerns in "stabilizing" directions—may achieve considerable size and prominence in a short period, sometimes much to the surprise of their leaders.[40] Organizations based on what appear to be religious, medical, health, or food fads illustrate this point especially well.

Some divisive organizations may be perversions of potentially useful social instruments. For example, ethnic differences help give a sense of identity and help bring to our country's life the enrichment of diverse backgrounds. Ethnic organizations—some of them religious or quasi-religious—may help us to remember and to benefit from the cultural heritage of one or both of our parents. But other ethnic organizations conspire to mobilize prejudice to protect special privileges in housing, employment, and education. They can be disastrous, and they have been. They include not only the Ku Klux Klan, the Black Panthers, and the Jewish Defense League, but also many "respectable" orgnizations whose conspiratorial services are more discreet but much more effective in their divisiveness.[41] Sunday morning, with its various religious services, has been called the most segregated part of the week.

Destructive efforts are often distortions of what might be useful social experimentation. For instance, while one-couple homes are still treasured by most parents and children, it may be that multi-family or communal-type homes can enrich the social experiences of their members. But publicity is typically given to such pathological examples as the California Manson "family" and other drug-ridden and promiscuous communes.[42] Instances of sane experimentation are becoming richly available, but they are in large measure ignored by the mass media.[43]

Similarly for more than fifty years, diligent students of courtship and marriage have been advocating an arrangement that has variously been called "the companionate," "companionate mar-

156   *Sociology for Whom?*

riage," "term" or "trial" marriage,[44] and more recently just "living together." It is put forward as a type of relationship that would permit a couple to experiment with living together, to have a relatively easy means of separation, but also to be obliged to act judiciously and with responsibility for the health and welfare of each other and of possible offspring. But such a sane pattern of experimentation is blocked many times not only by bigotry but also by overblown and misinformed publicity about casual and transient liaisons which are said to be similar but which represent greater hazards to the misinformed and unwary. Responsible experimentation is needed here as elsewhere in human relations in order to assure the continued viability and flexibility of our reproductive, socialization, and day to day routines.

Along with other divisive and destructive tendencies, public leaders and the mass-media are helping to create or at least to exacerbate conditions that destroy the moral integrity of public functionaries. Police officials do not modify situations in which rookie policemen often quickly have to learn to "make it" by getting themselves assimilated into a graft subculture.[45] Administrators often find that institutionalized corruption among teaching, health, legal, and engineering professionals makes such specialists more "flexible" and less expensive. Heads of institutions shrink from the complications associated with trying to bring professional mores into congruence with vaunted professional morals (a question probed at greater length in the next chapter). Professional self-policing and public licensing and control are supposed to maintain professed professional standards, but these precedures are notably ineffective.

4. Federative unification and scientific sharpening of mass-manipulative media are points touched on especially in the preceding chapter. The diversion of social-scientific efforts from consumer-protective propaganda analysis to producer-oriented mass communications as well as increasingly sophisticated experimentation are providing the scientific sharpening. As with each of the other negative and positive points listed, an adequate treatment of federative unification would require space far beyond that available here. In this case, perhaps a few more comments plus citations of more extensive discussions in references will suffice.

Throughout society in any given country East, West, or Third

World, mass-media of education and communication preen themselves on being moral, orthodox, legitimate, respectable, and thus—*in terms of local criteria*—in controversy only with the unorthodox and on purely negative terms. For example, despite conflicts between Federal administrations and the bulk of press-radio-television over the control of news and thus presumably over its credibility, the media present an overwhelmingly similar front on all significant social issues. The two major newsgathering agencies, the producer-cooperative Associated Press and the privately owned United Press International, join with a great web of other instruments to maintain such orthodoxy.

What freely dissenting media still exist in the "free world" consist chiefly of classroom lectures and discussions of certain autonomous teachers, of books for which certain relatively independent publishers can visualize profitable sales potentials, and of publications and classes of relatively independent voluntary organizations (religious, political, and other). Such efforts are constantly criticized and subjected to pressures or infiltration by the establishment media as "substandard," "irresponsible," and even "immoral," but in the United States at least such dissenters do not depend so much on an "underground" market as they do in the Soviet sphere and in many parts of the Third World.

5. Supranational corporate empires continue to grow as autonomous networks. Their development gives the impression that states may eventually continue to exist just to the extent that they serve as instruments useful to basically stateless corporation conglomerates. With international Communist (Soviet and Chinese) industrial and distributing entities operating more widely, the state may eventually take the same secondary role actually in the Soviet Union and in the People's Republic of China that it already has many times in the United States and in the rest of the world. At the same time, it is doubtful that controllers of great aggregates of world economic power will try to seize directly and openly the formalities of political power. They are likely to continue to play it safe and, except for occasional publicity by accident or by a parvenu, to enjoy the fruits of their exploits in private and thus to remain unavailable to serve as political scapegoats. A critic of the multinationals, R. J. Barnet, points out: "Because there are no effective world public authorities, no community-based planning

in the United States, the managers of the multinationals in their daily operations have by default become the principal planners for the U.S. economy."[46] Lee A. Iacocca, president of a multinational, the Ford Motor Company, takes a sharply contrasting view:

The myth says the multinational corporation, if not rigidly controlled, would take all and give nothing to host countries. And the myth too often finds expression in unrealistic government policies that prevent resident multinationals from doing the job they could be doing for these countries, or that drive off foreign investment altogether. . . .

No one benefits if multinationals are welcomed with one hand and cut to pieces by the other.[47]

Thus, as on the domestic scene, Iacocca and other business leaders see untrammeled plutocrats as the only dependable trustees of society's future; the modest concessions made by politicians and political bureaucrats to their constituencies are the dangers to be fought against. Labor unions also try to operate internationally in order to cope with shifts in industrial operation from country to country in search of cheaper labor markets, but they have as yet obtained only slight gains against the multinationals in this regard, even within the European Common Market.[48]

6. Warfare in a corporately imperialistic and neo-feudal world is not of a novel character. Business imperialism and its ramifications and machinations go far back in human history—probably even beyond Rome, Phoenicia, Greece, and Egypt. What appears to be developing as a novelty is the maintenance of selected markets for industrial war materiel through insurrections and other limited wars that do not disrupt seriously the multinational network interests in the great centers of neo-feudal power. Intrigue, bribery, the placing of agents and agencies in strategic decision-making positions, the agitation of reforms and rebellions or opposition to them, and all the other forms of business interpower-bloc competition and conflict are continuing. They are merely adapted to changed technological and social conditions. Even though in such a framework of endless struggle a major international war appears to be a declining possibility, irrational political entrepreneurs can still arise, beguile financiers and industrialists in a variety of countries (including the United States) as did Adolf Hitler, and precipitate chaos.[49]

With this brief and depressing view of selected negative tendencies and resources held in mind, let us turn to the five positive ones mentioned above that we have not yet discussed:

2. The expansion of the power of the people and the vertical invasion of the seats of power by their representatives during the past five hundred years appear to accelerate rather than to diminish. Educational and other mass-communications facilities continually expand to meet the challenges of that invasion. Even though power elites constantly scheme to convert such mass media into media of manipulation or at least of tranquilization, they do not succeed even with their increasingly sophisticated methods. Levels of popular aspiration rise, and they are implemented through the focusing of popular ferment, leadership, and organization upon all types of decision-making in society. One is reminded of a prescient statement by William Berkeley (1606-1676), who was governor of Virginia from 1642 to 1676 and whose policies led to Nathaniel Bacon's rebellion of planters against taxation in 1676. In response to inquiries from the Lords of the English Committee for the Colonies in 1671, he asserted, "I thank God we have not free schools nor printing, and I hope we shall not have these hundred years; for learning has brought disobedience and heresy into the world, and printing has divulged them and libels against the government. God keep us from both."[50]

Fortunately for humanity, Berkeley's type of regime passed. Many a subsequent elitist, viewing mass aggression, wrings his or her hands and moans in terms similar to those of José Ortega y Gasset:

European civilisation . . . has automatically brought about the rebellion of the masses. From one viewpoint this fact presents a most favourable aspect. . . : the rebellion of the masses is one and the same thing as the fabulous increase that human existence has experienced in our times. But the reverse side of the same phenomenon is fearsome; it is none other than the radical demoralisation of humanity.

He illustrates his latter point by saying that "America . . . is a primitive people camouflaged behind the latest inventions."[51] Ortega and others like him lament that the rising masses are not content to put their necks into pre-existing yokes—that they do not merely infiltrate the classes formerly above them. Such infiltration would mean that the vertically invading "barbarians" would willingly accept the formal and informal cultural controls to which others have accustomed themselves. Such social structures

160   *Sociology for Whom?*

and moral conceptions assure the continuance of the world views current among literate elites; in other words they assure the continuance of those elites' perquisites. Such structures and conceptions at the same time are obstacles, not aids, to aggressive leaders from among the invaders. Such leaders have internalized other values, other bases of social control.

The current upward invasion of the masses has been called "the blueing of America,"[52] but that expression is not accurate. It gives the impression that only now are the children of the blue-collared replacing the children of the white-collared in high-status positions. It also implies that the blue-collared are "ethnics" and that the white-collared are white Anglo-Saxon Protestants ("WASPs"). In our relatively open society, such class circulation has been continual and sometimes much more actual than apparent. People with "ethnic names" achieving high status now offer the healthy novelty chiefly that not so many of them "de-ethnicize" themselves and their names in the process of upward mobility. The actual practice of ethnic mobility, with *and without* name changes, dates in this country among "British" settlers back to the Jamestown colony of 1607[53] and in England itself much further.[54]

The rise in the scale and the standard of living of the mass of the people involves agitation and struggle against socially accepted, traditional "understandings" about special privilege based upon racial, ethnic, religious, class, educational, and sex ties and categories. To absorb this rising tide means that a lot of middle- and upper-class people have to move over, give ground, and even revise downward their ambitions and their way of living. Thus a great many people have to revise what modish social technicians like to call their "game plans" or their "social scenarios,"[55] in other words their *modi vivendi*.

This push upward is a broadly revolutionary movement to which the past century's migrations and technological changes gave great impetus. It contains within it the dynamic with which humanity may well be able to cope with the environmental and related crises of our period. This forceful striving toward upward social mobility is undermining the power of crystallized wealth derived from physical resources and from the control of labor and technology maintained through entrenched social structures. It is turning powerseekers more and more into political channels, towards the possibilities of controls apparently representative of people. People-centered power can scarcely make power-seekers happy if they are wedded to more derived forms of wealth; such power-seekers often cannot adopt a new "scenario" or "game-plan." Thus the struggles leave behind many broken and nostalgic individuals and groups, their bards and apologists.

The extent to which Americans have managed to defuse the racial, ethnic, religious, class, and sexist time-bombs of our society still leaves a great deal to be desired. The strides we have made to do so demonstrate, however, the virtues of such defusings to the enlightened here and elsewhere in the world. People are still often hired because of their racial, ethnic, religious, or sexual ties, but there is a growing body of law, wisdom, and sentiment in opposition to such practices. People are still treated prejudicially by misguided school officials, but pressures against such oppressive acts are perhaps more effective today than they are in employment and certainly in housing. Religious as well as racial and ethnic restrictions still keep tenants and customers from obtaining desirable homes, but the restrictive "understandings" among realtors, other business men, and pressure-group leaders are under attack from civil rights organizations—albeit not with enough force and consistency. In the society that is coming, dominated by the great body of the people, such restrictions cannot persist.[56]

What we have of general public education plus the beginnings of desegregation, of "open enrollments" in higher education, and of more general and informed use of the ballot all point to considerable changes in education and in politico-economic controls. Faced with absorption of masses of people, schools and colleges are ceasing to be chiefly instruments for the training and certification of technicians, specialists, and, peripherally, of aristocrats (American model). Types of intellectualism strange to middle-class teachers are being forced into the academies. These include attention to the social history of the diverse American ethnic groups, to Marxist and other radical ideologies, to practical career problems, and to alternative styles of living. Types of political entrepreneurism strange to a plutocratically controlled society are forcing a reorganization of society. These include rank-and-file revolts in trade union ranks and the development of political leaders who seek only the support of their constituencies and refuse subsidies from special interests. Surges of radicalization during the 1960s are followed by surges of repression and reaction during the 1970s, but the long-term trend is a promising one. Repression leads to "things getting out of control" in fresh aggressive actions.

Increasing people-power means that power values are shifting more and more, as noted, from control through domination of crystallizations of wealth (money or credit based chiefly upon entrenched structures that control physical resources, production, and markets) to leadership through control of living wealth, of well-motivated talent and labor. Tools and physical resources will remain socially useful to the extent to which they magnify and serve talent, labor, and the quality of life and living. It will become more of a sin against society to waste or to degrade talent and labor than to waste materials or money. From this will come a better quality of life for mothers, fathers, and their children.

Ability to maintain or to improve the quality of life in society and to raise the levels of aspiration of children to meet the challenges of a changing society and to modify society will become more and more the test of a leader's ability to stay in power as well as of society's viability. Leaders with such abilities are most likely to be products of the common people. Overwhelming evidence, variously stated, offers little hope for leadership for change to be provided by established elites.[57]

3. The revolt of the young against exploitation, complacency, and irrelevant education combines something quite old with something else that seems significantly new. In Homer's *Odyssey* a young man is portrayed as meekly recognizing the generation gap: He says that for him "to interrogate an old man seems disrespectful." Innumerable quotations over the three millenia since then illustrate that point. Even so it is not accurate to assume that parents have always been entirely out of sympathy with their rebelling children. That is something that appears to be significantly new in the situation, but it is not. Homer has the goddess Athena prod the young man, "Not the least shyness, now, Telémakhos. . . . Reason and heart will give you words" with which to question "old Nestor."[58]

What is giving impetus to our periodic youth revolts is that gradually and willy-nilly our middle-class groups are becoming politicized and in part radicalized. Resistant to change and wedded publicly to a compromising stance, middle-class elders hide behind the generation gap, but—like Athena—they are restive and prod youngsters to experiment, to express the elders' hidden reactions to frustration. Thus middle-class youth are finding it easier to accept analyses of society's problems that are more basic, incisive, and less traditional than those publicly held by their parents. They also actively accept responsibility to organize, agitate, and otherwise effectively to bring to bear upon policy-makers contentions for change.

Middle-class groups such as professionals and bureaucrats, technicians and salespeople, and small shopkeepers and farmers have long served to maintain society's stability through compromise and through compensating between upper-class and lower-class activists. Middle-class identification with society as a whole and with its stability has traditionally been such that from childhood its members learn to fit themselves for roles as intermediaries, to avoid unorthodox and disruptive controversy, to "make friends and influence people" in the manner recorded and advocated by the late Dale Carnegie.[59]

That was all very well when middle-class groups were relatively small and obviously recognizable. Then their dedication to stability and tradition posed no great threat to societal survival. On the contrary, they probably did much to make human survival possible as well as more attractive; they could not put it into a straightjacket—even though they tried. In addition, among middle-class professionals and shopkeepers and farmers in those days were a few eccentrics—such as atheists, religious fanatics, and "wild talkers" about politics and business—to provide some leaven within our communities.[60]

But the upward invasion of the masses has expanded the middle-class until old forms and controls are crumbling. The vast proselytizing media of the middle-class—the public schools and the other mass-communications agencies—are changing in the persisting drift toward egalitarianism. Upper-class renegades such as Thomas Jefferson and F. D. Roosevelt become less available for positions of leadership. Potentially aggressive lower-class agitators of change are likely to have accepted a middle-class brainwashing before they are old enough to decide what they want to accomplish and to learn how to do it. Meanwhile, middle-class disenchantment with their own "rat race" is appearing in parent-supported revolts by middle-class youth. Thus, instead of an expanded middle-class making for the kind of rigidification and complacency the older middle-class might have led one to anticipate, the far more numerous disenchanted members of the new middle-class are spawning children with new or renewed visions and leverages for change.

The expansion of and vertical invasion or upward social mobility of the United States people thus combines with the partial radicalization (or at least politicalization) of the middle-class through its youth to increase the drive toward the humanization of social controls and of social options. Thus hopefully will individuals come to attach less value to material wealth and nations come to be less distinct entities, changes that are necessary to lessen struggles for domination and to save humanity from extinction in those struggles.

4. Increasing individual autonomy, rather than the mindless "one-dimensional man,"[61] is emerging as part of the two preceding humanizing developments outlined. This autonomy is symptomized by successful struggles for the shortening of the on-the-job work week and the privatization of living, by turnings away from the conservative controls of institutionalized religion, by revolts of women against traditional belittlement through the aid of technological change, education, and organization, and by continuing egalitarian pressures and revolts by nonwhites and by a wide range of other underprivileged groups. The latter include the organization for self-determination of mental patients, other patients, prisoners, people receiving public assistance, the blind, the deaf, the homosexuals, and all other controlled and manipulated groups.

We may be vividly aware of the shortcomings we see in commercialized mass media, in the manipulative tricks and social irresponsibility of product and service advertising, and in the boring ritualism and traditional propagandizing of most education, but let us face it: Their consequences are mixed. The deprived see on television how "good Americans" should be able to live, and they have their sights raised. They demand a "piece of that action."

Advertising prods all groups to be dissatisfied with aspects of how they are currently living. Its fads and fancies waste untold human energies. Its models of "excellence" or "success" or "the good life" are made of tinsel. But it does combat dead-level habituation not only in the material but willy-nilly in associated non-material aspects of life. For instance, despite all the trashy music "consumed" in this country, Americans probably also listen to more hours of classical and of freshly innovative music than people ever have elsewhere. When human dissatisfactions are stimulated, no one can predict where they will lead. Even in unlikely schools and churches, with outworn curricular ideas, dedicated teachers do sometimes open vistas of personal expression and accomplishment of worth both to pupils and to society.

The periodic revolts of youth on behalf of themselves and against the situation in which their parents have placed them are parts of a broad social process of struggle that give us needed individual autonomy with which individually and collectively to meet the changed conditions of the environmental crisis and to find more durable and satisfying ways of life.

5. The inefficiencies and inconsistencies of huge corporations have been hidden to most employees and customers, voters and soldiers, even most investors and many administrators, but thoughtful people are beginning to be aware of them. They are learning that the dehumanization necessary to create and develop and maintain gigantic human collectives is not only not worth the price but is also self-defeating to the corporations in the not very long run. Effective efforts to cope with the environmental crisis and with other prime social problems must come from much more decentralized and humanized types of operation.

The inefficiencies of huge organizations worry our compulsive bureaucrats—administrators, engineers, and accountants—to the extent that they are aware of them. As operations become more vast, costs skyrocket from employee thefts, from anti-management understandings and conspiracies, and from blunders. Administrators' anxieties about how to assure the personal loyalty to them of their underlings lead them to overlook mere incompetence, waste, and dishonesty ("within reasonable limits"). A business person who believes press reports of "bureaucratic inefficiency" in government has a surprise in store if he or she comes "across the street" and takes a job in a government agency. After the "crossing," it becomes apparent that dedication, competence, honesty, and efficiency are about as common in government as in business, albeit not adequately encouraged or rewarded anywhere.

Costs of such inefficiencies are often described, but think of what the costs to society would be if huge organizations could be made as efficient as their technicians and apologists now contend they can and should become. In addition to the massive unemployment throughout our society that such "efficiency" would immediately create, think of the human costs of the necessary controls, of the extent to which creative, humanizing choices would be ruled out, of the lack of pleasure in working under "Big Brother's" constant surveillance, and of society's consequent loss of benefits from sometimes casual and intended or unintended experimentation. The proposal would thus project the dehumanizing processes of organizational gigantism to a point beyond human toleration.

The inherent inconsistencies of huge organizations fret the tidying bureaucrats who are administrators, lawyers, personnel specialists, computer programmers, and public relations analysts. For example, as *Business Week* points out, both government and business now utilize vast numbers of computers, but there is a "growing threat to computer security." Donn B. Parker, a senior management systems specialist at SRI International (formerly Stanford Research Institute) who has given especial attention to computer fraud, admits, "Fundamentally, we do not know how to protect large-scale, multi-access computer systems."[62] That inherent inconsistency of huge organizations is estimated to be costing American business and government more than one-half billion dollars a year. On the contrary, such inconsistencies are taken in stride by entrepreneurs in the same hierarchies. After all, such wheeler-dealers believe only in themselves. All else counts in their reckonings only as their own more or less useful instruments, those of other "players," or instruments not yet "in play." But the bureaucrats worry about inconsistencies in the organization they hope will remain the pillar of their life and of their way of living.

Inconsistencies are everywhere in huge organizations, and yet they are hopefully swept aside with one of a stock of well-worn rationalizations. Advertising inconsistencies are the easiest to demonstrate: Everything is the cheapest, the greatest, the best—but not really. Such inconsistencies are scarcely the most significant ones from the standpoint of organizational operation in spite of their great social costs. Think of all the interests, aspirations, and needs of personnel and publics a huge organization must somehow appear to satisfy in at least a minimal sense. In connection with our discussion of social scientists, we mentioned their division into those devoted to life-patterns somewhat arbitrarily characterized as entrepreneurial, bureaucratic, technical, and innovative—types found in many other occupations and on all class levels in our society. Any huge private or public organization must depend upon services from all four such types of careerists. In addition, the huge organization must somehow handle the conflicting visions of it and of its services and other functions that are held by various class, regional, ethnic, and even national publics outside of it and relevant to its operations.[63]

Whether an organization is involved in manufacturing and distributing or in a nation's foreign service, and even though its ambiguities may be veiled by secrecy and by social distance, its inconsistencies constantly threaten its stability and force critical readaptations if it is to persist. Only rarely, when a corporation is at or near bankruptcy or a power-bloc take-over or when a political party stands as naked as it usually does at its convention, are the range of inconsistencies and manipulations adequately revealed.

Among other possibilities, the inconsistencies of huge organizations are forcing them to undertake steps to absorb or blunt the most pressing demands for wider democratic participation of relevant human interests in their policy-making. The dynamics of large organizations being what they are, it is a hopeful eventuality that such bodies may be democratized and, in the process, decentralized and humanized.

The personalization of organizations also involves the humanization of their goals. As the sociologist William R. Burch, Jr., puts it,

If we must be concerned with population explosions of human beings, let us be even more concerned with the population explosions of automobiles, missiles, and other bedrock junk of our industrial growth. To point at the automobile and war industries is to consider the two most significant providers of jobs, living standards, mobility, and adman eroticism in industrial societies; it is also to point at two of the least important and least significant activities yet invented by man. There is no crucial need to make sure Americans, Russians, Chinese, or whomever, are killed ten times over, nor is there any survival need to speed through ten national parks in five days.[64]

Only as organizations for production, distribution, financing, and government become more democratic, human, and decentralized in their operations and their goals can they meet the challenges of the environmental and related social crises of our time.

6. Pressures to achieve a more rational and tenable basis for participatory community, as they work themselves out, suggest strongly that function is more significant than form in achieving such a tendency. The social wisdom of leadership and the insistence of members upon sharing constructively in decision-making can do much more to encourage participatory democracy than mere constitutional structure.

Here are some old but sound axioms of participatory democracy:

a. The views of each individual are to be sought and to be treated with respect.

b. Communication within an easily recognizable unit of organization should be full and free.

c. That unit should not be too large for face-to-face consultation or so small as to appear to its members to be comparatively trivial.

d. Each individual in such a unit should have a realistic sense of counting in decision-making.

e. Intercommunication between each local unit and those with greater and with less power should be convincingly a two-way matter, with expressed views given the weight due them for their cogency rather than for the apparent power vested in the unit or its spokesperson.

f. No major policy change should be undertaken prior to a thorough process of fact-finding and consultation during which the policy is recognizably shaped and then modified.

g. On all levels, tricks manipulative of personnel need to be recognized as being delusory—now more and more transparently so—and thus not used.

h. In an informed and participatory community, decisions concerning such basic issues as population limitation, pollution, resource conservation, and a better quality of living should be reached on the basis primarily of a consensus as to human values rather than primarily on the basis of class or property values as is now so often the case.

Participatory democracy can permeate all levels and functions of society. It is a spirit facilitated but not assured by structural changes. It would be predicated upon providing adequate attention to such human problems and goals as those associated with the environmental crisis at all levels. It would do much to offset the inefficiencies and inconsistencies now apparent in huge organizations by substituting democratic socialism for plutocratic "democracy."

Admittedly, participatory democracy would not furnish the melodramatic shifts in policy and the colorful social manipulations that characterize so much of human history and thus of human misery. But participatory democracy would crystallize popular support and morale to achieve goals as does no other procedure.

Hopefully cocktail parties and women's and men's luncheons will one day hum happily with the good news that mass manipulation is not only not necessary but that it is also too costly to human beings and thus inexpedient. Hopefully, soon enough to help us cope with our environmental and related crises, we will learn the arts of democratic leadership, of facilitating social discussions and decision-making—even along the most unanticipated lines. These are arts that resemble in consequence far more those of a midwife than those of a ruthless entrepreneur or field marshall.[65]

notes

[1]This is one of many formulas that have "failed" business men. The enthusiasm with which business leaders sometimes seize oversimplified and misunderstood scientific findings and then their subsequent "disillusionment" with them were both given classical illustration by their reactions to Herbert Spencer, William Graham Sumner, and Friedrich A. Hayek. All three delighted business people by talking about the evils of excessive governmental controls over business. Then Spencer also pointed to the disastrous nature of "commercial cannibalism." Sumner analyzed the social destructiveness of plutocracy and especially of plutocratic imperialism. Hayek's talk about the "totalitarians in our midst" included both Left and Right in his condemnation. See J.D.Y. Peel, *Herbert Spencer* (London: Heinemann, 1971), M. R. Davie, *William Graham Sumner* (New York: Thomas Y. Crowell Co., 1963), and F. A. Hayek, *The Road to Serfdom* (Chicago: University of Chicago Press, 1944).

[2]Earth Day originated with Wisconsin's U.S. Senator Gaylord Nelson and other Congressional conservationists. *New York Times*, April 20, 22, 23, and May 4, 5, 1970.

[3]W. A. Williams, *The Roots of the Modern American Empire* (New York: Random House, 1969).

170 Sociology for Whom?

[4]Paul and Anne Ehrlich, *Population, Resources, Environment* (San Francisco: W. H. Freeman & Co., 1970), p. 129. Cf. W. R. Burch, Jr., *Daydreams and Nightmares: A Sociological Essay on the American Environment* (New York: Harper & Row, 1971), chap. 1.

[5]See "A Message to Our 3.5 Billion Neighbors on Planet Earth From 2100 Environmental Scientists," *Society for Social Responsibility in Science Newsletter*, 1971, no. 3 (Bala Cynwyd, Pa.), pp. 1-2. See also *Fellowship*, vol. 31, no. 5 (May 1971), pp. 16-19.

[6]Fellowship of Reconciliation, "Petition for Disarmament," leaflet, 1976.

[7]M. Q. Sibley, contributor to "Eighteen Leading Social Critics Comment," K. A. Kirkpatrick and L. K. Northwood, eds., *Journal of Sociology and Social Welfare*, vol. 4 (1976-1977), pp. 323-38; p. 335 quoted.

[8]Burch, op. cit., pp. 22-29; Ehrlich, op. cit., pp. 321-22.

[9]Fellowship of Reconciliation, op. cit.

[10]B. Bruce-Briggs, Hudson Institute, "The Energy Crisis," *Worldview*, vol. 19, no. 4 (April 1976), pp. 52-53; p. 53 quoted.

[11]Brendan Jones, "Antipollution Overseas Stirs Fears in Business," *New York Times*, June 7, 1971, pp. 1, 48; p. 1 quoted.

[12]K. E. Boulding, *Beyond Economics* (Ann Arbor: University of Michigan Press, 1968), p. 281.

[13]T. S. Kuhn, *The Structure of Scientific Revolutions* (Chicago: University of Chicago Press, 1962), pp. 15, 24.

[14]A. McC. Lee, "Institutional Structures and Individual Autonomy," *Human Organization*, vol. 26 (1967), pp. 1-5; *Multivalent Man*, new ed. (New York: Braziller, 1970), esp. chaps. 14-17; *Toward Humanist Sociology* (Englewood Cliffs, N.J.: Prentice-Hall, 1973), esp. chap. 5.

[15]S. E. Deutsch and John Howard, eds., *Where It's at: Radical Perspectives in Sociology* (New York: Harper & Row, 1970); A. W. Gouldner, *The Coming Crisis in Western Sociology* (New York: Basic Books, 1970).

[16]For an attempted glorification of technicianism, see special number on "Sociological Research and Public Policy," *American Sociologist*, vol. 6 (1971), June.

[17]The lives of Georg Simmel and Willard Waller illustrate problems of innovators in social science. Both paid in lack of professional preferment for their innovativeness. Only in death have their great contributions started to receive more adequate recognition. K. H. Wolff, "Fragments of Simmel's Life and Mind," in *The Sociology of Georg Simmel*, trans. and ed. by Wolff (New York: Free Press, 1950), pp. xviii-xiv, and W. J. Goode, F. F. Furstenberg, Jr., and L. R. Mitchell, "Willard W. Waller: A Portrait," in their edition of Waller, *On the Family, Education, and War* (Chicago: University of Chicago Press, 1970), pp. 1-110.

[18]Jean-Paul Sartre, *Existentialism*, trans. by Philip Mairet (London: Methuen, 1947); Nicola Abbagnano, *Critical Existentialism*, trans. and ed. by Nino Langiulli (Garden City, N.Y.: Anchor Books, 1969); Karl Marx, *Early Writings*, trans. and ed. by T. B. Bottomore (London: C. A. Watts, 1963); Marx, *The German Ideology*, R. Pascal, ed. (London: Lawrence & Wishart, 1938); F. W. Matson, *The Broken Image* (New York: George Braziller, 1964).

[19]Daniel Bell, "Adjusting Men to Machines," *Commentary*, vol. 3 (1947), pp. 79-88.

[20]As, e.g., by Jacques Maritain, *Existence and the Existent*, trans. by Louis Galantière and G. B. Phelan (1948; New York: Greenwood, 1975).

[21]Mel Elfin, H. L. Trewhitt, Lloyd Norman, and others, "The Secret History of Vietnam," *Newsweek*, June 28, 1971, pp. 12-22, 25-27, 30-31; p. 16 quoted. See Neil Sheehan and others, eds., *The Pentagon Papers* (New York: Bantam Books, 1971), a book digest from New York *Times*; for a longer version, see *The Pentagon Papers:*

The Senator Gravel Edition, 4 vols., and vol. 5, *Critical Essays,* Noam Chomsky and Howard Zinn, eds. (Boston: Beacon Press, 1971). Vol. 5 contains index to 4 vols.

22See A. McC. Lee's reports as president of the American Sociological Association in *Footnotes,* vol. 3, no. 9 (December 1975), p. 8; vol. 4, no. 1 (January 1976), pp. 1, 3; no. 3 (March 1976), p. 6; no. 5 (May 1976), p. 8; no. 9 (December 1976), p. 4; E. B. and A. McC. Lee, "The Society for the Study of Social Problems: Parental Recollections and Hopes," *Social Problems,* vol. 24 (1976–1977), pp. 4–14.

23See A. McC. Lee's reports on the American Sociological Association in *Social Problems,* vol. 9 (1961–1962), pp. 289–92, 386–89, 400–401; vol. 10 (1962–1963), pp. 97–100, 293–97, 409–11; vol. 11 (1963–1964), pp. 319–21; vol. 12 (1964–1965), pp. 356–60; and his reports on the International Sociological Association in *American Sociologist,* vol. 2 (1967), pp. 248–50; vol. 3 (1968), pp. 349–50; vol. 4 (1969), pp. 362–63; and vol. 6 (1971), pp. 361–63. See also his "Ph.D.s for Whom at 42nd Street?" *Action* (United Federation of College Teachers), vol. 7, nos. 4–5 (January–February, 1970), p. 4.

24The sociology of knowledge as a conception (not so labeled) is often traced to Karl Marx's preface to his *Contribution to the Critique of Political Economy,* trans. by N. I. Stone from 2nd German ed. (1859; New York: International Publ. Co., 1904), esp. pp. 11–12. Marx's conception is in line with "propaganda analysis" as the term is used here.

25See *Sociological Practice,* vol. 1 (1976) et seq.; I. L. Horowitz, *Professing Sociology* (Chicago: Aldine Publ. Co., 1968), chaps. 9–11, 14–15; Duncan MacRae, Jr., "A Dilemma of Sociology: Science Versus Policy," *American Sociologist,* vol. 6, suppl. no. 1 (1971), pp. 2–7; R. W. Friedrichs, *A Sociology of Sociology* (New York: Free Press, 1970), chap. 12.

26Read Bain, "Natural Science and Value Policy," *Philosophy of Science,* vol. 16 (1949), pp. 182–92; p. 184 quoted. See also Bain, "Man, the Myth Maker," *Scientific Monthly,* July 1947, pp. 61–69.

27B. T. Hunter, *Consumer Beware* (New York: Simon & Schuster, 1971); see also *New England Journal of Medicine,* April 22, 1971.

28Ehrlich, op. cit., esp. chaps. 6 and 7; B. T. Hunter, *Gardening Without Poisons* (Boston: Houghton Mifflin Co., 1964); Robert and L. T. Rienow, *Moment in the Sun* (New York: Dial Press, 1967), esp. chaps. 15–16; Burch, op. cit., esp. chap. 1.

29Herbert Marcuse, *One-Dimensional Man* (Boston: Beacon Press, 1964), chaps. 1–4.

30B. F. Skinner, *Beyond Freedom and Dignity* (New York: Alfred A. Knopf, 1971); Richard Sennett's cogent review of the Skinner volume, *New York Times Book Review,* October 24, 1971, pp. 1, 12, 14, 16, 18; E. O. Wilson, *Sociobiology: The New Synthesis* (Cambridge, Mass.: Belknap Press of Harvard University Press, 1975); Skinner, *About Behaviorism* (New York: Random House, 1976); M. D. Rosenthal, "Sociobiology: Laying the Foundation for a Racist Synthesis," *Harvard Crimson,* February 8, 1977, p. 3.

31H. R. Cayton, *Black Workers and the New Unions* (College Park, Md.: McGrath Publ. Co., 1969); J. D. Greenstone, *Labor in American Politics* (New York: Alfred A. Knopf, 1969); Daniel Bell, *The End of Ideology* (New York: Collier Books, 1961), esp. chaps. 10–12.

32Arvid Brodersen, *Soviet Worker* (New York: Random House, 1966); Robert Conquest, *Industrial Workers of the Soviet Union* (New York: Frederick A. Praeger, 1967); G. V. Osipov, ed., *Industry and Labour in the U.S.S.R.* (New York: Barnes & Noble, 1966).

33C. O. Jones, *Clean Air: The Policies and Politics of Pollution Control* (Pittsburgh: University of Pittsburgh Press, 1975); Ralph Nader *et al., What to Do With Your Bad Car* (New York: Grossman, 1971).

[34]A. R. Andreasen, *The Disadvantaged Consumer* (New York: Free Press, 1975); Ralph Nader *et al.*, *The Consumer and Corporate Accountability* (New York: Harcourt, Brace & Jovanovich, 1973).

[35]Annedore Leber *et al.*, *Conscience in Revolt: Sixty-Four Stories of Resistance in Germany 1935–45* (London: Valentine, Mitchell, 1957); Hannah Vogt, *The Burden of Guilt* (New York: Oxford University Press, 1964), esp. chap. 11; J. W. Wheeler-Bennett, *The Nemesis of Power: The German Army in Politics 1918–1945* (London: Methuen & Co., 1964), esp. part 3, chap. 7; Roger Manvell and Heinrich Fraekel, *The Canarsis Conspiracy: The Secret Resistance to Hitler in the German Army* (New York: David McKay Co., 1969).

[36]Gene Sharp, *The Politics of Nonviolent Action*, ed. by Marina Finkelstein (Boston: Sargent, 1973); Robert Cooney and Helen Michalowski, eds., *Active Nonviolence in the United States: The Power of the People* (Culver City, Calif.: Peace Press, 1977); Anders Boserup and Andrew Mack, *War Without Weapons* (New York: Schocken, 1975); L. H. Pelton, *The Psychology of Nonviolence* (New York: British Book Center, 1976).

[37]J. C. Jones *et al.*, "The Attica Tragedy," *Newsweek*, September 27, 1971, pp. 22 ff.; Derrick Morrison and Mary-Alice Waters, *Attica: Why Prisoners Are Rebelling* (New York: Pathfinder Press, 1972).

[38]P. M. Blau, *The Dynamics of Bureaucracy*, 2nd ed. rev. (Chicago: University of Chicago Press, 1973); Richard Cornelle, *De-Managing America: The Final Revolution* (New York: Random House, 1976).

[39]William Gellerman, *The American Legion as Educator* (New York: Teachers College, Columbia University, 1938); Raymond Moley, *The American Legion Story* (1966; New York: Greenwood, 1975).

[40]J. R. Howard, *The Cutting Edge: Social Movements and Social Change in America* (Philadelphia: J. B. Lippincott Co., 1974).

[41]J. A. Ladner, ed., *The Death of White Sociology* (New York: Vintage Books, 1973).

[42]Vincent Bugliosi and Curt Gentry, *Helter Skelter: The True Story of the Manson Murders* (New York: W. W. Norton Co., 1974); G. D. Bartell, *Group Sex* (New York: New American Library, 1974).

[43]P. Abrams and A. McCulloch, *Communes, Sociology and Society* (New York: Cambridge University Press, 1976); Patricia Baum, *Another Way of Life: The Story of Communal Living* (New York: Putnam, 1973); Michael Gordon, ed., *Nuclear Family in Crisis: The Search for an Alternative* (New York: Harper & Row, 1972); Keith Melville, *Communes in the Counter Culture* (New York: William Morrow & Co., 1972).

[44]E. C. Parsons, *The Family* (New York: Putnam, 1906), pp. 348–49; M. M. Knight, "The Companionate and the Family," *Journal of Social Hygiene*, vol. 10 (1924), pp. 257–67; B. B. Lindsey and Wainright Evans, *Companionate Marriage* (New York: Boni & Liveright, 1927), chaps. 7–9.

[45]The New York City Commission to Investigate Alleged Police Corruption, chaired by William Knapp, after an 11-month study aided by a staff of thirty, reported July 1, 1971: "The commission is persuaded that the underlying problem is that the climate of the department is inhospitable to attempts to uncover corruption and protective of those who are corrupt. The consequence is that the rookie who comes into the department is faced with a situation where it is easier for him to become corrupt than to remain honest." (Quoted July 2 by David Burnham, *New York Times*) The present author's unpublished observations on police behavior in Pittsburgh, New Haven, Cleveland, Detroit, Chicago, and other cities over the past half-century indicate to him that the Knapp committee findings are typical of much of the American police "climate" of the period.

[46]R. J. Barnet, "Multinationals: A Dissenting View," *Saturday Review*, February 7, 1976, pp. 11, 58; p. 58 quoted.

[47]L. A. Iacocca, "Myth of the Big, Bad Multinational," *Newsweek*, September 12, 1977, p. 21.

[48]Joseph Schumpeter, *Social Classes/Imperialism*, trans. by Heinz Norden (New York: Meridian Books, 1955), esp. pp. 64–98; William Hoffman, *David: Report on a Rockefeller* (New York: Lyle Stuart, 1971); R. M. MacIver, *Power Transformed* (New York: Macmillan Co., 1964), esp. chap. 13; V. I. Lenin, *Imperialism, the Highest Stage of Capitalism*, 1917 (Moscow: Progress Publishers, 1970).

[49]R. S. Lynd, "Foreword" to R. A. Brady, *Business as a System of Power* (New York: Columbia University Press, 1943); Dennis Eisenberg, *The Re-Emergence of Fascism* (London: MacGibbon & Kee, 1967); Danilo Dolci, *Non Sentite l'Odore del Fumo?* (Bari, Italia: Laterza, 1971).

[50]William Berkeley quoted in S.N.D. North, *History and Present Condition of the Newspaper and Periodical Press of the United States* (Washington: Government Printing Office, 1884), p. 4.

[51]José Ortega y Gasset, *The Revolt of the Masses*, authorized trans. (1930; New York: W. W. Norton & Co., 1957), pp. 125, 139.

[52]P. L. and Brigitte Berger, "The Blueing of America," *New Republic*, vol. 164 (1971), pp. 20–23.

[53]Louis Adamic, *A Nation of Nations* (New York: Harper & Bros., 1945), pp. 288–90, 294, 315; C. E. Hatch, Jr., *The First Seventeen Years: Virginia, 1607-1624* (Charlottesville: University Press of Virginia, 1957).

[54]S. L. Thrupp, *The Merchant Class of Medieval London* [1300-1500] (Ann Arbor: University of Michigan Press, 1948), esp. chaps. 5-7.

[55]Melvin Dresher, *Games of Strategy* (Englewood Cliffs, N.J.: Prentice-Hall, 1961); F. B. May, *Introduction to Games of Strategy* (Rockleigh, N.J.: Allyn & Bacon, 1970); Anatol Rapoport, *Strategy and Conscience* (New York: Schocken Books, 1969); Douglas Basil and C. W. Cook, *The Management of Change* (New York: McGraw-Hill Book Co., 1974); Karl Marx, *On Society and Social Change*, N. J. Smelser, ed., (Chicago: University of Chicago Press, 1975).

[56]Pamela Roby, ed., *The Poverty Establishment* (Englewood Cliffs, N.J.: Prentice-Hall, 1974); J. B. Williamson, ed., *Strategies Against Poverty in America* (New York: Halsted Press, 1974); F. F. Piven and R. A. Cloward, *Regulating the Poor* (New York: Pantheon, 1971).

[57]Barrington Moore, Jr., *Social Origins of Dictatorship and Democracy* (Boston: Beacon Press, 1967), esp. chap. 9; Gaetano Mosca, *The Ruling Class*, trans. by H. D. Kahn, Arthur Livingston, ed. (New York: McGraw-Hill Book Co., 1939), esp. pp. 63–64, chaps. 4, 12, 15-16; Vilfredo Pareto, *The Mind and Society*, trans. by A. Bongiorno and Livingston, Livingston, ed. (New York: Harcourt, Brace and Co., 1935), 4 vols., esp. vol. 4.

[58]Homer, *Odyssey*, trans. by Robert Fitzgerald (Garden City, N.Y.: Doubleday & Co., 1961), p. 48 (lines from book 3).

[59]Dale Carnegie, *How to Win Friends and Influence People* (New York: Simon & Schuster, 1936).

[60]The early lives of Mark Twain and Clarence Darrow give the flavor of that Midwestern American world to which reference is made. See *The Autobiography of Mark Twain*, Charles Neider, ed. (New York: Harper & Row, 1959); Maxwell Geismar, *Mark Twain* (Boston: Houghton Mifflin Co., 1970), esp. chaps. 2-5, 11; Irving Stone, *Clarence Darrow for the Defense, a Biography* (Garden City, N.Y.: Doubleday & Co., 1941).

[61]Herbert Marcuse, op. cit., chaps. 1-4.

[62]"The Growing Threat to Computer Security," *Business Week*, August 1, 1977, pp. 44-45; p. 44 quoted.

[63]A. McC. Lee, *Multivalent Man*, op. cit., chaps. 14-17.

[64]W. R. Burch, Jr., op. cit., pp. 168-69.

[65]This chapter is in part adapted from the author's "Modern Civilization and Human Survival: A Social-Scientific View," *Philosophy Forum*, vol. 12 (1972), pp. 29-66, by permission of Gordon and Breach Publishers Ltd., London, England.

eight

---

*Responsibility
and Accountability
in Sociology*

Morality and its systematization as ethics make great social promises and raise difficult problems for all human beings. Those who try to be both sociological scientists and social engineers are far from being exceptions to this general circumstance.

The moral patterns of our societal culture are crystallized in such documents as the Ten Commandments, the Federal Bill of Rights, the United Nations Universal Declaration of Human Rights, and a variety of other ethical codes. The principles these and other legal and voluntary documents set forth appear to hold our society together, to undergird our institutions, and thus to make our "civilization" possible.

Typically, moral precepts are vaguely stated in summary formulas: "Thou shalt not steal." "Congress shall make no law respecting an establishment of religion, or prohibiting the free exercise thereof; or abridging the freedom of speech, or of the press; or the right of the people peaceably to assemble, and to petition the Government for a redress of grievances."

The Eighth Commandment and the First Amendment to the Federal Constitution place a tremendous burden upon four and forty-five words. Such terms as "steal," "religion," "freedom," and "grievances" have definitions that readily become points of controversy in struggles for social control. Like other expressions of moral principles, those few words require interpretation and indications of their applicability in specific cases for them to be practically meaningful. For guidance in their application we can turn to traditional social usage, to laws and judicial precedents, to exemplifications by esteemed individuals, and to ethical theories dealing with what the philosopher T. V. Smith characterizes as "the organization or criticism of conduct in terms of notions like good, right or welfare."[1] As the sociologist Emile Durkheim points out, a systematic consideration of "morals and rights should be based on the study of moral and juridical facts. These facts consist of rules of conduct that have received sanction."[2] Thus an ethic is not a product of special revelation once and for all. As cross-cultural data richly indicate, an ethic does not consist of precisely definable universals. It is a social conception in a specific time, place, and culture of what conduct is broadly acceptable and useful.

In addition to rhetorical formulas, we can also turn for guidance to specialists in applying, in adjusting to, and in avoiding the implications of current moral principles. These include the clergy, lawyers, psychiatrists, social workers, personnel counselors, social engineers, and social scientists. Their aid might be idealistic, compromising, casuistic, or machiavellian. It depends upon the conception of their social roles held by individual specialists, by informal groups of them, and by their formal organizations. Especially it depends upon their notions as to whom they owe responsibility and accountability.

One typical definition of a social practitioner's professional ethics highlights the contrast between such ethics and those of scientists: According to the philosopher, C. F. Taeusch, "The immediate objective of [a practitioner's] professional service is the welfare of the client or patient, and any realistic as well as justifiable system of professional ethics [for practitioners] should be similarly oriented." Taeusch adds that major problems in this area "arise when this objective fails of attainment or when it is incompatible with the public interest, as in keeping inviolate confidential communications, or with the interests of the practitioner, as in subordinating fees to the proper performance of services."[3] In contrast, a scientist's loyalty is owed ideally only to her or his conception of truth and of social welfare. She/he may participate in social action through providing guidance as an independent consultant or an independent researcher, but the relationship for a scientist is one aligned with her/his conception of social welfare. It cannot be a controlled or a dependent, mercenary one. No client influences her/his research or advice. In the social sciences, orientation toward the needs or desires of a client or patient often takes the form of grant or contract research. This creates responsibilities far more in conflict with those to which scientists ideally commit themselves than are those of a teacher to student needs.

Professionals—whether in applied or contract work or independent scientists—typically claim that they adhere to high traditions of private and public service and that there is no conflict between the private and the public.[4] A broad range of professionals and especially of those who are in applied or contract work now possess impressive codes of ethics replete with rules of procedure and with personnel designated to implement those rules. Their professional associations allege that fidelity to their codes is best assured by the individual scientist's or practitioner's personal dedication and by the association's collective self-governance. Although professionals typically benefit from some form of governmental certification, their leaders jealously maintain their right to autonomy. They assert that their codes do not result from or require implementation by outside social pressures, by litigation, or by governmental action. These contentions underscore the likelihood that ethics codes will be developed and used primarily as public relations instruments for practitioners rather than as guides for conduct. Scientists as such have shown little need for such codes. Their disciplines themselves provide methods for exposing charlatanism or poor work.

The words "responsibility" and "accountability" in relation to professionals as practitioners remind many of the scene at university graduation exercises when new M.D.s promise to uphold the ancient Hippocratic oath. Thus, through public affirmation of an idealistic ethical code do new physicians signalize their taking on of a priestly societal role, their donning of their ideological robe of office. Other professionals in one way or another earn similar certification by their peers and by the state and then are clothed in a moral cloak of societal respectability and authority.

This all sounds quite proper and rather noble, but many incidents in the professions during this century suggest that twisted values and corruption are commonplaces in the many aspects of our lives in which professionals are involved. Watergate was just one such incident that happened to penetrate the mass-communications media. It became visible through an accidental tear in the curtain of legitimacy that usually screens such incidents from our public inspection. Before World War I, Lincoln Steffens stirred public concern with his accounts of corruption that he called "the shame of the cities."[5] A Steffens today would have at least as much material and perhaps stir even greater concern if he were to write on the shame of the professions. In doing so, the new Steffens would assess the changes in the roles of professionals wrought by our integrating monopolistic capitalism and particularly by our multinational conglomerates. These changes have glorified more and more the so-called "higher morality" of the "bottom-line ethic," the ethic oriented toward the accountant's line that totals up an enterprise's profit or loss. Ignoring as it does what happens to people, this ethic is more accurately called the "higher immorality." To the extent that it prevails, professionals shrink in significance and in the sense of social worth and thus of self-worth.

Evidences of fraud, corruption, neglect of duty, and unfair appropriation and exploitation of the work of others may not be as spectacular in social scientific circles as in political, industrial, legal, military, or medical, but may have far-reaching significance. Some sociologists have recognized this, and they have thus interested themselves and their professional organizations in such problems of their discipline. Let us look at how the principal professional sociological society has tried to engage in discussions of ethics and in efforts at self-governance in this respect since the 1950s.

In 1951, a Committee on Standards and Ethics in Research Practice of the American Sociological Society grew out of a committee established the previous year on problems of the individual researcher.[6] In its first sentence, a report of that Committee suggests the motivation for much of the subsequent activity of sociological leaders in considering ethical problems: "Sociology finds itself in a position of increasing importance and also, as a part of this, of greater and greater exposure to criticism and even attack."[7] Renamed the Committee on Ethical Principles in Research, that Committee continued until 1955.[8]

In terms of the increasing emphasis among sociological association leaders upon subsidized or contract team research, upon social engineering and consulting, these committees were somewhat anachronistic or—as some then said—professionally naïve. In terms of the interests of teachers and students in unfettered scientific investigation, the concerns of those committees were timeless. The first committee urged "especial attention to (a) the rights and needs of graduate students and [to] (b) competition between academic and commercial research agencies."[9] The chairperson of the second committee, Jessie Bernard, was especially concerned about the difficulties of graduate students. For example, she stated that they should have "considerable freedom in choice of dissertation problems" and that they "should be kept on as assistants not longer than two or three years."[10]

The next move toward providing the American Sociological Association (as it was by then called) with an ethics document arose in 1959 in the ASA's Committee on the Profession chaired by Talcott Parsons. Parsons had read a paper at the 1958 convention in which he observed that "the creation of codes for the professionally proper ways of organizing . . . the applied role . . . will . . . constitute one major task of our profession."[11] To further this idea, his committee appointed a Subcommittee on Ethics of the Profession to study "critical incidents which either directly or indirectly raise ethical questions involving the behavior of sociologists." This study, it was hoped, would result eventually in "a code of ethics with a solid empirical basis in case experience."[12]

Robert Cooley Angell chaired that subcommittee and from 1961, the subsequent Committee on Professional Ethics. Angell and his associates labored in this vineyard until 1964. Then the ASA Council formally received and filed "the revised version of the Draft Code of Ethics with thanks for the effort of the Committee." The Council minutes noted that the Committee's "report has made all Association members more sensitive to their ethical responsibilities as professional sociologists."[13] The Angell committee had not dealt with "problems that concerned university teachers in general since the American Association of University Professors had already formulated ethical standards in this field."[14] Thus it did not appear to share with preceding committees an active concern for the exploitation and neglect of sociology students and particularly of sociology graduate students.

The Angell Committee document did not remain very long on the so-called "back burner" of the ASA Council. Project Camelot made the question of an ethics code again a hot issue right in the sociological field.

In the early 1960s, members of the Army Research Office of the U.S. Department of Defense developed an idea eventually to be called Project Camelot. In consultation with chosen social scientists, those "operators" devised a plan for a three- to four-year contract with the Special Operations Research Organization (SORO) at a cost of some $4-6,000,000. The plan was to collect intelligence on insurgency and revolution in a range of underdeveloped countries around the world beginning with Chile. SORO existed under the academic cover of American University in Washington, D.C.; it had been carrying on other research projects under contract for the Department of Defense.

A SORO document distributed December 4, 1964, to recruit selected social scientists pointed out that Project Camelot would seek to "make it possible to predict and influence politically significant aspects of social change in the developing nations of the world." It added that the "U.S. Army has an important mission in the positive and constructive aspects of nation building in less developed countries as well as a responsibility to assist friendly governments in dealing with active insurgency problems."[15] In other words, in the guise of mounting a social-scientific investigation from an academic base, social scientists under the leadership of the sociologist Rex D. Hopper were being invited to take part in an imperialistic venture. The letter of invitation spelled that out clearly enough.

By June 1965, the U.S. Ambassador to Chile faced so much anti-American agitation as a consequence of Project Camelot that he demanded that it—whatever it was—be stopped. Latin Americans did not take it to be important to distinguish between social-scientific investigations useful to the military for the purpose of influencing social change and out-and-out military espionage and manipulation—if there were any differences. Anti-American agitation similar to that in Chile rapidly swept through other Latin American capitals.[16]

J. William Fulbright, as chairperson of the Senate Foreign Relations Committee, disapproved bluntly of the project's imperialistic intent: "Implicit in Camelot, as in the concept of 'counter-insurgency,' is an assumption that revolutionary movements are dangerous to the interests of the United States and that the United States must be prepared to assist, if not actually participate in, measures to repress them."[17] When the popular election of Marxist President G. S. Allende in 1970 posed a threat to the copper and other Chilean operations of multinational corporations based in the United States, the support of insurgency rather than of a government in power became American policy there, as it had been in many places before.

On July 8, 1965, the day on which the Defense Secretary put an end to Project Camelot, the SORO director was informing a Congressional committee that the name of King Arthur's legendary palace site had been chosen because "It connotes the right sort of things—development of a stable society with peace and justice for all."[18] He did not mention that Camelot also connotes feudalism. Some social scientists were impressed, they said, by the SORO director's sincerity on this and other occasions as he tried to make a case for his conception of social science applicable to public policy. Sincerity is scarcely an acceptable defense for sociologists who become mercenaries of a project serving plutocratic multinational corporations in the exploitation of underdeveloped countries.[19]

In discussing probable reasons why social scientists in the United States did not comment much on the life and death of Project Camelot, the sociologist Irving L. Horowitz mentioned first that "many 'giants of the field' are involved in government contract work in one capacity or another. And few souls are in a position to tamper with the gods."[20] For example, W. J. Goode wrote an apologia for Camelot in which he stated his conviction "that CAMELOT was intellectually the most significant research project under way during the past decade. Even now, I would accept its challenge and devote the next ten years of my professional life to its execution, if given sufficient research freedom."[21] That last clause would be a rare attribute for a military research contract; with it added, many would vie for such a research opportunity. All too many social scientists, however, would justify their involvement by claiming against all contrary evidence that such freedom did actually exist.

Camelot, like Watergate, was only a symptom of change. Old-fashioned social-scientific ideals of a William Graham Sumner, a Charles Horton Cooley, a W.E.B. Du Bois, or a Willard Waller were being replaced among sociological elites by ideals of social engineers for hire, by the so-called "bottom-line" operators. To the extent that young sociologists are inspired by models of scientific integrity, social responsibility, and productivity, the field does not need a code of ethics. Camelot made the problem of professional self-justification a pressing one for those who felt that their grants or contracts were threatened. As one observer, the educator L. J. Carter, put it, "The reverberations of *Camelot* are still being heard [a year later] and seem sure to influence the proposals to be made in the next few years to safeguard, in appearance as well as fact, the scholarly independence of government-sponsored research done in the United States and abroad."[22]

Thus, when the ASA Council in January 1967 authorized President Charles P. Loomis to appoint a new Committee on Professional Ethics, it asked that the committee "consider those issues currently in the center of public interest . . . the sociologist's role as scientist and researcher, not as practitioner."[23] This assignment's wording appears confused, but the chairperson of that committee, Edgar A. Schuler, referred to the committee's task as the drafting of a code of professional ethics. In sociology that would include the professional's roles as scientist and researcher and also as practitioner and social engineer. Carrying out this task in any literal sense was as impossible as trying to draft a single code of ethics that would cover both physiologists and physicians or both physicists or mathematical theorists and mechanical engineers. A preamble and a code of ethics went through many committee and Council revisions and then were adopted by the membership in a referendum in the fall of 1969, just sixty-four years after the establishment of the organization.[24]

So far as it goes, the ASA code is a noble document. Its tone is set by a preamble which combines notes of practical realism with echoes of the traditional idealisms and assertions of autonomy so long nurtured by the older professionals of the cloth, the law, and medicine. The preamble is worth quoting at length:

Sociological inquiry is often disturbing to many persons and groups. Its results may challenge long-established beliefs and lead to change in old taboos. In consequence such findings may create demands for the suppression or control of this inquiry or for a dilution of the findings. Similarly, the results of sociological investigation may be of significant use to individuals in power—whether in government, in the private sphere, or in the universities—because such findings, suitably manipulated, may facilitate the misuse of power. Knowledge is a form of power, and in a society increasingly dependent on knowledge, the control of information creates the potential for political manipulation.

For these reasons, we affirm the autonomy of sociological inquiry. The sociologist must be responsible, first and foremost, to the truth of his investigation. Sociology must not be an instrument of any person or group who seeks to suppress or misuse knowledge. The fate of sociology as a science is dependent upon the fate of free inquiry in an open society.

At the same time this search for social truths must itself operate within constraints. Its limits arise when inquiry infringes on the rights of individuals to be treated as persons, to be considered—in the renewable phrase of Kant—as ends and not as means. Just as sociologists must not distort or manipulate truth to serve untruthful ends, so too they must not manipulate persons to serve their quest for truth. The study of society, being the study of human beings, imposes the responsibility of respecting the integrity, promoting the dignity, and maintaining the autonomy of these persons.[25]

A fourteen-point code of ethics then spells out certain implications of this preamble so far as sociological research is concerned. The code deals with (1) objectivity, (2) integrity, (3) the research subject's rights to privacy and dignity, (4) protection of subjects from personal harm, (5) preservation of confidentiality of research data, (6) presentation of research findings, (7) misuses of research role, (8) acknowledgement of research collaboration and assistance, (9) disclosure of sources of financial support, (10) distortion of findings by sponsor, (11) disassociation from unethical research arrangements, (12) interpretation of ethical principles, (13) applicability of principles, and (14) interpretation and enforcement of ethical principles.[26] As had been officially stated, emphasis on research activities "was not to deny the importance of standards relating to teaching and consultation; rather the plan was to attempt to deal with most urgent matters first, then to evolve a more comprehensive ethical statement as later circumstances and experiences might indicate."[27]

The Committee on Professional Ethics to implement the code was appointed in 1969 before the membership had formally adopted the code. With Lewis A. Coser in the chair, the Committee learned from an attorney that the code could not legally be applied to a case at hand until the membership of the ASA had formally approved not only the code but also a formal set of rules of procedure. In consequence, such rules were drafted and, after a referendum, became effective September 1, 1971. Meanwhile, this Committee, as the ethics committees of the early 1950s had in effect predicted, discovered that "a number of cases which were formally or informally brought to the attention of the Committee involved charges of the unauthorized use of academic work of graduate students by their instructors."[28] The Committee called this "crass exploitation and . . . contrary to professional ethics. It deserves the sharpest censure."[29]

In commenting on the ASA code, the sociologist Robert W. Friedrichs notes that "it may serve to quiet the growing unease that spokesmen for the body politic have evidenced of late regarding social research." In other words, the code might serve as a useful public relations device. At the same time, Friedrichs predicts that the code "will in fact contribute to divisiveness rather than unity in the house of sociology itself." He contends that it will do this by baring even more the conflict between the "value-free" and the normative among sociologists.[30]

Friedrichs also suggests that the allegedly value-free sociologists themselves—those who claim that they can serve clients and yet be indifferent to client interests and involvements and relations to public welfare—can scarcely be happy with codifying normative standards even though they may try to do so "out of whole empirical cloth," as had been requested by Parsons[31] more than a decade earlier. This sort of thing, Friedrichs observes, is what "value-free" sociologists "had for some time been energetically professing to be quite impossible."[32]

What kind of social phenomenon then is or should be a code of ethics? To what sort of social interests does a code assure some degree of responsibility and accountability as well as authority—if it does—among those in a profession such as sociology? What practical significance does it have in a person's role as scientist or professional? What about the sociologists in so-called "research universities" which now pressure their professors to establish institutes and to accept grants and contracts for "research"? What about the influence of job-hungry students with specific industrial, therapeutic, actionist, and governmental goals? To what extent do

186   *Sociology for Whom?*

sociologists amorally join in the common effort of other professionals to make a less than moral world look moral?

As one pair of sociologists, D. S. Dorn and G. L. Long, analyze the ASA ethics code, it

is (1) a result of the increasing professionalism of the discipline and (2) a set of strategic rules which are functional for three related purposes: the maintenance of a "value-free" image of sociology, upward mobiltiy, and the protection of the discipline and members of the Association from external pressures and threats that might undermine professional autonomy and private interests.

The writers of the quoted statement call it naïve "to imply that the Code is (a) an instrument for protecting the interests of research subjects, however inadequately; (b) a mechanism for internal, professional social control; and (c) an appropriate vehicle for shaping the values and research orientations of sociologists."[33] Thus, the code serves principally goals of the wheeler-dealers and not of scientists as students, researchers, or teachers. Those dedicated to sociology as a search for knowledge create the tenable substance of the discipline. The wheeler-dealers or "bottom-line operators" develop and package for the market the salable items they find in the discipline.

Just how the ASA's standing Committee on Professional Ethics handles cases brought to its attention necessarily remains confidential. In 1973 it "voted to urge members of the Association to make use of its machinery for the review of ethical problems." At the same time it recognized "that certain issues and dilemmas facing the sociologist today have not been adequately covered by the present Code." It therefore sought "recommendations for amendment to the present Code."[34] In a subsequent report, Cynthia Fuchs Epstein as chairperson of the Committee asserted, "This notice did not bring forward more than a very few cases."[35] Later she summed up "cases brought before the Committee" during her period in its chair as being in four "major areas of ethical concern." These were: student freedom from professional and emotional exploitation; due credit to students and to peer colleagues for efforts contributed to a research project; the right of first publication of data by the person gathering them; and misrepresentation of academic credentials.[36] On the whole, however, the brevity and even paucity of its reports have done little to characterize positively

Responsibility and Accountability in Sociology   187

the Committee's activities and thus to elicit confident applications for its services.

Another problem for the ethics committee of any professional association is that ethical problems pervade all aspects of a discipline, of a profession, and of its organizations. The ASA has, for example, standing Committees on Freedom of Research and Teaching, on the Status of Women in Sociology, and on the Status of Racial and Ethnic Minorities in Sociology, as well as an *ad hoc* Committee on Information Technology and Privacy and another on Problems of the Discipline. All these committee titles suggest ethical concerns. The three standing committees came into existence as a result of the social and academic ferment of the 1960s, which reached peaks in sociological circles at the ASA's 1968 Boston and 1969 San Francisco conventions under the leadership of the Women's Caucus, the Black Caucus, and the Sociological Liberation Movement. These groups were the predecessors respectively of the continuing Sociologists for Women in Society, the Association of Black Sociologists, and the Radical Caucus, the collective which publishes *The Insurgent Sociologist,* and the Section on Marxist Sociology of the ASA.

The ASA's members are at times confused by the overlap among some of the committees involved in ethical problems. The committees themselves further complicate distasteful or difficult cases or situations by claiming that their assignment from the ASA Council is unclear.[37] Notably, the least productive Committees have been those on Professional Ethics and on Freedom of Research and Teaching. After all, they are the ones called upon to defend nonconformists. With better organizational support than the nonconformists, women and the nonwhites have had a difficult enough time defending their rights, especially in the face of employment cutbacks by both academic and non-academic employers during the 1970s.

The Committee on Freedom of Research and Teaching was added to the 1969 roster of ASA groups. The 1970 report of its first chairperson, Robin M. Williams, Jr., indicates the complications of the committee's assignment in these terms:

Our primary concern is with sociological *research and teaching,* not with any and all problems of academic and professional tenure, promotion, dismissal, and the like. It seems plain also that a serious and continuous effort to investigate all instances in which alleged interferences have occurred would require an augmented staff in the Executive Office and would involve other heavy expenses. For the time being, the Committee expects to be able to work only with those major cases that may establish precedents or principles.[38]

Subsequent activities of the committee could not always be reported because of their confidential nature. The members found, too, that some cases "are easy to dispose of on grounds that our Committee does not have jurisdiction or because the issue is more properly considered by another committee." The annual report making this admission contains these significant generalizations:

. . . the position of the untenured faculty member in the usual university setting is a very vulnerable one. In most cases, a department does not have to even inform a faculty member of the grounds for his dismissal or non-renewal. Coupled with the fact that few departments have clear and well defined criteria for hiring, promotion, or retention, the procedures are easily subject to abuse, at worst, and subject to misinterpretation on the part of a disappointed faculty member, at the least. Secondly, many departments sought out young persons of a very liberal or radical bent or with looser teaching and research styles during the period of student discontent and unrest [in the 1960s] in the hope that such appointments would be responsive to the demands for increased relevance in sociology courses. These recent appointments are not now as attractive with the decline of student activism. Such persons are especially vulnerable to dismissal since their styles are most uncongenial to the "straighter" predominant styles of senior faculty.[39]

Reports of the Committee on Freedom of Research and Teaching make it clear that the members may occasionally (with ASA Council supporting action) censure the top administration of a school in order to support a department's position[40] but that it will not act to help a competent nonconformist sociologist denied reappointment by "the 'straighter' predominant . . . senior faculty."[41]

Since so many sociologists are employed academically, a good brief summary of what their ethics committees reflect in their operations can be found in the statement of Fred M. Hechinger, *New York Times* education specialist: "In truth, education's ethics more often than not merely mirror society's social climate. It may therefore appear unreasonable to expect more of the Ivory Tower than of the White House." Nevertheless he believes that higher social responsibility by such academics as sociologists is still "essential to the peace of mind of those who have not abandoned

Responsibility and Accountability in Sociology   *189*

their love affair with education or turned their backs on Jefferson's conviction that democracy depends on the integrity of an educational system."[42] Fortunately for the future of sociology and that of sociology's contribution to social welfare, a gratifying number of sociologists of all ages still have that "love affair" both with education and with their discipline. They are the ones to whom sociology is a search for new insights useful to humanity and not just a profession of technicians available to those who can provide attractive stipends.

Let us look at five incidents which suggest what ethics and an ethics code appear to mean among certain entrenched social science leaders. These incidents have to do with (1) separation of church and state, (2) busing to equalize educational opportunities, (3) fakery in a closely related discipline, (4) nonrenewal of a teacher's contract because of politico-economic views, and (5) sex discrimination in academic promotion.

At the March 1976 meeting of the ASA Council a proposal "to recommend the inclusion of questions on religion in the 1980 Census" was discussed at length and then referred to the ASA Committee on Government Statistics for further study.[43] On September 1, 1976, the chairperson reported back to the Council for his committee as follows:

Data on religious identification and participation that could be yielded by items in a decennial census would have great value for sociology and demography. In voicing this judgment, COGS [the Committee on Government Statistics] does not presume to judge the merits of political, ideological, and theological arguments on the issue of including religion items in the decennial census. COGS does note that some of these arguments make fact judgments on which data may be adduced.[44]

Failure to answer decennial census questions is a punishable offense. Asking about religious membership or belief not only yields questionable results[45] but is an invasion of personal privacy when it is done as a matter of legal obligation and record by a governmental agency. Memories of bloody interreligious conflicts and persecutions led the promoters of the First Amendment to seek to assure the separation of church and state in the Federal Constitution. Apparently ignoring the terms of the ASA ethics code, as minimal as it is, as well as the provision of the Federal Constitution, the committee thus did not take into consideration the protection of the rights of subjects and informants.

I trust that R. L. Hagan, the acting director of the Bureau of the Census, reflects continuing United States policy when he wrote to me in 1976 that his agency "will not ask a question on religion in the 1980 census because of legislative action that prevents this under conditions where responses are mandatory, as they are in a decennial census." His organization had considered asking such questions on "the Current Population Survey [an interim sample survey] where responses are voluntary," but, he continued, "after considering at length the arguments on both sides of this issue a decision has been reached not to do so in the foreseeable future."[46]

The question is for the present settled, no thanks to the ASA Council or its committee. But why did the ASA leaders fail to take into consideration the social history of this matter which was brought to their attention? Why did they not take into account the great gains for public tranquility in this country by our somewhat effective separation of church and state? Why did they forget the statement in the ASA ethical code's preamble that sociologists "must not manipulate persons to serve their quest for truth"[47]? In what sort of social vacuum do these sociologists presume to live and operate?

The second incident mentioned has to do with busing to equalize educational opportunities. It also raises significant ethical issues. In a communication dated December 30, 1975, I asked the ASA Council and the ASA Committee on Professional Ethics to give serious consideration to the unsubstantiated statements being put forward by James S. Coleman of the University of Chicago and the Urban Institute of Washington, D.C., before legislative, judicial, and other public forums. These statements presented findings against the use of busing for educational-opportunity equalization which were called sociological. In making my request, I had in mind the statement in the ASA ethical code's preamble that "Sociology must not be an instrument of any person or group who seeks to . . . misuse knowledge."[48]

In response to my communication and without considering Coleman's reports and speeches, the ASA Council at its March 1976 meeting took the following action:

The Council rejects President Lee's recommendation that it ask the Ethics Committee to consider Professor Coleman's testimony on school busing and related issues. The Council reaffirms Professor Coleman's right of freedom of expression and conscience.[49]

I, too, reaffirm Coleman's right to freedom of expression and conscience. Freedom of expression and conscience was not at issue in this matter. Coleman had had considerable freedom of expression before the Massachusetts State Legislature, before many other governmental bodies, and in the mass media.

At the same time, I would not free Coleman from critical review by his fellow sociologists. I insist that his pouring of what amounted to flammable propaganda on the conflict situations in South Boston and in other American cities[50] requires some judicious consideration by responsible agencies of our professional association. As Marie Haug, a member of the ASA Committee on Professional Ethics, wrote to me in this connection: "It is an unfortunate fact that *sociology*, not simply one of its practitioners, is viewed by the public, both nonacademic and academic, as having validated a particular policy stance on the basis of 'scientific' evidence."[51]

Thomas F. Pettigrew of Harvard University and Robert L. Green of Michigan State University prepared a 53-page analysis of Coleman's activities, published in the February 1976 *Harvard Educational Review*. They summarize their findings thus:

Throughout the furor created by Coleman's statements, there has been confusion about where his limited research ends and his sweeping opposition to court-ordered desegregation begins. When critics questioned his views, they repeatedly suffered *ad hominem* abuse [in other words, attacks in terms of personal matters in order to avoid dealing with issues]. Some critics have hurled such abuse at Coleman. They make good copy for the mass media, perhaps, but they cheapen the debate, lower the public's respect for social science, and divert public attention from real issues. Indeed, the whole episode goes beyond racial issues or attacks on personalities, to raise painful ethical questions about the relationship between social science and public policy.[52]

ASA Footnotes, the association's official news publication, provided Coleman with ample space in November 1976 to make an irrelevant personal attack upon me for having raised the issue, as it had for his friends William Foote Whyte of Cornell University and Jackson Toby of Rutgers University in its August 1976 issue. Its editor did not give equal space to the many anti-Coleman letters he also received. In fact many he just refused to publish at all. Nor did he publish a publicly released letter to Coleman from his former student, Dean Robert A. Dentler of Boston University, part of which follows:

Your speech before the Massachusetts Legislature revealed to me . . . the extent to which you have lost touch with the very touchstones of social research in recent years. . . . The enrollment figures you cited are figures that have been discredited again and again in the course of this community conflict, which is now 11 years in the making. Contrary to the premises of your own seminal work on community conflict, you never researched the social facts or analysed the content of communications about this one, and yet you have spoken out in the name of sociology on the merits of the case![53]

Freedom of expression does not mean freedom from criticism. Critical consideration of such matters is the least we can and should expect from the sociologists in control of our professional association. We did not receive it.

The third incident to be mentioned has to do with spectacular fakery in a closely related field (psychology), fakery influential in some sociological circles and even more in the shaping of public policies. It is a case which persisted because of the lack of prying curiosity and courage to disagree with a prestigious figure upon the part of both psychologists and sociologists.

Genetic determinists scored policy-shaping successes on both sides of the Atlantic for several generations[54] in large part on the basis of what Nicholas Wade, a writer for Science, characterized as Cyril Burt's "unrivaled collection of data on heredity and IQ which he gathered as research psychologist to the London school system from 1913 to 1932, and later as professor of psychology at University College, London."[55] His reported findings aided particularly class-oriented and racially segregated tracking systems in education.[56] Since he had "proved" that intelligence is largely innate, children might well be placed at age eleven, without recourse, upon a single educational track leading to a profession, a trade, or unskilled labor. The results of more stimulating motivation, instruction, and facilities and the possibility of "late blooming" were judged to have relatively minor influence.[57] Thus Burt was deemed deserving of becoming the first knighted psychologist in England, and the American Psychological Association gave him its 1971 Thorndike award.

Then, after Burt's death, one of his followers, Arthur R. Jensen of the University of California at Berkeley, an influential and controversial hereditarian, gathered together Burt's scattered contributions to psychological literature and discovered in them a curious constancy in statistical correlations despite many changes in sample size. Jensen reluctantly concluded that "20 such instances unduly strain the laws of chance and can only mean error, at least in some of the cases."[58] He was being kind. Another psychologist, Leon Kamin of Princeton, was less protective. He reacted to Burt's class and race biased work thus:

The absence of procedural description in Burt's reports vitiates their scientific utility. The frequent arithmetical inconsistencies and mutually contradictory descriptions cast doubt upon the entire body of his later work. The marvelous consistency of his data supporting the hereditarian position often taxes credibility; and on analysis, the data are found to contain implausible effects consistent with an effort to prove the hereditarian cause. The conclusion cannot be avoided: The numbers left behind by Professor Burt are simply not worthy of our current scientific attention.[59]

When Philip Vernon of the University of Calgary, Alberta, a former Burt collaborator, was asked after the Jensen and Kamin revelations why no one had taken exception to Burt's findings earlier, he claimed that "there were certainly doubts although nobody dared put them into print, because Burt was enormously powerful. . . . He would write a 50-page paper denouncing any criticisms."[60] An irrelevant counterattack in terms of personalities rather than issues, as we have seen, is at times the recourse of such persons.

Liam Hudson of Edinburgh University offers an important lesson for social scientists in this incident: "The sober fact is that scholarly penetration of the literature, and endless delving into primary sources, occurs only rarely."[61] To this, Kamin adds: "Every professor knew that his child was brighter than the ditch-digger's child, so what was there to challenge?" He sees the moral of the Burt performance as: "Caveat emptor! The people who buy social science should remember that those who have collected the data may have axes to grind."[62] In other words, we recur to: Social science for whom?

Burt exerted tremendous pressure toward genetic determinism among susceptible sociologists and other social scientists as well as policy-makers in education and government. No ethics committee in any discipline on either side of the Atlantic made any contribution to his discreditment. As such committees are constituted and with the personnel typically available, no ethics committee of any professional association is likely to deal with such crucial instances of charlatanry upon the part of a prestigious member of its own profession. Such a discreditation depends—as it did in this case—upon the unconfined curiosity and courage of individual scientists.

The fourth incident to be outlined deals with the nonrenewal of a teacher's contract allegedly because of his lack of *relevant* competence but actually because of his nonconformist politico-economic views. Such a case as this, that of the sociologist Paul J. Nyden at the University of Pittsburgh, quickly becomes very complex. Charges on both sides build up countercharges. Efforts to inject extraneous issues further muddy the situation. Shortly only a highly motivated and experienced person can or will sort out what is happening.

Senior "colleagues" and administrators now find excuses other than "liberalism" or "radicalism" for excluding an offending or "uncongenial" person from a campus position. It is usually an alleged violation of some formal regulation or an alleged failure to meet some standard of competence or activity in teaching, research, publication, campus activities, or community service. That is what formal sets of university rules or "standards" are for: They are to be used to discipline or dispose of those who "make waves," and they are to be overlooked in the case of the upholders of the local view of disciplinary or politico-economic orthodoxy. If all else fails, an administrator can usually count on a conspiracy of fearful colleagues in a department to team up against an innovator or upon an array of disgruntled students who will want to get even for poor grades.

So many things come down to biased definitions of terms, to sociology for whom? Or it might be the willingness of professorial mice to sacrifice one of their number to help ward off a raid by the campus cat! Casuistry is not at all a new art in human affairs—nor is "brown-nosing"!

In a struggle between a professorial David and an institutional Goliath, it takes a lot more than one practiced throw with a slingshot for the David to win. Nyden had a vast number of well-wishers on campus and in the Pittsburgh community who pushed hopefully for his retention. The issues in the case were well summarized in a resolution at a regular membership business meeting of the American Sociological Association on September 1,

1976, which I chaired. The resolution, to which a very large share of the 300 members in attendance subscribed, is as follows:

Whereas the Department of Sociology of the University of Pittsburgh has denied Dr. Paul J. Nyden a second three-year contract as Assistant Professor because of his political views and activities—especially his research and writing on rank-and-file movements in the coal and steel industries and his activities in support of affirmative action and against militarism on the University of Pittsburgh campus, and

Whereas that Sociology Department has refused to release at least four secret reports giving the reasons for Dr. Nyden's termination and has repeatedly refused to specify its academic standards for contract renewal and tenure, both of which run counter to recommendations made by the American Sociological Association's Committee on Freedom of Research and Teaching,

Therefore be it resolved that the American Sociological Association calls upon the Sociology Department of the University of Pittsburgh to release all documents that relate to the case of Dr. Paul J. Nyden to the American Sociological Association's Committee on Freedom of Research and Teaching, to Dr. Nyden, and to any other groups Dr. Nyden might designate, and

Be it further resolved that the American Sociological Association calls upon the Sociology Department to demand that the administration of the University of Pittsburgh award Dr. Paul J. Nyden a second three-year contract as Assistant Professor immediately.[63]

This overwhelmingly positive resolution by the general business meeting of the ASA is not to be taken as a final endorsement by the Association as such of Nyden's position. Such action can be taken only by the Council, even though it is quite likely that the 300 members present at the business meeting—self-chosen though they were from among the ASA's some 8,000 voting members—represented a far broader cross-section of the whole voting membership than do the eighteen Council members. Except for an occasional person nominated like myself by petition or by a write-in campaign on ballots, and elected as a result of a membership revolt against the controlled nominating committee, the Council is an ideologically self-perpetuating body that represents in large part the same military-industrial interests as do those people who dominate the University of Pittsburgh and its Sociology Department. They are people far more interested in the entrepreneurial games of grants and contracts for corporations, governmental agencies, and foundations than they are in building a humane scientific discipline of sociology of service to people.

The University of Pittsburgh had first employed Nyden as of January 1, 1973, on a sixteen-month contract as an instructor. Then, in the spring of 1974, his doctoral committee at Columbia University *unanimously* accepted his dissertation and recommended him for the doctor of philosophy degree with distinction and for a special Universtiy prize. In consequence of this, the University of Pittsburgh placed him under a three-year contract as an assistant professor. This contract began in September 1974 and continued until April 30, 1977.

Before the Nyden case came up for consideration in the ASA Council at its March 1977 meeting, representatives of its Committee on Freedom of Research and Teaching had visited Pitt and prepared a 28-page report. Crucial sentences in this report as presented to the Council are the following:

We find that there is no substantial evidence that the decision not to renew Nyden's appointment was politically motivated and deceptively cloaked by procedural and substantive decorations. Insofar as our investigation could provide evidence about it, the department's evaluation process appears to have been motivated and carried out by a good faith effort to evaluate Nyden. We find no evidence of a calculation by the tenured faculty, or some segment of it, to conceal an ulterior agenda of procedures and reasons for "getting rid" of Nyden. . . . Quite intentionally members of the subcommittee [entrusted with the on-site investigation] avoided reading Nyden's work. Evaluation of colleagues is a department's affair. It alone is responsible to carry out this difficult task.[64]

A motion in the ASA Council to accept the report carried with only two dissenting votes. V. P. Singh,[65] as acting chairperson of the Pitt department, asserted that the ASA action "vindicates the department from various charges Nyden made during his campaign over the last year."

This "victory" of the department's senior faculty members was short-lived but it helped to bolster the chancellor's eventual arbitrary decision. As Nyden[66] notes, "Since my scholarly work is at the heart of the controversy, the ASA subcommittee, by avoiding this question, made its report irrelevant at the outset." The Council particularly discussed this aspect of the situation, and many members agreed that the quality of Nyden's work should be ignored. They said that the department should define as it saw fit what it looked upon as defensible sociological work. Council members contended that the department could take as narrow a position on sociology as it wished and that that decision could not be the concern of the ASA. Thus, once again the Council chose to ignore a dictum of its own code of ethics: "The fate of sociology as a science is dependent upon the fate of free inquiry in an open society."[67] How could a like-minded department reinforcing its restricted and ideologically biased conception of the discipline be serving "free inquiry in an open society"?

As a result of continuing student and public pressures, Pitt's chancellor took the unusual step of setting up a prestigious university professorial hearing board to take another look at the case and to listen to expert witnesses acquainted with Nyden's scientific work and with his activities at Pitt. On April 29, 1977, that board of six, after many days of hearings and of deliberations, transmitted to the chancellor this unanimous decision:

Our conclusion . . . is that the procedures followed by the Department of Sociology were not customary and proper, that the procedures were defective, and that the defect was material. It bears repetition that in that unanimous opinion of this Board the Department of Sociology used strictly professional criteria in its deliberations. Our decision is based solely upon the procedural defect in failing to communicate adequately to Dr. Nyden, under circumstances which would assure effectiveness, the criteria for the renewals decision and the evidence of professional productivity to which they would be applied. . . .

Given our conclusions that there exists a material procedural defect, we unanimously believe there is no alternative but to recommend that Dr. Nyden receive a new appointment as an Assistant Professor.[68]

Upon receiving this report, the Pitt chancellor, who had the power to make the final decision in the case, responded by asserting that

it should be emphasized that the hearing board, while finding a procedural defect on one of seven issues presented to them, completely cleared the actions of the dean of the Faculty of Arts and Sciences in all respects and the actions of the Department of Sociology in all but one respect, that one pertaining to communication of information regarding professional standards.[69]

From the evidence of both friends and critics, it is clear that Nyden devoted himself to activities that would have earned him a three-year contract renewal in a comparable university with a sociology department oriented to student needs and to independent scientific research.

198   Sociology for Whom?

The "procedural defect" apparently arose from the fact that the leaders of the Pitt department found it expedient to communicate *informally* to Nyden the following mandates: He was to aid a senior staff member with that professor's contract research for the military. He was to forget his doctoral study of rank-and-file organizing within the miners' union. He was to learn the desirability of becoming involved in contract research projects for some part of the military-industrial complex. All that could not be spelled out frankly in written instructions. Such frankness is not good academic form. It would give too accurate a conception of the activities of the department's predominant members. It would not have been the kind of document the department or the university would wish to place in public circulation.

In formal statements, proper academic language deals with conformist pressures in glittering generalities. In the chancellor's letter of May 12, 1977, finally offering Nyden a 15-month *extra-departmental* contract as Assistant Professor of Sociology, the language takes this form: "Your prospect for further renewal and promotion will be based upon a total view of your past performance and your demonstrated competence as they reveal existing and prospective strengths as a scholar, teacher, and constructive contributor to the intellectual life of the University." Nyden was to report to and be given instructions by the dean of his college and two sociologists selected by the dean. The final evaluation of his work at the end of a year would "be made directly by the senior faculty of the Department of Sociology or be delegated by them to the Dean of the Faculty of Arts and Sciences and the monitoring committee, who may employ the advice of other scholars in your field," to quote further from the chancellor's[70] letter of appointment to Nyden. In other words, the people who had fired Nyden before would have an opportunity to do so again.

The term "procedural defect" is academic doubletalk for the failure of the department's leaders to impress Nyden formally with the kind of role model he would have to accept to be assimilated into their group. This was the very issue on which the ASA committee and Council failed to take a position through refusing to consider what Nyden's and the department's standards for professional behavior might be and how defensible they should be considered. In view of the relatively low scientific research "productivity" rating of many of the tenured professors in the University of Pittsburgh department, a comparison of any formal "communication of information regarding professional standards" with existing exemplifiers of those standards in the department would have made the task of writing such a "communication" difficult if not embarrassing.

In this case, the nonconformist temporarily won a nominal or token contract renewal at a great cost in energy, time, and funds, with no thanks to more than several of his sociological colleagues at Pitt or to his professional association's hierarchy. He had, however, great support from his students, rank-and-file sociologists around the country, and leaders of Pittsburgh civic, religious, and labor organizations. The professional integrity of the Hearing Board of six made the difference in their recommendation to the chancellor, but that recommendation led only to the nominal or "sop" contract offer outlined.

In responding to this contract offer, Nyden stated in the first paragraph of a seven-page analytical letter: "I am accepting it [your offer] with requests for clarification and with serious reservations. I had hoped that you would not set the specific terms of my contract until the full transcript of the Hearing Board's proceedings was available and reviewed by you."[71] Chancellor Posvar's reaction to this letter was to withdraw his contract offer. As a writer for the *Pittsburgh Press* summarized it, "The University of Pittsburgh has, in effect, fired left-wing teacher Paul J. Nyden again."[72]

The case did not stop there. Having exhausted recourses within the University of Pittsburgh, Nyden petitioned the U.S. District Court to have himself reinstated in the University as an assistant professor of sociology. During hearings and negotiations in the District Court on August 29 and 30, 1977, Gerald J. Massey as president of the University of Pittsburgh Faculty Senate acknowledged that faculty power in such cases can legally be overridden by the Board of Directors and by its representative, the University Chancellor. He contended, however, that academic custom and moral authority as well as the fact that Posvar had appointed a Hearing Board should give the unanimous decision of that Hearing Board decisive weight. The Federal judge hearing the case, Daniel Snyder, was apparently impressed by legal obligations implied by the Hearing Board's decision and by Posvar's contract offer. He therefore worked out an agreement between the lawyers representing Nyden and the University. This gave Nyden a cash settlement without the nominal academic status previously offered to him. According to a reporter for the *Pittsburgh Press,* David Nilsson, the cash settlement was for the equivalent of about three years' salary with no allowance for legal costs. Nilsson stated that this settlement included a "gentlemen's agreement" not to reveal the amount of the payment, but he added: "The $50,000 settlement figure . . . was contained in a transcript of the lawyers' verbal agreement made before Snyder and obtained by The Press."[73]

Some of Nyden's backers were disappointed that he did not fight the case further in the Federal District Court, but it is doubtful if he could have accomplished any more through that medium for the cause of academic freedom than he already had during his well-publicized campus struggle. With the case settled and with his appointment in September 1977 to a teaching position in Antioch College's Beckley, West Virginia, branch, Nyden said, "My primary desire is to get back to my work. I've been upset that I haven't been able to do my research and writing for 18 months." The book on which he is working, based on his doctoral dissertation, is entitled "Miners for Democracy." According to a staff writer for the *Pittsburgh Post-Gazette,* "Nyden reiterated his belief that the dissertation . . . was the crux of his problems with Pitt officials."[74]

The fifth and last incident to be described involves sex discrimination in academic promotion. Margaret Cussler, an associate professor of sociology, brought formal charges against five former and current administrators of the University of Maryland "for refusing to grant her rank, salary and other rewards commensurate with her qualifications and performance." An account of this case in the *Newsletter* of Sociologists for Women in Society outlines its outcome as follows:

> The jury ruled under a [century-old] Reconstruction-era statute that the five defendants had not deliberately and maliciously discriminated against Cussler in denying her benefits.
> In a separate decision, federal Judge Edward S. Northrup ruled that actions taken by the university itself had also not resulted in any discriminatory treatment. The judge further ruled that Cussler was not entitled to back pay or compensatory damages.[75]

How did such a case become the subject of a Federal court suit filed in 1972? How did the judge and jury come to agree in 1977 with the university's male-biased administrators and sociology department controlling group and to disagree with the assessment of many leading sociologists?

As to the quality of Cussler's work, the District of Columbia Chapter of Sociologists for Women in Society reported:

Her credentials have been reviewed and compared with those of male full professors in the same department by Robin Williams [Cornell, ASA past president], William J. Goode [Columbia, ASA past president], Carle C. Zimmerman [Harvard], and others; all have judged her to be equal or better than her male counterparts.[76]

In addition, on May 25, 1977, the District of Columbia Sociological Society gave her its coveted Stuart A. Rice Merit Award "for her achievements in qualitative sociological research, her creative use of film in sociology, her service to the discipline, and her contributions to sociology and society through her insightful and sensitive studies of dentistry, food and nutrition, and, especially, the woman executive."[77]

Lewis A. Coser, ASA president, Arlene Kaplan Daniels, president of Sociologists for Women in Society, and six other representative leaders of the discipline pointed out in 1975 that the

. . . important issues involved in the [Cussler case] . . . resulted in a resolution passed at the December meeting [1974] of the ASA Council, following its unanimous approval by the membership present at the annual business meeting of the Association last August. The resolution censures the administration of the University of Maryland for attempting to obstruct the enforcement by HEW [the Federal Department of Health, Education, and Welfare] of laws against discrimination in employment.

They further recounted that from 1962 to 1972, Cussler

. . . exhausted all remedies open to her within the University. Two faculty committees found in her favor and recommended relief. University inaction forced her to file suit in 1972. Thereafter, HEW issued a letter of findings in her favor after three on-site investigations, and called upon the University to provide remedies, whereupon the University filed suit against HEW.[78]

This communication asked sociologists to contribute to Cussler's expenses of some $30,000 for bringing the case to trial in 1975.

The *Newsletter* of Sociologists for Women in Society reported that the impressive evidence outlined above came to naught "because of the judge's bias, his final instructions to the jury, his refusal to admit crucial evidence into the trial and the difference in financial resources available to the plaintiff and the defendants." The judge appeared to give special weight to the testimony of certain selected sociologists and administrators willing to oppose Cussler's case. The *SWS Newsletter's* account of the trial also makes these points:

Judge Northrup . . . frequently napped and read magazines during testimony. On many occasions he expressed general irritation at discrimination cases resulting from "ridiculous and utterly inhuman statutes passed by Congress." In his opinion, academic matters have no place in the courtroom. . . .

He did not allow any reference to two university review committee reports which supported Cussler's promotion. [Sylvia] Roberts [Cussler's attorney] was handicapped in her efforts to prove a pattern of discrimination because the judge neither allowed references to situations prior to 1969 nor allowed her to ask witnesses to compare Cussler's qualifications with those of male full professors in the department. Furthermore, while the defense was allowed to present witnesses who claimed there was no sex discrimination in the department, the plaintiff was not allowed to introduce counter-testimony regarding the treatment of other women faculty members. Also excluded as evidence was a supportive resolution passed by the ASA Council. . . .

The judge told the jury not to consider whether the university's procedures were discriminatory, but whether the university's criteria were "rational" and if it had followed its own procedures. If so, the jury should find for the defendants.[79]

The impressive support for Cussler did not prevent many sociologists from appearing in court against her. These included an ASA past president, Ralph H. Turner of UCLA, and Dean Helen Gouldner of the University of Delaware. Gouldner "claimed that only full professors, not judges and juries, are qualified to make promotion decisions, that 'well-prepared' women have no trouble securing good university positions, and that teaching is considered equally with publications in promotion decisions." Another woman sociologist, Jeylan T. Mortimer of the University of Minnesota, "had been hired as an assistant professor at Maryland at a lower salary than a man hired at the same rank at the same time from a less prestigious graduate department." She "testified that she had never been treated unequally and had never observed discrimination against women at the University of Maryland."[80] Other sociologists who sprang to defend the administrators were

Gerald Leslie (University of Florida), Michael Schwartz (Kent State University), Jerome K. Myers (Yale University), and Edward Z. Dager, Robert W. Janes, and Peter P. Lejins (full professors at the University of Maryland). Leslie claimed "that it is 'virtually unheard of' for peer review ever to result in discrimination, and he had never seen any hint of it in departmental considerations for hiring, tenure or promotion." In order to brush aside prior favorable testimony for Cussler, Leslie even went so far as to assert "that the testimony of William Form [then ASA secretary and professor at the University of Illinois in Urbana] and John Pease [University of Maryland associate professor of sociology] was not valid because they were 'radicals and identified with the counter-culture.'" This summary of the trial continues:

> Schwartz and Myers, in their testimony, compared Cussler with Edward Dager, who had been hired as a full professor while Cussler was being denied that rank. They, like Turner, praised Dager as a scholar with a national reputation who has made major contributions to the discipline, and denigrated Cussler's work as trivial and poorly done.
>
> Dager, Lejins and Janes defended their votes by condemning her teaching, relations with colleagues, research, publications, professorial judgment and service to the field of sociology.
>
> Robert A. Ellis, one of the five defendants, took the stand in his own defense. He said he could not investigate prior discrimination against Cussler because the file cabinets were in disarray. He did not accept the letters of recommendation from: Carle Zimmerman [Harvard]—because a graduate advisor is too closely associated with the student to give an accurate evaluation; Robin Williams—his evaluations had been unreliable in the past; or Harold Hoffsommer, the former head of the [Maryland] department—because he "was the reason the department needed upgrading." Ellis also claimed, on the basis of his expertise in social stratification, that women are always equally rewarded on the basis of merit.[81]

And after this defeat, what can Cussler now do? The grounds are ample enough for an appeal to a higher Federal court, but the costs of such a procedure present a high obstacle. To have a necessary transcript prepared of the first trial would cost some $40,000. If Judge Northrup were to declare Cussler a pauper of the court, the Federal government would have to assume her court costs. Efforts by Cussler, her attorney, and representatives of national women's organizations to arouse interest in further action within the Department of Justice have failed.

As we can see from the earlier discussion and from these five incidents, our ideas about responsibility and accountability in sociology as in other disciplines and aspects of life are shaped only superficially by written codes of ethics. Such codes are fashioned from social hopes, fears, aspirations and pretentions. To the extent to which our role exemplifiers come transparently to use an ethical rationale as a mask for exploitative activities, the professional organizations they control try to make those masks more opaque. They do this by attempting to strengthen—to give greater plausibility—to such masks by promulgating noble codes and by setting up impressive but only tokenly effective enforcement arrangements.

Actual human behavior in a profession or elsewhere in society is what counts so far as human welfare is concerned. That is influenced a great deal more by several overlapping groups of social and cultural factors than by formal moral mandates or ethical codes. These groups of factors are (1) the moral principles currently held to be *obligatory* in our community and society, (2) our role exemplifiers, (3) the mores of childhood, adolescent, and adult groups into which we are assimilated or with which we have to deal, and (4) our habit patterns resulting from our own individual experiences in coping with social realities as we perceive them. The resulting impact of all this upon actual individual and group behavior is much more complex than one ordinarily finds made relevant to statements of moral mandates or codifications of ethical principles. In consequence, disquisitions on ethics or morality often appear one-dimensional in our multi-dimensional, multivalent society.

In connection with these groups of influences, two points in particular need to be stressed: First, among our role exemplifiers we have many and diverse types whom we admire or detest. There are many possible pathways to many possible life styles, and our role exemplifiers are among our guides or deterrents. Second, the mores of our prototypical socializing groups of childhood and adolescence are still embedded in our attitudes and behavior patterns, even though we may now be adults. Many times a key to understanding the behavior typical of a women's or a men's play or work group can best be found in the behavior patterns of childhood and adolescent groups common to the social class, ethnic background, physical environment, and time period of its members. No wonder that it is so easy for members of a given group to have ideas about responsibility and accountability that may vary widely from that of other groups. It is also easy for the ethical ideas of individuals to change as they move from one group context to another.[82]

This humanist conception of the patterning of thought and action is relatively amorphous, contradictory, and changeful. It discredits the neatly determinable structure-and-functionalism or systemic theorizing of many positivist social scientists. It places the development of socially acceptable responsibility and accountability where it has always been—in the individual and the individual's perceived social and cultural setting.

What then can be done to help sociologists discern that to be scientific includes being responsible and accountable to humanity rather than merely to special vested interests? As the sociologist George Simpson contends, sociologists "are the keepers of the conscience of the social sciences."[83] To fulfil such an assignment, which I take to be the basic social expectation concerning sociologists, the ASA ethical documents and organizational arrangements have provided little service, and its committees and Council some notable disservices. Behavior, as is so often and so correctly intimated, speaks more loudly than words. For example, as the *New York Times* education specialist Fred M. Hechinger reminds us: "Students become aware that some much-published professors reap the fruits of some of their best students' unacknowledged services. Inevitably, some students respond by charting their own shortcuts."[84]

Perhaps if ethical documents were to be produced through a broadly participatory process, common understanding and agreement would give them greater influence than is apparent now. This would mean participation in their formulation by people who work in and also by those who benefit from social-scientific research, consultation, and teaching. Unless moral principles become looked upon as more compelling, as less superficial and ritualistic, however, even a broadly conceived code becomes merely another façade behind which the usual special-interest understandings and conspiracies find shelter. Unless prominent role exemplifiers perform wholeheartedly in terms of a code's principles in their own behavior as well as in their rhetoric, the code is meaningless.

The mores of intimate groups readily furnish the shortcuts to circumvent limitations of any such code unless somehow the code's higher morality can be shown to contain greater wisdom—to be more expedient socially—than the immoral mores so commonly learned in our intimate play and work groups and in individual experiences. The future of sociology as a scientific discipline in the service of humanity thus rests on the creative scientists, upon their curiosity, courage, integrity, and concern for the human condition.[85]

notes

[1]T. V. Smith, "Ethics," *Encyclopaedia of the Social Sciences,* vol. 5 (1931), pp. 602–7; p. 602 quoted.

[2]Emile Durkheim, *Professional Ethics and Civic Morals,* trans. by Cornelia Brookfield (Glencoe, Ill.: Free Press, 1958), p. 1.

[3]C. F. Taeusch, "Professional Ethics," *Encyclopaedia of the Social Sciences,* vol. 12 (1934), pp. 472–76; pp. 472–73 quoted.

[4]P. L. Berger, "The Human Shape of Personnel Work," in C. P. Hall, ed., *On-the-Job-Ethics* (New York: National Council of the Churches of Christ in the U.S.A., 1963), pp. 79–91, esp. pp. 90–91.

[5]J. L. Steffens, *The Shame of the Cities* (1904; New York: P. Smith, 1948).

[6]A. McC. Lee, chair, "Report of the Committee on Problems of the Individual Researcher," *American Sociological Review,* vol. 16 (1951), pp. 863–64.

[7]A. McC. Lee, chair, "Report of the Committee on Standards and Ethics in Research Practice," *American Sociological Review,* vol. 18 (1953), pp. 683–84; p. 683 quoted; see also his "Implementation of Opinion Survey Standards," *Public Opinion Quarterly,* vol. 13 (1949–1950), pp. 645–52; "Responsibilities and Privileges in Sociological Research," *Sociology and Social Research,* vol. 37 (1952–1953), pp. 367–74; and "Social Pressures and the Values of Psychologists," *American Psychologist,* vol. 9 (1954), pp. 516–22.

[8]Jessie Bernard, chair, "Report of the Committee on Ethical Principles in Research," *American Sociological Review,* vol. 20 (1955), pp. 735–36.

[9]Lee, op. cit., 1953, p. 684.

[10]Bernard, op. cit., p. 736.

[11]Talcott Parsons, "Some Problems Confronting Sociology as a Profession," *American Sociological Review,* vol. 24 (1959), pp. 547–59; p. 559 quoted.

[12]Talcott Parsons, chair, "Report of the Committee on the Profession," *American Sociological Review,* vol. 25 (1960), p. 945.

[13]Talcott Parsons, secretary, "Minutes of the First Meeting of the 1964 Council, Montreal," *American Sociological Review,* vol. 29 (1964), pp. 890–91; p. 891 quoted.

[14]R. C. Angell, chair, "Report of the Committee on Professional Ethics," *American Sociological Review,* vol. 27 (1962), p. 925.

[15]Johan Galtung, "After Camelot," in I. L. Horowitz, ed., *The Rise and Fall of Project Camelot* (Cambridge, Mass.: M.I.T. Press, 1967), pp. 281–312; p. 281; see also Horowitz, "The Life and Death of Project Camelot," in *Professing Sociology* (Chicago: Aldine Publ. Co., 1968), chap. 19.

[16]Henry Raymont, "U.S. Is Due to Drop Study of Latin Insurgency," *New York*

Times, July 8, 1965, p. 11; Richard Eder, "Pentagon Drops Insurgency Study," *New York Times,* July 9, 1965, p. 8.

[17]J. W. Fulbright quoted by Horowitz, op. cit., 1968, p. 288.

[18]Horowitz, ibid.

[19]Cf. K. H. Silvert, "American Academic Ethics and Social Research Abroad: The Lesson of Project Camelot," in Horowitz, op. cit., 1967, pp. 80–106.

[20]Horowitz, op. cit., 1968, p. 296.

[21]W. J. Goode, "Communication to the Editor," *American Sociologist,* vol. 1 (1966), pp. 255–57; p. 255 quoted. See also Gino Germani, "In Memoriam: Rex D. Hopper," *American Sociologist,* vol. 1 (1966), p. 259.

[22]L. J. Carter, "Social Sciences: Where Do They Fit in the Politics of Science?" *Science,* vol. 154 (1966), pp. 488–91; p. 488 quoted.

[23]E. A. Schuler, "Toward a Code of Professional Ethics for Sociologists: A Historical Note," *American Sociologist,* vol. 4 (1969), pp. 144–46; p. 144 quoted.

[24]P. H. Rossi, secretary, "Minutes of the 1969 Council Meeting," *American Sociologist,* vol. 5 (1970), pp. 58–59; p. 58 cited; L. A. Coser, chair, "Report of the Committee on Professional Ethics," *American Sociologist,* vol. 5 (1970), p. 413; D. S. Dorn and G. L. Long, "Brief Remarks on the Association's Code of Ethics," *American Sociologist,* vol. 9 (1974), pp. 31–35, esp. p. 32.

[25]American Sociological Association, "Preamble," "Code of Ethics," and "Rules of Procedure," effective September 1, 1971 (leaflet).

[26]Ibid.

[27]Anon., "Toward a Code of Ethics for Sociologists," *American Sociologist,* vol. 3 (1968), pp. 316–18; p. 316 quoted.

[28]L. A. Coser, chair, "Report of the Committee on Professional Ethics," *American Sociologist,* vol. 6 (1971), p. 353.

[29]American Sociological Association, "Statement of the ASA Committee on Professional Ethics," *American Sociologist,* vol. 6 (1971), p. 57. See J. F. Galliher, "The ASA Code of Ethics on the Protection of Human Beings: Are Students Human Too?" *American Sociologist,* vol. 10 (1975), pp. 113–17, esp. p. 113.

[30]R. W. Friedrichs, "Epistemological Foundations for a Sociological Ethic," *American Sociologist,* vol. 5 (1970), pp. 138–40; p. 138 quoted; cf. J. A. Roth, "A Codification of Current Prejudices," *American Sociologist,* vol. 4 (1969), p. 159.

[31]Parsons, op. cit., 1959, p. 559.

[32]Friedrichs, op. cit., p. 138.

[33]Dorn and Long, op. cit., pp. 32, 31; cf. J. F. Galliher, "The Protection of Human Subjects: A Reexamination of the Professional Code of Ethics," *American Sociologist,* vol. 8 (1973), pp. 93–100, and op. cit., 1975.

[34]Anon., "Committee on Professional Ethics Calls for Cases," *ASA Footnotes,* vol. 1, no. 8 (November 1973), p. 5.

[35]C. F. Epstein, chair, "Report of the Committee on Professional Ethics," *ASA Footnotes,* vol. 2, no. 6 (August 1974), p. 15.

[36]C. F. Epstein, chair, "Ethics Committee Concerns Cited; Reactions Invited," *ASA Footnotes,* vol. 3, no. 2 (February 1975), p. 1.

[37]Anon., "Council Takes Action on Ethics, Conditions of Research & Teaching," *ASA Footnotes,* vol. 4, no. 2 (February 1976), p. 1.

[38]R. M. Williams, Jr., chair, "Report of the Committee on Freedom of Research and Teaching," *American Sociologist,* vol. 5 (1970), pp. 407–8; p. 408 quoted.

[39]P. H. Rossi, chair, "Report of the Committee on Freedom of Research and Teaching," *ASA Footnotes,* vol. 2, no. 6 (August 1974), p. 15.

[40]"Summary of the Report of the Sub-Committee Concerning Simon Fraser University," *American Sociologist,* vol. 6 (1971), pp. 58–60; American Sociological Associa-

tion, "History of Committee on Freedom of Research and Teaching," 3 pp. mimeo., esp. p. 2.

[41]"Update on Paul Nyden," pp. 69-70, A. McC. Lee, "The Nyden Case: An Alumnus Revisits Pitt," in *Insurgent Sociologist*, vol. 7, no. 1 (Winter 1977) pp. 70-73; Jack Ladinsky, W. V. D'Antonio, and Paula Goldsmid, "Report of the Committee on Freedom of Research and Teaching of the American Sociological Association on the Case of Dr. Paul J. Nyden and the Department of Sociology, University of Pittsburgh," March 4, 1977, as accepted March 26 by ASA Council, xerox, 28 pp.

[42]F. M. Hechinger, "Watergating on Main Street: Education," *Saturday Review*, November 1, 1975, pp. 27, 56-57; p. 57 quoted.

[43]W. H. Form, secretary, "Minutes of the Third Meeting of the 1976 ASA Council," *ASA Footnotes*, vol. 4, no. 5 (May 1976), pp. 8-9; p. 9 quoted.

[44]Robert Parke, chair, "Report of the Committee on Government Statistics to the Council, American Sociological Association," offset copy, September 1, 1976.

[45]John Darby, *Conflict in Northern Ireland* (Dublin: Gill & MacMillan, 1976), p. 115.

[46]R. L. Hagan, letter to A. McC. Lee, December 23, 1976.

[47]American Sociological Association, "Preamble," etc., op. cit.

[48]Ibid.

[49]W. H. Form, secretary, "Minutes of the Third Meeting of the 1976 ASA Council," *ASA Footnotes*, vol. 4, no. 5 (May 1976), pp. 8-9; p. 9 quoted.

[50]F. H. Levinsohn and B. D. Wright, eds., *School Desegregation: Shadow and Substance* (Chicago: University of Chicago Press, 1976); J. A. Ladner, *The Death of White Sociology* (New York: Vintage Books, 1973).

[51]Marie Haug, letter to A. McC. Lee, February 10, 1976.

[52]T. L. Pettigrew and R. L. Green, "School Desegregation in Large Cities: A Critique of the Coleman 'White Flight' Thesis," *Harvard Educational Review*, vol. 46 (1976), pp. 1-53; p. 50 quoted; J. S. Coleman, S. D. Kelly, and J. A. Moore, *Trends in School Segregation, 1968-73*, with insert (Washington: Urban Institute, 1975); J. S. Coleman, "Letter to the Editor," *ASA Footnotes*, vol. 4, no. 8 (November 1976), p. 4.

[53]R. A. Dentler, letter to J. S. Coleman, April 6, 1976, as released to the press.

[54]L. J. Kamin, *The Science and Politics of I.Q.* (New York: John Wiley & Sons, 1974), pp. 1-34.

[55]Nicholas Wade, "IQ and Heredity: Suspicion of Fraud Beclouds Classic Experiment," *Science*, vol. 194 (1976), pp. 916-19; p. 916 quoted.

[56]See A. R. Jensen, "How Much Can We Boost IQ and Scholastic Achievement," *Harvard Educational Review*, vol. 39 (1969), pp. 1-123, and "Reducing the Heredity Environment Uncertainty: A Reply," *Harvard Educational Review*, vol. 39 (1969), pp. 449-83; R. J. Herrnstein, *I.Q. in the Meritocracy* (Boston: Atlantic Monthly Press, 1973).

[57]Cyril Burt, "The Genetic Determination of Differences in Intelligence: A Study of Monozygotic Twins Reared Together and Apart," *British Journal of Psychology*, vol. 57 (1966), pp. 137-53, and "Mental Capacity and Its Critics," *Bulletin of the British Psychological Society*, vol. 21 (1968), pp. 11-18.

[58]A. R. Jensen, "Kinship Correlations Reported by Sir Cyril Burt," *Behavior Genetics*, vol. 4 (1974), pp. 1-28; p. 24 quoted.

[59]Kamin, op. cit., p. 47.

[60]Philip Vernon quoted by Wade, op. cit., p. 918.

[61]Liam Hudson quoted by Wade, ibid.

[62]L. J. Kamin quoted by Wade, ibid.

[63]"Resolution in Support of Dr. Paul J. Nyden," adopted in two parts at membership business meeting, American Sociological Association, September 1, 1976, mimeographed.

Responsibility and Accountability in Sociology 209

[64]"Report of the Committee on Freedom of Research and Teaching . . . on the Case of Dr. Paul J. Nyden," op. cit., pp. 15–16.

[65]V. P. Singh quoted by MP, "Sociological Association Clears Pitt of Nyden Charges," *University Times* (University of Pittsburgh), March 31, 1977.

[66]P. J. Nyden, letter to editor, *Pitt News*, April 8, 1977.

[67]American Sociological Association, "Preamble," etc., op. cit.

[68]R. H. Seeburger, chair, and others, report of Hearing Board "concerning the non-renewal of Mr. Paul Nyden" to Chancellor W. W. Posvar, April 29, 1977, 8 pp.; pp. 7–8 quoted.

[69]W. W. Posvar quoted by Gabriel Ireton, "Nyden Rehiring Urged by Pitt Faculty Panel," *Pittsburgh Post-Gazette*, April 30, 1977.

[70]W. W. Posvar, public letter to P. J. Nyden, May 12, 1977.

[71]P. J. Nyden, public letter to W. W. Posvar, May 26, 1977.

[72]William Wisser, "Pitt Drops Nyden Offer," *Pittsburgh Press*, June 7, 1977.

[73]David Nilsson, "Pitt 'Settles' $50,000 on Nyden," *Pittsburgh Press*, September 16, 1977.

[74]Fritz Huysman, "Nyden OKs Pitt Offer: Cash, End of Job Bid," *Pittsburgh Post-Gazette*, August 31, 1977.

[75]"The Cussler Suit: A 'No-Win' Fight," *SWS Newsletter*, vol. 7, no. 2 (June 1977), pp. 1–2.

[76]District of Columbia Chapter of Sociologists for Women in Society, letter, *ASA Footnotes*, vol. 5, no. 2 (February 1977), p. 4.

[77]"Cussler Receives Stuart A. Rice Award," *SWS Newsletter*, vol. 7, no. 2 (June 1977), p. 2.

[78]Herbert Blumer, L. A. Coser, A. McC. Lee, A. J. McQueen, Stanton Wheeler, Charlotte Wolf, A. K. Daniels, and C. W. Smith, "Cussler Legal Defense Fund" (communication), *ASA Footnotes*, vol. 3, no. 4 (April 1976), p. 6.

[79]"The Cussler Suit," op. cit., p. 2.

[80]Ibid.

[81]Ibid.

[82]A. McC. Lee, *Multivalent Man*, new ed. (New York: Braziller, 1970); Lee, *Toward Humanist Sociology* (Englewood Cliffs, N.J.: Prentice-Hall, 1973); Lee, "Northern Irish Socialization in Conflict Patterns," *International Review of Modern Sociology*, vol. 5 (1975), pp. 127–34.

[83]George Simpson, *Science as Morality* (Yellow Springs, Ohio: American Humanist Association, 1953), p. 43.

[84]Hechinger, op. cit., p. 56.

[85]This chapter is an expansion and adaptation of an address with the same title given before the Seventh Annual Alpha Kappa Delta Research Symposium, February 18, 1977, at Richmond, Va. The original address was copyright 1977 by Alfred McClung Lee.

nine

What Future Has a Humane Sociology?

As the foregoing chapters suggest in a variety of ways, the current forms of sociology and their possible future constantly raise the question: Sociology for whom? In narrowing the focus of consideration in this final chapter to the future of a sociology for people, of a humane or humanist sociology, we still have problems associated with the questions: Whose conception of "humane"? "Humane" in what perspective?

In the preface to his book on sociological theory, Leon H. Warshay confesses to an "earlier appreciation of humanist broader conceptions of experience, and of humanist innovations and supplements to neo-positivist and mathematical methodology." He then recalls that he became "chastened by the growing realization that positivist narrowness, prejudice, and intolerance were matched by humanist self-indulgent subjectivity, terminological debates, and cult behavior."[1] This is a strange statement for an analyst of social theories to make. No approach to social thought and to sociological investigation appears to be free of persons and groups who exhibit narrowness, prejudice, and intolerance and also self-indulgent subjectivity and scientism, endless quarrels over terms and rhetoric, and thus cult-like behavior. Any theory raises this question: What are its personal, social, historical, and other origins and settings? This means especially and briefly: Sociology by and for whom?

As long ago as the thirteenth century, Roger Bacon, in his *Opus Majus,* concerned himself with the implications of that question. He warned against "four chief obstacles in grasping truth, which hinder every man, however learned, and scarcely allow any one to win a clear title to learning, namely, submission to faulty and unworthy authority, influence of custom, popular prejudice, and concealment of our own ignorance accompanied by an ostentatious display of our knowledge."[2]

Sociological practitioners are not alone in confronting and attempting to overcome those obstacles, but sociological literature is so vast that the individual mind is overwhelmed by its ramifications. It is easy to trim the literature down to one or several authorities, to be a Weberian or a Marxist or a Sumnerian or a Parsonian and to quote the master's "holy writ." It is much more difficult to go out into society and to try to understand social relations and manipulations at first hand and upon the basis of a wide range of personal observations and tested data and ideas. Custom and prejudice are obstacles to perception and understanding that everyone acquires during socialization into the multivalences of a complex, competitive, and contentious society.[3] Ignorance of human affairs is hidden behind trick terms and the playing of pretentious games with "sophisticated" methodological ploys in so many sociological monographs that it does not need further illustration here.

Instead of struggling against the obstacles Roger Bacon outlines, sociologists all too often share what Mark Twain calls "that large defect in your race—the individual's distrust of his neighbor, and his desire, for safety's or comfort's sake, to stand well in his neighbor's eyes."[4] They write what they think the peer-review readers for journals or for book publishers will accept. Their efforts more often than not verge on artful plagiarism than on innovative effort. Mark Twain adds: "It is curious—curious that physical courage should be so common in the world, and moral courage so rare."[5] Few are the sociologists who have the courage to do disturbingly creative research on the really crucial social problems of our time.

Sociologists tend to give theories simplistic characterizations, then to insert them into neat pigeon holes, and to ignore the interrelations and overlappings among them. They are also prone to stereotype major theorists and to insert them into those same tight little holes along with what are taken to be their theories. They thus package both theory and theorist for easy assimilation by students and for ready legitimation, trivialization, or condemnation. The only exceptions to this procedure are ordinarily the one or a few theories and theorists that are recognized by a given group of sociologists to be "basic" or "seminal." It is so much easier to attribute ideas to one or a few revered writers than to explore their antecedents and their competitors.

Few sociologists also wish to permit their theory and history to become further complicated by considering the changes through which a sociologist's theories might go in forty or fifty years of active investigation and thought. Yet the sociologist's intellectual life history—to the extent that it is revealed in her/his writings and in memories of associates—can often tell us more about social science as a process of exploration and discovery than can any of her/his individual products. We could thus follow, as best we might, her/his intellectual movements in response to confrontations with social events, social climate, personal experiences, and contrasting theorists. The creative mind would be seen modifying or scrapping inherited ideas, perceiving aspects of "reality" ("facts") in a variety of terms or perspectives, reaching out beyond habitual barriers for different data, ideas, syntheses, and wisdom.

As we have seen, sociologists often tend to preoccupy themselves with theories sufficiently narrow, technical, and verbally idiosyncratic to distinguish their discipline from others, and to reinforce its status as an autonomous social science whose turf is readily defensible against incursions from other specialists. But sociology—like cultural anthropology, social history, human geography, social psychology, social and moral philosophy, education, and humanistic belles-lettres—is at the major crossroads of investigation and thought about the human condition. All these disciplines intertwine and can enrich one another. Humanist sociologists recognize this broad perspective as the challenge of their discipline, but positivistic purists see that perspective as either naïve or as treachery against the autonomy of their profession.

What general attitude should sociologists now take toward their probings of human society? In response to this question, it is clear that few sociologists approach their inquiries with a preconception similar to that of George Moore as expressed in his *Confessions of a Young Man* (1888): "Humanity is a pigsty, where liars, hypocrites, and the obscene in spirit congregate."[6] Without Moore's bitterness as a disillusioned young man but with curiosity about the widespread occurrence of hypocrisy, let us discuss how humanist sociologists try to turn their concerns into contributions to sociology and to human welfare.

Social phenomena that intrigue humanist sociologists include the personal and institutional façades that disguise multidimensional, multifaceted people and groups. More than 2500 years ago, Aesop[7] pointed to this situation with his tale about the wolf in sheep's clothing. More generally stated, this wisdom often takes the form it does in Gilbert and Sullivan's "H.M.S. Pinafore": "Things are seldom what they seem."[8]

The phenomena characterized by this folk sagacity—the endless contrasts between what people say and what they do, between the promises of social institutions and the actual behavior of their functionaries—fascinate humanist sociologists. On the whole, however, novelists and psychologists give more persistent attention than do a great many sociologists to what personal masks and organizational façades may hide or disguise. Too many sociologists assume that offhand expressions of opinion by a person to a casual interviewer can be used as data upon which to predict the probable behavior of the person.[9] Too many presuppose that a person or group behaves in terms of the same set of values or uses the same procedures in different social contexts. Too many work on the basis of the inaccurate notion that the public image a person or institution projects is dependably something more than a mask or a façade. Too many think that they can learn about the nature of social behavior without empathy, without participant observation of a patient and continuing sort, and without testing generalizations in actual social practice.

Too many teachers believe that they serve their students and society best by helping those in their classes to become dependably formed technicians who have assimilated details and methods without learning to suspect the limitations or even the validity of those details and methods. Such teachers are often fearful of the consequences to themselves and to their students of encouraging the young to reach out for new perceptions and new insights. Such teachers would deny that they dread novelty or creativity, but they are highly protective of the existing "system."[10] They do not wish to suggest that they would shake the apple cart. They do not comprehend that they are serving not their students and society but the needs of entrenched power manipulators for an oversupply of indoctrinated tools. Whether wittingly or unwillingly or unconsciously, the teachers themselves have long since come to serve as minions for power manipulators. Thus too many sociologists are little more than routine collectors of techniques and data, and they are comfortable with students who hope to emulate them.

Teachers need to understand better and to accept readily what might be accomplished by helping students perceive and experience contrasts between the superficial or transient on the one hand and the many-faceted wholeness of personal behavior or of social processes on the other. They can do this by stimulating their students to seek new experiences. They can arouse enthusiasm for social exploration with a poem or other work of art, with a hypothesis, or with opportunities for fresh investigation into diverse social situations. They can encourage creative efforts at interpretation and explanation. It is too easy merely to try to cram student minds with textbook details, classifications, characterizations, and methods.

A sociology teacher can help open up new worlds of experience for students by encouraging them to perceive empathetically and thus to understand the thoughts and activities of people in groups different from their own, for instance, in age, religion, or ethnic background. Then the behavior of their own group and of many others can become vivid to them in terms of each group. How much more useful are such experiences than classroom exercises with methodologies that trivialize social problems and those with jargonized restatements or traditional justifications for the current social class structure.

What does all this discussion mean in terms of the sociological discipline and profession as a human enterprise faced with the bureaucratic, technocratic, plutocratic, and imperialistic problems of the closing decades of this century? How do our professional and scientific societies help sociologists face these problems—if they do? Or have such organizations become merely a part of the problems? What kind of professional body should humanist sociologists now help to create which can mean something more to the whole discipline of sociology and to society at large than the organizations existing in the field? What can such an effort mean to the sociological discipline in general and to its own members as sociologists and as people? These are complex questions. They depend upon so many human variables. They can be answered in many ways. They require serious and continued consideration.

Our oldest and largest professional body, the American Sociological Association, has been in existence since 1905. In all these years it has never represented the needs and interests of American society generally and even many of the concerns of those working in the discipline. Constructive pressures from groups of social problems researchers and activists,[11] from radicals,[12] from Blacks and other nonwhites,[13] and from women[14] have gradually forced the ASA to become somewhat more representative scientifically and socially, but the ASA and its journals and other projects are still largely in the hands of entrepreneurs of "research" institutes preoccupied with grants and contracts.

Since myths of legitimacy have powerful influence over the ill-informed and conformist, far too many sociologists accept and permit the ASA and regional organizations to define the terms of status scrambles within our profession. The ASA elite names the peer-review committees who pass on manuscripts for ASA publication and for non-experimentally minded editors of periodicals and of book-publishing firms otherwise owned. This elite also attempts to control review committees for other professional plums, such as grants and contracts. In fact, it tries to give the impression that it holds the keys to all the gates to paths upward in the sociological profession. These claims are nonsense.

American society is too complex for that loosely knit and individually competitive elite. There are a great many other journal and book publishers as well as experimentally minded foundation executives. From my own experiences as department chairperson and as a participant and critic in sociological professional societies, I would assure those in doubt that the control claims by the ASA ideological elite have some substance but that many people have gotten ahead and even gained great distinction in sociology while by-passing the ASA gatekeepers.

As we saw in the previous chapter, the American Sociological Association is deeply enmeshed in aspects of the control structure of our society. Its ruling cliques are dedicated consciously or unconsciously to the reinforcement of our social structure, self-destructive though that structure be. The existing social-scientific societies are a part of the social problems sociologists should be probing in their effort to make human society more livable and hopefully more self-fulfilling for a greater number of people.

What will be useful at this time is a scientific body that will bring together those who are not impressed by the deceptive appearances of exclusive control of sociological legitimacy by our existing organizations. The Association for Humanist Sociology is such an organization. It seeks to affiliate people whose curiosity is constantly roused by the realization that "things are seldom what they seem." It is attracting sociologists committed to the service of humanity, to the age-long highroad of humanist social investigation and social theory. Its sociology implies acceptance of a humanist ethic as a self-imposed mandate. That ethic implies not only service to broad human interests and concerns but also accuracy in observation, mistrust of formulas and methodologies, use of statistics not as irrefutable "hard facts" but as a medium for the summarization and analysis of human observations, search for the most tenable and practical theories, and freedom from an acceptance of outside controls over one's scientific work.

The rationalizing and even the justifying of outside control over "scientific research" projects has become, as we have seen, a sophisticated and organized activity. Thus, all too often, the "ethics" committees in sociological and other societies devote themselves to the construction of public relations casuistries from which to fabricate profitable public images for the service of special interests. They try to rationalize or obscure propagandistic distortions of data, as currently in the desegregation and intelligence testing controversies, rather than to define and maintain scientific ideals.[15] The Association for Humanist Sociology is trying to provide an alternative to such hypocrisies. Its founders hope its members will criticize freely unethical practices now taking place in the sociological discipline. This will uncover sharply conflicting views of ethics, and that is so much the better for the future of sociology's role in society.

The building of an Association for Humanist Sociology is not easy. It is controversial. Like the Society for the Study of Social Problems in its early days,[16] it may be looked upon as a threat to the discipline's alleged "integrity," that is to say, to sociology's repute with administrators fearful of any novelty that might conceivably rock a community's or a college's "boat." Hopefully, members of the Association for Humanist Sociology will long be more concerned with developing a socially useful sociology than with trying to take seats at the tired old entrepreneurial games played by the cliques who rule so many of our organizations.

Those who are creating the Association for Humanist Sociology might learn much from both the successes and the failures of the Association for Humanistic Psychology. The AHP cannot well be taken as a model for the AHS. The two disciplines are too dissimilar. But the history of the AHP can help guide those building the AHS. For example, in a communication for the *AHP Newsletter* in 1972, Rollo May warned his fellow humanistic psychologists not to attempt merely to form a Division of Humanistic Psychology within the American Psychological Association. As May put it, the AHP members "represent the New Underground in psychology, and I think that is a crucial function, as necessary for APA as for ourselves."[17]

Many humanist sociologists would surely agree with Rollo May and other humanistic psychologists that both groups can make their greatest impact upon their disciplines through forming autonomous organizations. But I would not take a position parallel to that stated by May that humanist sociology—like humanistic psychology—is a "New Underground" movement in sociology. Quite the contrary. Humanist sociologists represent the great traditions of social philosophy and social science as far back as those traditions reach.

The partial eclipse of humanist social science in this century and especially since the depression of the 1930s has not driven humanist sociologists "underground." It takes more than the faddish scientism of the sociologists Lester F. Ward, George A. Lundberg, Paul F. Lazarsfeld, and Samuel A. Stouffer to displace the great contributions to social thought and human welfare of the humanist theorists and activists. Now that the various forms of neo-positivism have thoroughly demonstrated their dehumanizing character, their class orientations and other special-interest proclivities, and their propagandistic uses, humanist sociology is staging a great come-back for which the Association for Humanist Sociology provides a useful medium and focal point. The sociologies of Karl Marx and Frederick Engels, of Sigmund Freud, of the older W. G. Sumner (the anti-plutocrat and anti-imperialist), of Florian Znaniecki and W. I. Thomas, of Pitirim A. Sorokin, of C. Wright Mills, of W.E.B. Du Bois, and of Willard Waller—not to mention the many out-standing humanist sociologists now still alive—represent no "un-derground" movement in sociology. Neglected though they may be by ASA "establishment" figures, trivialized though they may be by their so-called interpreters in textbooks, and whether or not one agrees with them at all or in part, they are great lights of the sociological discipline.

The communication of Rollo May about the Association for Humanistic Psychology quoted above contains another warning that is probably not necessary for humanist sociologists. At least I hope not. May was concerned especially with an anti-intellectual tone he said he detected in certain AHP circles, a tendency "to leave out the thinking, reflecting, historical man and put in only the feeling, touching man."[18]

The great differences between sociology and psychology make this possibility less a threat to the AHS. At the same time, in comparing relations of the AHS with the ASA to those of the AHP with the APA, I would put what anti-intellectualism there may be on the ASA side, not on that of the humanist sociologists. So many current sociologists are heedless of historical, cultural, and some-times even situational contexts, but humanist sociologists have often been notably sophisticated about social processes through time, about cultural differences among societies and among groups and classes within a society, about control structures and class conflict, and about the significance of environmental and techno-logical changes. Humanist sociologists are also aware that they must perceive people and groups as totally as possible in their changing social environments: They must try to see whole people who feel, experience, decide, think, and reflect as well as act.

The Association for Humanistic Psychology originated with a

small group of deeply concerned psychologists who were vividly aware of the artificialities and dehumanizing tendencies of "regular"psychology as exemplified by the APA and its current divisions. Its permissive experimentalism made it grow rapidly. As A. H. Maslow listed his own suggestions "for maintaining openness and flexibility"in that organization, he expressed the hope that AHP would: "(1) retain a shifting and fluctuating organizational structure; (2) define the organization in terms of the problems; (3) develop an intellectual movement *without* a leader."[19] In other words, AHP was founded by psychologists who wanted to provide a more personalized organization as a means of transforming psychology into a science more relevant to people.

Then a variety of appliers, therapists, and even enjoyers, watchers, and sympathizers joined themselves to the original corps of researchers and analyzers. They now even include various types of "mystics"and other cultists. As Maslow also suggested, there should be no effort to exclude any one who might wish to join the organization, but he pointed out that AHP "could have 'scientific' members and meetings and *other* meetings for trying out new techniques."[20] That would avoid a confusion of goals.

The Association for Humanist Sociology plans to be equally open and permissive in its membership and programming. Whether or not this will mean that it will have to find ways to live with a variety of cults remains to be seen. Humanist sociology does not have the wide range of clinical organizations in its sphere which might seize upon AHS as a medium for publicity and recruitment. There are cultish religious-humanist sociologists, but they may continue to find themselves more at home in such bodies as the Association for the Sociology of Religion and some denominational societies. The possible consequences of its inclusiveness do not alarm those who are building the organization, so long as the AHS maintains a firm commitment to broad humanitarian concerns.

From the psychologists the AHS can certainly borrow such key conceptions as Maslow's "self-actualization," a human goal to be sought and achieved through "peak experiences."[21] This calls for a struggle toward human identity, dignity, and self-expression to which humanist sociologists can contribute significantly but differently from humanistic psychologists, belletrists, social philosophers, musicians, poets, painters, and novelists.

This is a great challenge for sociologists. To spell out some challenges related to this one, challenges for building a future for a humane sociology, here are concerns to which sociologists might well give their attention:

1. They can develop first of all a society of cooperative friends in search of social knowledge rather than one of competitive "prima donnas."

2. They can be critical of the abuses of privilege and power in their discipline, especially of the exploitation of junior colleagues and of graduate students.

3. They can refuse to look upon the published work of any author as "holy writ." They can be wide-ranging in their search for facts and ideas.

Merely because a given sociologist of the past could not transcend racist, sexist, or class-centered conditioning does not mean that she or he might not have left behind some challenging ideas and possibly collections of data. For example, it is easy and I believe justifiable to make a case against Herbert Spencer or Vilfredo Pareto, but it is also profitable to study their writings *at first hand*. I am sure that Marx, Sumner, Cooley, and Weber would now regard a lot of their published ideas as "old hat" if they were still at work among us. It is ridiculous to get into long exegetical debates as to what some passage in the writings of Marx or Sumner or Cooley or Weber "really" meant. The important consideration is what given phenomena, actions, and processes can mean to people generally today and tomorrow. Fortunately there is a tool such as *Sociological Abstracts* and various other indexes and abstracts to help find in the international maze of sociological contributions what might be needed. *Sociological Abstracts* also brings abstracts of our own writings to the attention of those who use research libraries throughout the world.

4. They can examine critically the stylish fads and suspect theories, including the terminological repackagings of older theories, that sweep across the field.

Refer especially to the current resurgence of a sophisticated racism and classism led by certain academicians and echoed by those who are making political or economic capital out of so-called "reverse discrimination," agitations against the desegregation of housing and the use of busing for desegregation, and class-biased and ethnocentric IQ tests. Further, criminologists who dig deeply enough into the statistics of their field know that crime statistics are largely arbitrary fictions set by the current notions of expediency of those who compile them. The basic weakness of such statistics lies in the class and race biases in detection and recording of crimes. All sorts of loose generalizations are then based upon them.[22] And, for another example, marriage and divorce figures may be more accurate in a formal sense, but analyses of their significance often have little reference to actual human behavior.

5. They can try to see social problems as something more than developments that irritate the inhabitants of white suburban ghettos and carefully guarded urban highrises.

Visit the prisons. Talk at length with the guards and inmates. You will get the impression that criminals are disproportionately nonwhite. And yet it is no great secret that anti-social conspiracies, law violations, interpersonal violence, theft, and other crimes take place in all social circles, classes, neighborhoods. Those responsible get differential treatment. Our prisons are the end-product of a society shot through with white racism and middle-class-centeredness subservient to upper-class controls. Why do our newspapers and other mass media see housing desegregation and busing to end racial school segregation only from the standpoint of the alleged evils of white flight and not from the standpoint, among others, of Black deprivation in jobs, housing, health care, as well as education? Is a white, middle-class ghetto a fit place in which to raise children who will presumably be able to take their places one day as impartial judges, broad-minded educators, and intelligent and fair administrators in what is so often called our "democratic" society? Are educators concerned enough with the anti-intellectual roles, even the socially subversive roles that college social sororities and fraternities prepare our students to play in American society?

6. They can look at the worldwide problems of colonialist and neo-colonialist exploitation, at the millions who lack not only civil rights and dignity but food and shelter.

The problem centers where so much of world control centers, especially in the United States, and this is all the more reason for us to recognize it and to preoccupy ourselves with it. A visitor from Bombay, a sociologist of note, said to me recently, "Why do we Indians have to accept American sociology as if it were something

222   *Sociology for Whom?*

other than apologetics for American plutocracy and for plutocratic imperialism?" When I lectured abroad in such countries as Bangladesh, India, Pakistan, Lebanon, Syria, and even parts of Europe, I had great difficulty in establishing my credibility—to the extent that I did so at all. Foreigners see the United States as the principal base for the multinational corporate conglomerates, and those conglomerates owe loyalty to nothing other than their own boards of directors who treat the United States and other countries' governments as instruments for domination and exploitation. I was thus suspected of being a propagandistic tool of a governmental agency in the service of those multinational operations. Certainly the Jews, Christians, and Muslims of the Middle East are not fighting each other in consequence of religion alone. They are struggling for human dignity, for civil rights, for reasonable security for themselves and their families, but their loyalties and their struggles are exploited by remote military-industrial interests to carry on their vast games of power manipulation. Humanist sociologists can help Americans see their share in those manipulations. They can suggest the disastrous future toward which we do not have to be drifting.

Many more challenges confront sociologists, but only one more will be mentioned:

7. They can explore more carefully and then publicize the manipulative strategies and propagandas to which so much of our mass media, politics, religious apologetics, and formal education are devoted. Who is selling what to whom and at what costs and for what purposes? Sociology textbooks appear to be giving less and less space to the nature of public discussion and opinion, to the ways in which specialists manipulate them, and to the ways people may defend and assert themselves. As Francis Bacon put it, the desirable goal of all the sciences is "that human life be endowed with new discoveries and powers."[23]

In preparing students to live effectively and constructively in a world that constantly experiences Watergates but only occasionally learns about them, sociologists need to discover all they can about how human beings are made into tools and societies subjected to costly and even catastrophic scenarios. Sociologists and their students can even work at discovering how human beings can initiate and then develop their own more livable scenarios.[24]

notes

[1]L. H. Warshay, *The Current State of Sociological Theory* (New York: David McKay Co., 1975), p. xii.

[2]Roger Bacon, *The Opus Majus*, trans. by R. B. Burke (New York: Russell & Russell, 1962), vol. 1, p. 4.

[3]A. McC. Lee, *Multivalent Man*, new ed. (New York: George Braziller, 1970), chap. 4.

[4]Mark Twain, *The Mysterious Stranger*, W. M. Gibson, ed. (Berkeley: University of California Press, 1969), p. 155.

[5]Mark Twain, *In Eruption*, Bernard DeVoto, ed. (New York: Harper & Bros., 1922), p. 69.

[6]George Moore, *Confessions of a Yound Man* (1888), Susan Dick, ed. (Montreal: McGill-Queen's University Press, 1972), p. 186.

[7]Stith Thompson, ed., *Motif-Index of Folk-Literature* (Bloomington: Indiana University Press, 1957), vol. 4, p. 344.

[8]W. S. Gilbert and Arthur Sullivan, "H.M.S. Pinafore," in *The Complete Plays of Gilbert and Sullivan* (New York: Modern Library, n.d.), pp. 101-37; p. 122 quoted.

[9]Irwin Deutscher, *What We Say/What We Do: Sentiments and Acts* (Glenview, Illinois: Scott, Foreman & Co., 1973), and *Why Do They Say One Thing, Do Another?* (Morristown, N.J.: General Learning Press, 1973).

[10]A. McC. Lee, "The Concept of System," *Social Research*, vol. 32 (1965), pp. 229-38, and *Multivalent Man*, op. cit., chap. 14.

[11]Richard Colvard, issue editor, "SSSP as a Social Movement," *Social Problems*, vol. 24 (1976-1977), no. 1.

[12]See esp. *Insurgent Sociologist*, 1969-.

[13]See esp. *CBS Newsletter*, 1971-1975, *Black Sociologist*, 1975-.

[14]See Sociologists for Women in Society, *Newsletter*, 1971-.

[15]W. H. Form, secretary, "Minutes of the Third Meeting of the 1976 ASA Council," *ASA Footnotes*, vol. 4, no. 5 (May 1976), pp. 8-9; A. McC. Lee, "Valedictory: A Report on the Year 1975-1976," *ASA Footnotes*, vol. 4, no. 6 (August 1976), pp. 1, 9-10.

[16]Colvard, op. cit.

[17]Rollo May, "Rollo May Writes," in Carol Guion and Tina Kelly, eds., *Satan Is Left-Handed* (San Francisco: Association for Humanistic Psychology, 1976), pp. 89-90; p. 89 quoted.

[18]Ibid.

[19]A. H. Maslow, paraphrased quotation in "Culled From the Archives," ibid., pp. 167-69; p. 167 quoted.

[20]Ibid., p. 168.

[21]A. H. Maslow, *Religions, Values and Peak-Experiences* (Columbus: Ohio State University Press, 1964).

[22]L. H. DeWolf, *Crime and Justice in America: A Paradox of Conscience* (New York: Harper & Row, 1975).

[23]Francis Bacon, "Magna Instauratio" (1620), in his *Essays, Advancement of Learning, New Atlantis and Other Pieces*, R. F. Jones, ed. (New York: Odyssey Press, 1937), pp. 239-363; p. 303 quoted.

[24]Adapted from the author's presidential address, "A Different Kind of Sociological Society," given at the founding conference, Association for Humanist Sociology, Miami University, Oxford, Ohio, October 30, 1976, published in *Humanity and Society*, vol. 1 (1977), pp. 1-9.

Index